Library of
Davidson College

# ETHICAL DILEMMAS IN ANTHROPOLOGICAL INQUIRY: A CASE BOOK

# ETHICAL DILEMMAS IN ANTHROPOLOGICAL INQUIRY: A CASE BOOK

by

G. N. Appell

CROSSROADS PRESS

African Studies Association
Epstein Service Building, Brandeis University
Waltham, Massachusetts 02154

© 1978
African Studies Association
All rights reserved

Printed in the United States of America

No part of this publication may be reproduced
or transmitted in any form or by any means,
including photocopy, recording,
or any information storage and retrieval system,
without permission in writing from the publisher.

CONTENTS

Preface

Introduction 1

*Section 1: Relations and Responsibilities to Host Community 13*
1.1 Involvement in a Local Dispute 17
1.2 Whether to Intervene in Infanticide 19
1.3 The Efficacy of Faith Healing 21
1.4 Providing a Storage Place for Weapons 23
1.5 Using a Disguised Role 24
1.6 Imposition of the Anthropologist on the Community 26
1.7 Firearms in the Field 28
1.8 How Does a Foreign Researcher Interfere to Stop Illegal Activities 30
1.9 To Take a Wife 31
1.10 A Problem of Political Identification and Co-option 33
1.11 Mediation of a Conflict 42
1.12 Breaking a Taboo 45
1.13 The Perceived Advantages of Being Studied by an Anthropologist 47
1.14 Problems and Consequences of Actively Helping the Host Community 49
1.15 A Problem of Involvement 60
1.16 A Challenge to Anthropological Inquiry on an Indian Reserve 61

*Section 2: Relations and Responsibilities to Respondents and Informants 65*
2.1 Participation in Illegal Activities 67
2.2 A Case of Privileged Communication 74
2.3 A Medical Emergency 75
2.4 The Ethical Problems of Doing Field Work in a Setting of Intense Socio-Political Conflict 76

vi    Contents

2.5   Disease and Death: Research in the Uguru District   83
2.6   Conflict in the Roles of Friend and Informant During the Feedback of Research Results   86
2.7   Death From a Wound   89
2.8   An Act of Compassion   90
2.9   The Consequences of Investigating a Sensitive Subject   92
2.10  Intervention in a Curing Session   93
2.11  Embarrassing Informants   95
2.12  Dealing with Theft   96
2.13  Dealing with Threats of Aggression   98

Section 3: Relations with Host Government   101

3.1   A Request for Informant Names by a Government Official   103
3.2   Field Work in a Restricted Region   107
3.3   Field Work in a Climate of Governmental Suspicion   108
3.4   Political Ramifications of Field Work Among the Klee   112
3.5   The Anthropologist as a Political Catalyst   115
3.6   Presenting Research Goals in an Acceptable Light to the Host Government   119

Section 4: Relations with Representatives of Outside Agencies and the Public with Respect to the Host Community   121

4.1   The Priest, the Mamaoans, and the Role of the Anthropologist   123
4.2   On the Horns of a Dilemma: A Problem of Intercession   127
4.3   Playing the Role of Intercultural Mediator   130
4.4   An Unwelcome Intrusion into the Host Community   132
4.5   Relations with the Peace Corps in Boroboro   134
4.6   A Confrontation with a Priest   137
4.7   How Far to Go in Deception: A Clash of Viewpoints   139
4.8   The Local Mission and Its Priest   141
4.9   The Trader and His Monopoly   144
4.10  Missionaries and Anthropologists   146
4.11  Competition for Access to the Community   151

Section 5: Relations with Other Social Scientists and Responsibilities to the Profession   153

5.1   A Proposed Restudy of New Butu   155

5.2 The Breaking of a Disguise 156
5.3 A Case of Poaching? 157
5.4 Competition for Host Communities 158
5.5 Tensions in a Northern Community 159
5.6 A Problem of Responsibilities 160
5.7 Field Work Among the Kinani Indians 161
5.8 In the Field with an Intelligence Agent 163
5.9 The Discovery of an Early-Man Site and Its Subsequent Excavation 164
5.10 Dealing with Animosity Arising from a Previous Study 165
5.11 Anthropologists Three 169
5.12 Politics, Permits, and Professional Interests: The Rose Case 174
5.13 Mind Assault 186

*Section 6: Dilemmas in the Use and Misuse of Social Science Knowledge 187*
6.1 Misuse of the Anthropologist's Information 189
6.2 The Discovery of Drugs: A Difficult Ethical Question 191
6.3 Whether or Not to Deposit Field Notes in an Archive 192
6.4 On the Preparation of Ethnic Handbooks for the Armed Forces 194
6.5 The Inadvertant Feedback of Research Conclusions 195
6.6 Differential Access to the Results of Anthropological Inquiry: A Dilemma in Professional Responsibility 196

*Section 7: Publication: Responsibilities and Liabilities 199*
7.1 Publishing and Bad Science 201
7.2 A Problem of Publishing on Identifiable Communities and Personalities 202
7.3 Problems in Urban Ethnic Research 205
7.4 An Attempt to Control the Contents of Publication 208
7.5 The Problem of Publishing on Illegal Activities 209
7.6 The Possible Effects of Publication on the Society Studied 210
7.7 Competition with One's Informants 214
7.8 *Social Organization of Manu'a* (1930 and 1969), by Margaret Mead: Some Errata 215

*Section 8: Relations and Responsibilities to Funding Agencies 225*
8.1 Should Funding be Accepted? 226
8.2 Dissembling on Sources of Funds 228

8.3 The Professor's Dilemma over Research Funds 229
8.4 A Failure to Prepare for the Field 230
8.5 A Request from the National Foundation to Review a Research Proposal

*Section 9: Issues in Teaching 233*
9.1 The Introduction of Deviant Ideas by the Instructor 235
9.2 A Professor Fails in His Promise 236
9.3 Whether to Write a Recommendation 237
9.4 A Student Recounts His National Foundation Interview 238
9.5 A Case of Uncredited Editorial Work 239
9.6 A Matter of a Teaching Contract 240
9.7 A Recommendation for a Fellowship 241

*Section 10: Miscellaneous 243*
10.1 Ethical Dilemmas in Anthropological Field Work 243
10.2 When a Research Proposal Turns Out to be a Flop 249
10.3 Difficult Childbirth in Africa 254
10.4 Cosponsoring Tourists 256
10.5 Intervention in a Matter of Belief 258
10.6 Archaeologists, Museums, and Indians 259

Appendix 1: Ethical Issues and the Use of Case Materials 265

Appendix 2: Sources of Extended Case Materials 276

Appendix 3: Materials from Professional Societies 279

Bibliography 281

# PREFACE

*For us* [Americans] *the making of mediocre things is the rule while the ability to detect mediocrity or anything else is rare.... Don't knock, boost! was the cry of Warren Harding. To which the corollary was plain: anyone who knocks is a bad person with a grudge. As a result, the American has always reacted to the setting of standards rather the way Count Dracula responds to a clove of garlic or a crucifix. Since we are essentially a nation of hustlers rather than makers, any attempt to set limits or goals, rules or standards, is to attack a system of free enterprise where not only does the sucker not deserve that even break but the honest man is simply the one whose cheating goes undetected.*

Gore Vidal (1974, p. 10)

Vidal has clearly identified one of the major themes in the American character. But he has neglected to note an opposing theme: the desire to build a just society, an ideal society. At various times in American history, one or the other of these themes has predominated. During the 1960's and the early 1970's, the hustler theme was more evident in the American character, and as a result, the social scientist as hustler was more prevalent on the landscape. It is toward the resurgence of the theme of a just society that this book is dedicated. For the hustler has no place in scientific endeavor, in which the basic ethic is the habit of the truth (cf. Bronowski 1965; Glass 1965a, 1965b). This ethical premise is particularly critical to the social sciences, because in social inquiry it is difficult, if not impossible, to duplicate an "experiment" in order to verify the original results.

In the introduction which follows, I discuss those changes which have occurred in American anthropology—and the social sciences in general—which have contributed to the emergence of the scientist as hustler. Although these changes have produced specific ethical problems, the fact remains that moral dilemmas are intrinsic to social inquiry, demanding extensive study and discussion. Social inquiry has the very real potential for violating the conditions of human freedom and contributing to dehumanization. An added complication in anthropological inquiry is that it takes place at an interface of ethical and epistemological systems, thereby posing unforeseen moral dilemmas for the anthropologist.

How can we sensitize the student of the social sciences to these issues? How can we teach each new generation of students the necessary skills and judgement to make appropriate decisions in the face of ethical dilemmas? This book addresses these problems by presenting a series of case materials on ethical conflicts in social inquiry, and, in particular, anthropological inquiry. They have relevance to research in all disciplines that involve cross-cultural inquiry, as well as in many instances research that takes place in our own society. The purpose of this collection of cases is thus to provide the basis for the training of anthropologists and social scientists in ethical decision making through the discussion of the issues presented in the cases. By this approach it is hoped that greater awareness of the range of ethical issues involved in social inquiry will be generated and skills and judgements refined to deal with these.

## WHY THE CASE METHOD?

Why a case book? The limitations of moral codes as guidelines for behavior in concrete decision-making environments are discussed in the introduction. But this only partially explains why the case method was chosen.

As a graduate student, I was appalled by an instructor's story of letting a baby die so that he could observe a funeral before leaving the field. Since then I have witnessed and heard a number of other incidents which have led me to believe that at times my vision of moral behavior differed from that of some of my colleagues (see Appell 1973a for an expanded discussion of the history of this project). But I found few guidelines available to inform one's actions. Therefore, I decided to make an ethnographic inquiry into the nature of ethics in the anthropological profession. The scope of the inquiry was later enlarged to include other social science disciplines. The problem was how to begin.

I had been impressed in graduate school at Harvard University and at the Harvard Business School by the use of the case method—which is essentially a clinical approach—to develop an understanding of human relations (cf. Dunphy 1967). I then found that Fletcher (1966) and Eckel (1968) were also using the case method as a means of developing skills in ethical decision making (cf. also Beck and Orr 1970). I thought that this approach could be applied to the same range of problems in social inquiry. I thus began to collect case materials on the nature of ethical conflicts in social science. I then tested these materials in discussion sessions to discover the range of ethical issues involved, the sensitivity of social scientists to these issues, and the possible solutions. The cases were thus used in two courses I taught and at a number of discussion sessions I was invited to hold at universities in the East and Midwest, as well as at several annual meetings of the American Anthropological Association and the Northeastern Anthropological Association.

Thus what began primarily as an ethnographic investigation into ethical dilemmas slowly grew into the use of the case method to explore these dilemmas for teaching purposes. In preparing this volume, I have also included certain substantive articles to enlighten and supplement the case materials.

The case method provides a unique learning climate to develop the skills and judgement necessary to react creatively to situations involving ethical conflict and ambiguity. It develops the ability to think when faced with unexpected situations of conflict in value and the faculty to respond effectively. The case method is a particularly appropriate technique for cross-cultural inquiry, where new challenges are constantly occurring in different and unexpected cultural contexts, and where clear standards of conduct are often difficult to formulate.

The case method also offers a wide variety of distilled experience. This is valuable for students and professionals alike. Even the most seasoned field worker may find himself in a new situation for which his past field experience provides no guidelines. He can increase his ability to deal with such situations through exposure to the experiences of other anthropologists provided by the case method.

In addition to its use as a training method, the approach has a heuristic function. The premises upon which anthropological inquiry has been based have been challenged, and the environment in which such inquiry has traditionally taken place is changing or has changed. Thus, a number of new issues are arising; some are still ill-defined and others are just beginning to be articulated. The case method provides a means by which the accumulated experience and judgement of a group of participants can be brought to bear on such issues, to delineate them and define the areas of conflict. This technique can also help identify the various facets of those dilemmas for which there are as yet no solutions, where the issues are still clouded. Eventually, this method may help contribute toward a consensus in the profession for dealing with some of these dilemmas. Finally, solutions can be tested in various cultural milieux and field situations by means of the case method.

There are some who will not agree with this approach. Some of these believe that the structure of human relations rises primarily out of the ongoing negotiations of social life, forgetting that every human act has its moral directions and constraints. This approach also may not be easy for those reared in the anomic milieu where moral considerations are seldom explicitly considered. Anthropology and the other social sciences are at times the inadvertant handmaidens to the cultural values of our society, and many thus realize that in seeking success and fame moral considerations can be a hindrance (cf. Clark 1975). We all know of careers impaired and health broken by an overcompetition that exceeds the limits of morality and the bounds of human dignity. It is odd that while we are organized to take action against many types of antisocial behavior, we have not considered controls for the overachiever who sacrifices personal and professional integrity, who selfishly strip mines the critical social assets of interpersonal trust, in order to win those merit badges that indicate success. Indeed we reward these individuals instead of those who sacrifice their own aspirations for the betterment of the common good.

It is my hope, however, that many readers will welcome this book as a useful method of sensitizing students and colleagues to the moral consequences of social inquiry. For it is one of the paradoxes of the social sciences that their moral stance has not been higher than the surrounding topography.

## ACKNOWLEDGEMENTS

In addition to those who have contributed case materials, I would like to thank the following people who have encouraged my efforts: Dell Hymes, Karl Heider, Robert Manners, George Hicks, Charles Frantz, Niels Braroe, Richard J. Preston, III, and Steven Polgar. I would particularly like to thank David L. Sills of the Social Science Research Council (SSRC) for his encouragement and for the opportunity to participate in an SSRC conference in May, 1975, entitled "Research into Ethical Issues in Social Science Research."

While guest professor at the Ethnographic Institute, Aarhus University, Denmark (1971-72), I led discussions of ethical dilemmas in anthropological inquiry based on the case materials I have collected. I would like to thank the students who participated in these discussions for their stimulating and useful comments. I would also like to thank Professor Gutorm Gjessing for inviting me to give a lecture at the University of Oslo on the problem of ethics in anthropological inquiry and the United States Educational Foundation in Norway for providing the funds for this. I am particularly grateful to Professor Gjessing, Alex Sommerfelt, and Per Mathiesen, all of the University of Oslo, for their useful comments.

I am also deeply indebted to those who participated in numerous case-discussion sessions I have held at various universities and professsional meetings of anthropologists in the United States and Canada. My debt to these individuals is immense, and I cannot thank them sufficiently.

To Dr. Theodore Dunham, Jr., President of the Fund for Astrophysical Research, Inc., I owe a special debt of gratitude. A broad-ranging scientist in two professions, medicine and astronomy, he has shown me the joys of the persistently inquisitive mind, the special grace of a selfless scientist who is constantly working to increase human knowledge for the benefit of all mankind, and a character that the Taoists would refer to as uncarved wood. Ingenuous and concerned, he practices the habit of truth with no conscious effort and inspires others by his example.

Authors frequently express a debt to their families for the sufferings they have had to endure. To Charity, Amity, Laura Parker, and my wife, Laura, I want to express my remorse for having put them through more than their share of suffering in trying to finish this book over a period of six years. It has been a beastly task.

Finally, I want to thank my secretary, Mrs. Joan N. Bubier, for her valiant and successful struggle in ordering the mass of information I collected for this book and putting up with the difficult task of typing and retyping the final manuscript.

# INTRODUCTION

The case method of instruction differs significantly from the lecture method. To aid those unfamiliar with this method, I discuss below the pedagogical techniques that have to be mastered and the role relationships between student and instructor that are necessary to make it a success. However, to put the case method in its proper perspective, I first discuss the limitations of moral codes in ethical decision making. I also discuss the changes that have occurred in anthropology that make the reexamination of ethical conduct necessary and the nature of cross-cultural research that poses special problems in ethical decision making above and beyond the ethical dilemmas inherent in social inquiry. The conclusions I reach stem from my own observations and those of participants in my case-discussion sessions.

## CHANGES IN THE CLIMATE OF ANTHROPOLOGICAL RESEARCH

Anthropology has been going through a period that occurs in the history of most disciplines when the shared moral base of its members begins to deliquesce. Without this base, the direction of the discipline appears to wobble. At such times, ethical discourse increases as the members attempt to redefine the boundaries of the discipline and articulate a new moral consenses that will justify new form of inquiry. Eventually, this period of exploration and redirection will affect the interests of all anthropologists, whether or not they are actively engaged in the effort.

These times of questioning arise in response to a variety of circumstances: when social inquiry moves into new environments so that a confrontation with past moral guides takes place, as in urban research; when social inquiry experiences a change in the old environments of research, such as has occurred in the new nations; and when a shift in epistemic paradigms takes place, as some now claim for anthropology.

Other internal processes can also challenge the traditional moral consensus. An increase in the size of a discipline, for example, can make the past mechanisms of social control ineffectual or inappropriate. And the introduction of new scarce resources, such as in research funding, can provoke new forms of competition which fall outside the traditional ethical purview. Both of these changes have occurred in anthropology during the past decade.

## CHANGES IN THE CHARACTER OF THE PROFESSION

Related to these changes in the structure of anthropological research have been significant changes in the character of the profession during the past two decades. My remarks here are based, to a certain extent, on random observation. But as in field work, one begins to sense a pattern emerging that warrants further inquiry.

One of the most significant changes in the character of the profession has been its enrichment. When I was a graduate student, some anthropology professors were forced to seek supplementary employment. Today one hears of villas along the Mediterranean and sailing yachts as the gains of anthropologists who have successfully exploited the media and funding institutions. Conversation among one's colleagues now has a very suburban flavor. Where once bourgeois values were detested and ridiculed, one hears colleagues talk of antiques, the problem of keeping a lawn, of stocks and bonds, and so forth. And I have found myself in the peculiar position of being attacked when I mention defects in the American social system.

With the entanglement of anthropologists in the economic reward system of the larger American society, there has been a subtle shift in anthropological goals. One begins to find evidence that the search for truth has been forsaken in favor of competition for profit and power. Interest in knowledge for itself has shifted more to what is promotable, what is saleable. As a result, the anthropological profession seems to have suffered a relative decline in introspection and self-awareness, which were formerly the hallmarks of anthropological inquiry.

Thus, the increase in ethical discussion in the profession during this period does not necessarily imply an increase in overall ethical awareness. Much of this ethical concern can be attributed to changes in the structure of anthropological inquiry rather than the growing sensitization to ethical issues by members of the profession. The institutionalization of professional ethics and the use of ethics in political discourse would seen to substantiate this observation. Bernard, Ottenberg, and Redl (1971) note in their discussion of the psychic mechanics of dehumanization that developments such as these in fact decrease one's emotional involvement with others and diminish one's sense of personal responsibility for one's own actions.

Ethical concerns imply an awareness and acceptance of the interdependency of human beings and the concomitant responsibilities. Yet one of the paradigms in American society is the independent, achievement-oriented individual with disposable social relations. It is perhaps not a coincidence that, in my observations, those individuals who are least concerned with the climate of ethical decision making in the profession are also theoretically oriented toward social strategems rather than social structure.

Fletcher sums up the consequences of a shift to opportunism: "Immorality occurs when things are loved and people are used" (1967, p. 36); "the essence of moral guilt lies in the failure or refusal to respond to the needs or calls of others" (1967, p. 233).[1]

While the changes in the climate of anthropological inquiry and the character of the profession have produced their own ethical problems, they have exacerbated the problems that are inherent in social inquiry—the possibility of limiting human freedom and encouraging dehumanization. They have also exacerbated many of the dilemmas that are characteristic of cross-cultural inquiry.

## THE NATURE OF CROSS-CULTURAL INQUIRY AND THE INHERENT MORAL DILEMMAS

No longer are anthropologists the only researchers interested in other cultural environments. Psychologists, sociologists, economists, historians, and political scientists now engage in field work in different societies. In some disciplines, such as psychiatry and psychology, the cross-cultural approach has attracted so much interest that separate subdisciplines have been developed to foster cross-cultural inquiry. Thus many of the cases in this book are as relevant to these other disciplines as they are to anthropology. To simplify the discussion and because my own field of inquiry is social anthropology, I have couched my considerations of ethical dilemmas in terms of anthropological inquiry. It should be remembered, however, that my observations are pertinent to all social inquiry.

By its very nature, cross-cultural inquiry takes place at an interface of ethical systems. As a result, the anthropologist is frequently forced to make a choice or select a plan of action in an environment of conflict between different customs, principles, and values that normally shape action. For many of these situations of conflicts in values, no obvious or immediate solution may exist. Furthermore, the investigator usually has to make a decision without adequate information or sufficient time to probe all the ramifications of the situation.

The anthropologist or social scientist also frequently finds that he is being used as a pawn in the conflict of interests between factions within the social system he is studying, or between members of the host social system and outsiders. Now that field work is no longer the isolated and encapsulated activity it once was, the manner in which the investigator resolves these complex issues may affect not only the climate for research in the area but for the profession as a whole.

Complicating the problem of decision making at an interface of ethical systems is the fact that the anthropologist occupies multiple roles: field worker, scientist, teacher, writer, guest in a foreign country, member of a different cultural tradition, and so forth (cf. Appell 1973a). All of these roles include moral expectations which can conflict and may be unreconcilable. As a result, an anthropologist characteristically must be able to tolerate a certain degree of moral ambiguity. In fact, the best field workers may well be those who can acknowledge and live with these moral ambiguities.

## THE LIMITATIONS OF MORAL CODES

The successful resolution of ethical dilemmas which arise in the course of social inquiry depends upon the degree to which the investigator's judgement has matured through knowledge, experience, and training. Unfortunately, the experience of seasoned anthropologists in dealing with such dilemmas is seldom passed on in any formal manner to the next generation of investigators. In fact, the process by which field workers come to terms with these dilemmas of moral ambiguity has yet to be extensively studied.

Furthermore, anthropological curricula as now structured provide primarily for transmitting what Alfred North Whitehead has called "inert knowledge." They do not develop the facility to act in response to new and unexpected experiences that arise during an inquiry. While developing skills in theoretical debate, the curricula seldom prepare students for making appropriate decisions in situations of moral ambiguity.

Unfortunately, codes of ethics, by themselves, are of limited value in resolving these moral dilemmas. There are a number of reasons for this which stem from the nature of such codes (cf. Cohen and Schwab 1965; Frankena 1963). First, no set of rules is free of exceptions to the rules or of conflict between them (cf. Frankena 1963, p. 23). Also, moral codes present only general principles to guide action. They are phrased in abstract language so that they can have broad application. Actual decision-making environments, on the other hand, are concrete, rather than abstract, and clouded with bewildering detail. The facts in such a situation are seldom clear-cut and are usually subjected to several interpretations. Consequently, the first problem in applying the tenets of a moral code to a situation of decision making is learning to recognize the situations in which an ethical issue is involved.

Second, there is the problem of choosing from a variety of ethical principles the one which applied to the particular situation; frequently, several principles are operative. If these conflict with one another, it must be decided which takes precedence (cf. Frankena 1963, p. 2).

Then to deal with specific situations, the investigator needs to develop skills for selecting the facts that are pertinent to the issues at hand, passing over those which are only peripheral. Judgement is also required in moving from a precept to its application, since a rigid application may produce unethical behavior in terms of other principles. And sensitivity to ethical issues is necessary, since the generalized terms in which principles are expressed may permit interpretations to justify a course of action that violates the spirit of the principle. The investigator must also develop an understanding of how and in what form a principle may be amended to fit the idiosyncrasies of the situation without destroying the validity of the principle.

Both in deciding which precept applies and in planning how to put it into action, one must learn to predict the probable consequences of an action. These consequences can provide clues to which principle might be most appropriate and what kind of application most satisfactory.

Finally, based on prior experience in dealing with difficult ethical decisions, the anthropologist should develop his own set of working rules for the selection and application of ethical precepts, and should develop the skills necessary to discern when a new situation demands the application of new ethical principles or revisions of old ones.

Thus, ethical codes can only provide rough guides to action. The development of skills and judgement in the application of such guides are critical to the resolution of moral dilemmas that arise in the course of social inquiry.

## THE CASE METHOD OF INSTRUCTION

The case method of instruction differs significantly from the lecture method.[2] Traditional education in both undergraduate and graduate schools is based on the memorization of fact, abstract argument, and idealized examples. As such it does not encourage the student to develop skills and judgement in dealing with human problems. The case method, by simulating the kinds of real-life situations that the student will eventually encounter, creates a learning climate where the student can test and refine his judgement and decision-making skills. This is not to imply that knowledge is not transferred to the student in the case method. Considerable knowledge is transferred; but it is in terms of acquiring the knowledge that will enable the student to solve a concrete problem requiring action.

Since the case method is centered on the student and his growth rather than on imparting knowledge, a different set of relationships are required in the classroom. The instructor must abandon his role of authority and participate with his students in what is essentially a cooperative effort to reach an understanding of complex human situations. Similarly the student must forego his role as passive receiver of knowledge in favor of active participation in the learning process. As a result of this unthreatening learning climate, the student's implicit assumptions and valuations about the world can be explored and analyzed, in terms of their influence on decision making, and weighed for their adequacy.

*The Student's Role.* In a case-discussion course, students are sometimes confused and lost for the first few weeks for a number of reasons. The case method, unlike preceptoral teaching, provides no answers. There are no facts to be memorized and repeated back to the instructor. There is no sense of a steady progression toward an explicit goal. Thus, in adjusting to the democratic approach of the case method, the students typically pass through at least four stages (Schoen and Sprague 1954, p. 79). The first stage is an initial reaction of frustration and an inability to grasp the purpose of the exercise. This is followed by an arousal of curiosity. In the third stage, the student develops insight. Finally, decision-making skills grow and are honed.

Part of the initial frustration may arise not only from the fact that there are no final answers but also from the realization that an individual cannot think of everything that his fellow students collectively can (cf. Gragg 1954, p. 13). Students must understand the need for cooperative approaches to the problems they confront and be willing to consult with others and draw on their ideas. As students thus accept the burden of case analysis and participate in the dynamics of the classroom discussion, they will develop confidence in their own abilities to think and judge.

*The Instructor's Role.* The instructor using the case-discussion method becomes a moderator of the students' discussion. He has to move from a superior position of imparting knowledge to that of a group member seeking insight and developing skills. For some instructors, this transition may be difficult; it is often tempting to retreat into an authoritarian role and provide answers to the problems presented in the cases. But this only destroys the unique learning climate of the method. The rewards are satisfying for the instructor who can make the transition successfully. One of the most exciting aspects of the case method is that new insights and ideas are generated each time a case is explored by a new set of students.

Thus, the success or failure of the case method depends on the relationship that the instructor is able to develop with his students. The instructor's goal is to encourage the students' uninhibited discussion of the facts of a case and the application of value judgements in analyzing these facts without fear of ridicule. The case-discussion method shares many features of the nondirective approach to counseling pioneered by Carl Rogers (cf. Rogers 1942, 1951).

Charles Gragg (1954, p. 12) discusses the instructor's changed role as follows:

> The more powerful are the students' arguments, the heavier is the burden on the instructor; he must understand and evaluate each contribution, many of which are new to him, regardless of how thoroughly he has studied the cases or how many times he has used them with previous classes. To the instructor, every class meeting is a new problem and a new opportunity both to learn and to help others learn. The important question under these circumstances is not whether the student pleases the instructor but whether he can either support his views against the counterattacks and disagreements of others in the group or, failing to do so, can accept cooperatively the merits of his antagonist's reasoning.

*Management of the Case Discussion.* In preparing for the class, the instructor must master the facts of the case. He may also wish to list the learning objectives that he would like to reach in the class, but in doing this he should be careful not to slip into the position of directing the discussion. One approach might be to list the key questions to be raised about the issues that he perceives in the case. But rather than lead the students to these issues and questions, he should let the students discover them and limit his own participation to the judicious use of questions that encourage the exploration.

The instructor begins the class by asking a student to present his own thoughts about the case. In the early stages of the course, it is important to focus on developing skills for the close analysis of the case materials so that the students can learn to appraise the structure of social situations carefully before considering possible solutions.

Sometimes there is premature closure on a case in that the discussion from the start focuses on what the person caught in the dilemma should do. If this occurs, or if the discussion moves too quickly to a consideration of possible courses of action, it may indicate both a lack of sufficient insight into the complexity of the case materials and a failure to develop the ability for an insightful analysis of the problem. It is thus important to develop early in the course the practice of careful analysis of the social situation presented and identification of the problem before moving to the last stage, the discussion of alternative courses of action and their consequences.

In addition to premature closure, there is also the danger that the discussion will turn into a heated debate of ideological issues. When this occurs, the instructor should encourage the participants to consider the possible consequences of each of the positions taken as they apply to the specific details of the case under discussion. This will move the discussion away from arguments about the "right" moral position. After weighing the consequences of a plan of action, the students can estimate its cost/benefit and thereby arrive at a more realistic consideration of the problem.

It is also important that the instructor, as moderator, refrain from expressing any value judgements. He should ask only questions which elicit the ramifications of a position or thought. If the moderator's own value judgements intrude, he will begin to influence the contributions from the class, encouraging certain views and discouraging the expression of others.

Initially, the instructor must be prepared for complaints from the students that a case discussed requires more information than provided. It is important to point out that this is in fact the usual state of affairs in decision-making situations. Sufficient information is seldom available. The students must learn to judge whether enough information is available to reach a sound decision to take action or whether the problem requires additional information and, if so, how it should be obtained.

If the discussion has wandered or if there are many points of view causing some confusion in the discussion, it may be useful to list on the blackboard some of the points that have been made. The instructor may also want to review the discussion from time to time, listing on the blackboard the major themes and issues expressed. In doing so, he might say, "Let me try to summarize what you have said to see if I understand you correctly."

At a later point, when the class is considering possible solutions, these can also be catalogued on the board, listing alternative interpretations and the choices of action for each.

The instructor must always be ready to ask a student what he means or to request that he expand on his statement in order to reveal his full intent. The instructor should also be careful to distinguish whether statements are opinions or facts by asking questions that bring out this distinction. On the other hand, if the instructor is asked a question, he can turn it back to the students by asking if they have any thoughts about it.

Thus, the instructor engages in three major activities. First, to stimulate discussion, he asks questions and rephrases arguments, but refrains from eliciting specific responses or directing the discussion. It has been found that an unfinished analysis may be more productive than a case wrapped up with a final solution provided by the instructor.

Second, the instructor attempts to link together various viewpoints and arguments made by the students. He should try to relate points brought up in the discussion not only to the specific case but also to previous cases where appropriate.

Finally, the instructor summarizes arguments to ensure a common understanding of what has been said. Summarizing also serves as a means of reviewing the progress of the discussion so that the class can ascertain whether it has been appropriate to the materials and the problem at hand. New insights and perspectives will often be gained as a result of these summaries.

I have made the point that the instructor should refrain from putting forth his own ideas, at least during the early sessions of the course, and retain his role as moderator. However, if he feels compelled to contribute his thoughts, he should only do so after the class has discussed the case thoroughly, so that the instructor's ideas do not substitute for the students' analysis of the problem. In addition, the instructor should offer his ideas with the expectation that they will be evaluated, discussed, and criticized with the same freedom as those of anyone else in the classroom. For example, he might preface his remarks with, "Could a case be made for . . . ?"

Kenneth Andrews (1954, pp. 98-99) summarizes the approach of the instructor in managing case discussions:

> . . . [The instructor] needs the sense of timing which tells him that a discussion is not moving fast enough to make good use of available time or is racing away from the comprehension of half the class. He knows what to do on such occasions. He exercises control over an essentially "undirected" activity, but at the same time he keeps out of the way, lest he prevent his class from making discoveries new also to him. Since unpredictable developments always distinguish real learning, he examines his class rather than his subject. His workshop is not the study but the classroom. He is the architect of a constantly complicating social structure, for a poorly integrated group cannot provide for itself much educational experience. He must himself be a student.

*Group Therapist.* The instructor should be aware of the shifting moods in the classroom, for at certain points he will be obliged to serve as a group therapist. During the initial stages, when the students are reacting to the frustrations of the case method and hesitate to take on the responsibility for the analysis and for reaching a decision, a negative feeling will rise to the surface. The course, and the instructor himself, may be the targets for these. The instructor's role is to detect these feelings and encourage their free expression. Otherwise, he will lose control of the conditions under which the class can work effectively (Andrews 1954, pp. 102-103).

David Ulrich (1953, p. 28) emphasized the value of discussing the students' conflicting expectations by raising the appropriate questions. This helps the instructor impart a useful point of view toward the materials and develop a rapport with the class which will give the students the necessary group leadership and yet free them to progress toward the independent exercise of judgement.

At times, the discussion may move on to a consideration of current issues of an ethical nature for which there are no case materials. The instructor should be alert to these growing concerns and attempt to locate relevant case materials.

## THE LIMITATIONS OF THE CASE METHOD IN DEVELOPING MORAL UNDERSTANDING

I do not want to create the impression that a simple case-discussion course grafted onto a traditional curriculum will completely solve the problem of developing moral concern on the part of social scientists. Moral education is an integral and ongoing part of the whole educational process (cf. Appell 1976; Wright 1971).

Thus, if the staff-student relationship is one of mutual hostility or indifference, antisocial behavior is encouraged; where self-esteem is threatened, moral controls are weakened (Wright 1971, pp. 239-244). If the teacher does not provide the proper role model if in his teaching he overstresses the objectification of man, ignores the crucial issues that are affecting ethnic groups throughout the world, he contributes to moral anesthesia.

While universities can encourage the development of moral concern by offering courses in ethical decision making and by designing the social relations in their departments to prevent dehumanization, the ultimate locus of moral responsibility lies with the individual. He must be willing to become sensitized to the interests of others, in both the conduct of his anthropological inquiry and the use of its results. He must become aware of the ways in which his actions may jeopardize the interests of others and be willing to sacrifice his own interests if humanity can be better served by doing so.

Ethical behavior is also expressed by the individual in his willingness to develop the habit of the truth, which forms the foundations on which scientific inquiry is built (cf. Bronowski 1965). Truth creates trust, which is the mortar of all social relations. It is clear that the present social disorganization in American society derives from a breakdown in trust. There has been a similar erosion of trust and concern for others within the anthropological profession for many of the reasons I have already discussed.

Thus, for the members of a science that deals with human beings, personal gain must be subordinated to an overriding commitment to others and the habit of the truth must be cultivated in the extreme. This is so not only because of the potential harm that an individual scientist can do, and not only because he otherwise betrays his own profession. But also it is because the anthropologist is his own primary instrument of observation. He must depend on himself, and the training that he has received, to make clear and accurate observations and scientific conclusions. It follows that the anthropologist must refrain from any deceitful or insincere social interactions with anyone. He must be completely honest with himself and others, no matter where the interaction takes place or with whom. Otherwise he corrodes his most precious scientific instrument, himself, and undermines the precision of his observations. Those who are less than honest in their social relations out of the field are also likely to be dishonest in their research. The ultimate responsibility for ethical behavior thus lies with ourselves.

"Responsibility cannot be laid down according to any set principles but must be ever again recognized in the depths of the soul according to the demands of each concrete situation" (Maurice Friedman, quoted in Fletcher 1967, pp. 232-233).

## ORGANIZATION OF THE CASE MATERIALS

I have organized the cases which follow in terms of the primary social relationships involved during the pursuit of an inquiry. There are two exceptions. One section presents a set of miscellaneous case materials. These are cases that I found difficult to classify in terms of social relationships because of their complexities. The second exception is the section of cases dealing with the misuse of the results of social inquiry.

I have classified the cases in terms of social relationships rather than ethical issues because the latter are sometimes less clear-cut. They tend to mutate or shift in focus, dissolving around one facet and growing in importance around another which might be shared with a different ethical issue. The cases also frequently deal with more than one issue. In addition, I do not want to influence the discussion of these cases by indicating which issues I believe they focus on.

However if the instructor wishes to select case materials in terms of ethical issues, Appendix 1 presents some of the more important issues underlying social inquiry and lists cases relevant to each issue, as well as supplementary readings.

### THE DISGUISE OF CASE MATERIALS

The majority of cases in this book have been disguised in terms of ethnic group, geographic location, actors, and even the time at which the events recorded occurred. The reader should be aware of this and should refrain from trying to unveil the disguises, which can lead to embarrassing results. In one case-discussion session which I conducted, an anthropologist I had never met before demanded to know how I had secured his case. In disguising the case in question, I had placed the events in an area in which he had worked, although they had actually occurred in another hemisphere. The sequence of events was apparently so similar to his own experience in the field that he had assumed I was describing his field work.

Case materials have been disguised not solely because of sensitive topics but also to prevent the intrusion of extraneous comments that might impede the discussion of the cases, as, for example, gossip about investigators or remarks about the culture of the ethnic groups.

### ATTRIBUTION OF CASE MATERIALS

In certain instances, contributors of case materials have asked that their names not be associated with this book in any form because of the sensitive nature of their cases. In other instances, authors have asked that they be acknowledged as contributors in the introduction only. Finally, there were those who wished to have their authorship identified with the case; the names of these contributors are included at the bottom of the first page of each case.

### CONTRIBUTORS TO THIS VOLUME

Cases have been contributed by G.N. Appell, Norman D. Ashcraft, James L. Brain, Jean L. Briggs, Matthew Cooper, James Dow, Dorothy E. Finnegan, Richard Franke, Morris Freilich, James W. Green, Carl M. Gussin, Judith Huntsman, Grant D. Jones, William Kelly, David Kertzer, Richard A. King, Brian Lang, Nancy B. Leis, Louis Lieberman, Robert Manners, Elmer S. Miller, Denise O'Brien, Stephen Pastner, G. James Patterson, Anton Ploeg, Jérôme Rousseau, Clifford A. Sather. Michael Scullin, Kevan Simon, Jeffrey Smith, Federico S. Vidal, Sally M. Weaver, Herbert L. Whittier, and Patricia Whittier.

## NOTES

1. See Thatcher (1975) for some brief but interesting observations on the decline of academic morality.
2. My discussion of the case method is based on my own experience in using it as well as on information and viewpoints provided in the references which follow: Glover and Hower (1953), Ulrich (1953), Bailey (1953), Fox (1953), Ronken (1953), Fuller (1953), Andrews (1953, 1954), Dewing (1954), Gragg (1954), Merry (1954), Schoen and Sprague (1954), and McNair (1954).

## SECTION 1
## RELATIONS AND RESPONSIBILITIES TO HOST COMMUNITY

**INTRODUCTION**

Gaining acceptance from a strange community can be difficult for the field worker and always involves various psychic stresses (cf. Wintrob 1969). The investigator must first obtain permission for his research, then find a role that is both acceptable to the community and compatible with his research goals. Finally, he must establish a system of exchanges with his respondents and informants to obtain the types of information that he wants.

The field worker enters the community as a stranger. Nash (1963) has significantly dissected the nature of this role drawing attention to the observational biases that it tends to create. The expectations that the members of the host community bring to the encounter also can contribute to a distortion of the field worker's observation. Field work is frequently conducted in communities that are remote, or at least far removed from the centers of power. And the field worker is thus viewed as one means of access to power. This can produce a structure of social relations which has a corrupting influence on the field worker, as individuals in the host community endow the stranger with greater influence and power than he actually has. In *Heart of Darkness* Joseph Conrad describes the personality changes experienced by Kurtz as the result of his isolation in a remote village, and this illustrates the psychic forces which can sometimes shape the behavior of the field worker.

In conducting field work, the investigator's presentation of self varies according to the audience involved (cf. Berreman 1962; Goldner 1967; Hanna 1965). To his host community, he selectively begins to reveal himself and the goals of his research. Eventually, as the field-work role is clarified, the investigator underplays his role of stranger and becomes a participant observer in the life of his host community.[1]

However, the consequence of the participant-observer role is involvement in social relationships that run the whole gamut from enmity to friendship. In particular, the inevitable growth of friendships presents a major source of psychic stress, as these may conflict with the research goals.[2]

The participant-observer role is thus fraught with conflicts of interest, moral dilemmas, unexpected pitfalls, and emotional strains (cf. Jarvie 1969 and Kloos

1969 for a discussion of these conflicts). The case materials here illustrate many of these problems. Wolff (1964) provides an extremely sensitive analysis of what it means for the social scientist to "surrender" to the field situation and become involved with the community he studies.

Friendships sometimes are viewed primarily in instrumental terms. They can be used as one of the counters exchanged in the business of establishing a system of reciprocity to gain information. Other counters include offers of help and assistance, but each of these has its psychic costs, particularly when they are overaccepted.

The involvement that can result from participant observation and the need to establish a set of exchanges can also take unusual forms. The cases in this section illustrate these. The research of Elliot Liebow and Laud Humphreys is also instructive. Liebow (1967) writes that his acceptance into the community of Negro streetcorner men was facilitated by his activity on behalf of one of them during a court case. Humphreys (1970 a and 1970b), in his study of homosexual behavior in public places, acted as a lookout for the police during his observation of these activities.[3]

In the last few years, the normal set of exchanges associated with field work has come under attack from various sources. Some demand that the field worker should do more for the community he studies than was customary in the past, since he benefits from the information provided him in terms of professional prestige and advancement and financial rewards. The claim is that the balance in this exchange has shifted away from the community to the scholar with the development of heavily funded science, increased professorial salaries, and larger audiences.

One of the methods of righting this perceived imbalance, it is argued, is to communicate the results of research to the community (cf. Crocombe and Spate 1969). I discuss some of the inherent ethical dilemmas involved in this feedback in Appendix 1, along with a list of case materials that pertain to the problem.

It has also been claimed that the field worker can correct the perceived imbalance in exchanges between himself and the host community by direct involvement in changing the structure of power relations between the larger society and the host community, when the community is at a disadvantage.[4]

Whatever the case, it is quite clear that to the host community the field worker is also frequently viewed as a resource to exploit. Two interesting problems arise as a result. First, various factions within the community may demand commitment to their causes. Henry (1966) discusses this problem in her own field work, and several of the case materials presented in this section illustrate the problem.

Second, members of the community often hope that by cooperating with field workers they will somehow benefit. This approach of raising the hope of betterment in return for cooperation can be a cruel hoax when there is no change and when a community is inundated with researchers. Mrs. Peter Challen, a social worker in South London, has recounted to me the problems that arise from using this set of exchanges to obtain information (personal communication):

I suppose that some families will have been interviewed by students or social scientists involved in community development a half dozen times. Those bloody clipboards! They will take two hours of a family's time and raise their hopes that something will be done. And the families get pretty disillusioned. They have bared their lives so many times, but they continue to acquiesce because deep down they think they will get something out of it.

In my view, the significant question to pose in each field situation is: How much does the field worker give of himself to the host community in return for invading the privacy of the community members and piercing the public veil of behavior? For in doing so, he subjects his friends, informants, and respondents to the risk of retaliation or punishment by community members or government officials who find the information elicited offensive or against their interests.

## RELATED CASE MATERIALS IN OTHER SECTIONS

*Section Two: Relations and Responsibilities to Respondents and Informants:* The Ethical Problems of Doing Field Work in a Setting of Intense Sociopolitical Conflict, Disease and Death: Research in the Uguru District; Conflict in the Roles of Friend and Informant During the Feedback of Research Results; Dealing with Theft.

*Section Three: Relations with Host Government:* Political Ramifications of Field Work Among the Klee.

*Section Four: Relations with Representatives of Outside Agencies and the Public with Respect to the Host Community:* On the Horns of a Dilemma: A Problem of Intercession; Playing the Role of Intercultural Mediator; An Unwelcome Intrusion into the Host Community; How Far to Go in Deception; A Clash of Viewpoints; The Local Mission and Its Priest; The Trader and His Monopoly; Competition for Access to the Community.

*Section Five: Relations with Other Social Scientists and Responsibilities to the Profession:* Tensions in a Northern Community.

*Section Six: Dilemmas in the Use and Misuse of Social Science Knowledge:* The Inadvertant Feedback of Research Conclusions; Differential Access to the Results of Anthropological Inquiry: A Dilemma in Professional Responsibility.

*Section Seven: Publication: Responsibilities and Liabilities:* Problems in Urban Ethnic Research.

## NOTES

1. Additional materials on the nature of the role of participant observer can be found in Becker and Greer (1960), Gans (1968), Glazer (1972), Gold (1958), Golde (1970), Henry and Saberwal (1969), F. Kluckhohn (1940), Humphreys (1970a, 1970b), Mead (1969), Jacobs (1970), Liebow (1967), McCall and Simmons (1969), Miller (1952), Pehrson (1966) and Schwartz and Schwartz (1955).
2. See Appendix 1 for a list of case materials in this book relating to this problem. The extended accounts of field work listed in Appendix 2 also provide many examples. In particular see Powdermaker (1966) and the authors in Golde (1970) for a discussion of the problems involved in the development of friendships in the field.

3. For further discussions of the nature of reciprocity in field work see Glazer (1972), Golde (1970), Gusfield (1960), Hessler and New (1972), New and Hessler (1973), and Wax (1960 a, 1960b).
4. Cf. Hymes (1972), Jorgensen and Lee (1973), Berreman, et al. (1968); see Appell (1973a) for a discussion of the implications of this argument.

## 1.1 INVOLVEMENT IN A LOCAL DISPUTE

David Jones was studying the method of agriculture used by the Yala. He had spent almost two months making an extended tour of various regions to find the field site that would best suit his investigation. Finally he found a village that met his requirements. It was prosperous, and the villagers maintained their traditional customs, at least as far as he could determine from his brief visit. They carried on the type of hoe agriculture that he was most interested in. The district commissioner of the region had approved his choice of village in which to conduct field work. Now permission had to be obtained from the village headman.

Jones spent one whole day discussing his research plans with the headman. He was not entirely sure that his position was being communicated clearly and accurately, since the interpreter lent him by the district commissioner seemed rather indifferent to the task at hand. Nevertheless, the headman was interested in the possibility of earning some cash for organizing the building of Jones's field house. Finally, the headman gave his permission, and Jones went back to the district capital to organize his field equipment and check out final details with the district commissioner and agricultural officer.

On his return to the village, Jones moved into a vacant house to await completion of his field house. His relationships with the villagers seemed to go smoothly, and there was no hint of dissatisfaction with his plan to study their system of agriculture.

When the field house was almost ready, Jones went back to the district capital to collect the rest of the supplies he needed and arrange for regular mail service through a local shopkeeper. The day before his return to the village to move into his new house, he received a visit from the headman and several of the village elders. The headman was no longer sure that he wanted Jones to conduct research in his village. He was obviously uncomfortable with the arrangement. Finally, the real reason for his change of mind emerged.

In a neighboring area, native land had been purchased by a large corporation for a plantation. The village headman was now concerned that Jones was planning to acquire land in his village, which would have limited the amount of land available for the Yala to cultivate. Jones assured the headman that he had no intention of applying to the government for land for a plantation; that once his field work was over he would be returning to his own country. The headman was not entirely convinced by Jones's statement. The district commissioner had told Jones that he could not reside in the village unless the headman and his council of elders approved. To try and prove to the headman the sincerity of his statements, Jones offered to declare in writing that he was not planning to purchase any land from the government to start a plantation or for any other purpose.

The village headman and his council representatives seemed satisfied with this offer. But Jones was somewhat shaken. He had been mistaken in assuming that he would be openly accepted in the village.

When Jones returned to the village to begin his field work, he seemed to have no difficulty establishing informal contact with the villagers, although he still had not yet found any reliable informants. About a month later, he was back in the district capital to get additional supplies. As he walked down the main street, he ran into two men from his village, who looked somewhat disturbed. They told Jones through an interpreter, that they had come to the capital to register their land with the government in order to receive title to it, as was now required. They had to put a cash deposit down, which they had had difficulty raising. But when they had given their money to the head clerk, he had not given them any receipt. Apparently this was not the first time that this had happened. They asked Jones for help.

Jones was at first reluctant to become involved. He maintained that he did not know how these things worked, and he thought it was a simple misunderstanding that they could sort out on their own. But they persisted in asking that he try to resolve the matter. Finally, Jones said he would do what he could. He needed the continued support and help of the villagers to conduct his research. If he refused to respond to their request for help, he might jeopardize his position in the village.

Jones went to the district commissioner and explained the circumstances. He also said that he did not want to become publicly involved, as he was new in the country and unfamiliar with this kind of situation. The district commissioner apparently had some inkling that something was wrong in the land office, for he made sure that Jones's remarks could not be overheard by any of his clerks. He assured Jones that he would be protected and requested that Jones tell the two men from the village to be in his office the next morning at 9 a.m. Jones conveyed this message and then considered that he was no longer involved in the affair.

In helping the two men, he had indeed established much better relations with the villagers, enabling him to complete his research for his Ph.D. dissertation. He later heard that the clerk involved had received a prison sentence for his illegal activities; Jones felt that he deserved it.

Just before he left the field, Jones learned that the clerk who had been imprisoned was the brother of an important figure in the administrative hierarchy, who was also a well-known extortionist. Jones was concerned about this, since the brother had considerable power in the region and could make trouble for the Yala if he wanted to. About a year after he had returned home, Jones heard that the brother of the imprisoned clerk had become the new district commissioner, and he wondered if he had in fact done a service to the members of his village.

## 1.2--WHETHER TO INTERVENE IN INFANTICIDE

The Iba formerly practiced twin infanticide. Regardless of sex, both twins were either thrown into the river immediately after birth or were placed in fishing baskets and allowed to die of exposure in the bush. There were also restrictions imposed on the activities and social contacts of the mother until she delivered a single child, as well as on the father until at least one of his wives gave birth to a single child. However, with the arrival of the British and the missionaries, infanticide became illegal, and mothers of twins now frequently resort to the more subtle method of allowing their newborn offspring to die from lack of nourishment.

There appears to be no functional reason for twin infanticide in traditional Iba society. When questioned, the only reason the people give to justify this custom is that their ancestors did it. Twins are believed to be inhuman, and the mother of twins is thought to offend the deities of the water and forest until she gives birth to a single child. Nevertheless, the Iba do not cite these beliefs as the justification for twin infanticide; and there appears to be no cogent functional reason for continuing the practice other than it is what their ancestors did.

The nonfunctional aspects of this practice are underscored by the fact that the Ibo both like and want children; large families are highly valued, and there is no problem of overpopulation. Furthermore, there appears to be no satisfactory psychological function for this behavior, although the explanation might lie in the realm of the cognitive. Twins are anomalies, as are breech births and children who develop upper teeth first. Therefore, twins are killed because they are "dangerous."

The village in which I lived had a number of Chrstianized Iba. However nominal their conversion may have been, these people were adamantly opposed to twin infanticide. They defended those who gave birth to twins by promising to send for the police if the twins should die unnaturally. And they expressed a desire for twins themselves, not only as a means to a large family, but also so that they could prove twins were not bad. This attitude toward twin infanticide united the Christian Iba.

My field situation was complicated by the fact that I am a twin. I couldn't let anyone know this, not even the Christianized Iba in my village, for they might have told the rest of the village.

Toward the end of my stay, twins were born to a pagan Iba woman in my village. The people were obviously very upset by this event. About three quarters of of them believed the twins should be killed; but they knew it was illegal and therefore felt it was up to the mother to decide what she wanted to do. The villagers sat in groups and discussed the rationale behind the custom of twin infanticide. It was interesting to listen to the questions being brought up of "Why do we do it?" Someone suggested that it was impossible for a woman to nurse two children at the same time and that this was why twins must be killed.

Then one of the pagan priests suggested, "Why kill both? You could kill one and not the other, and then the woman can still have one child." The people couldn't find any reason not to do this, except that it was the custom to kill both twins and the local deities did not like women who gave birth to twins.

The mother of these newborn twins claimed that she would not kill them. But the Christians suspected that she might do so surreptitiously by not nursing them. Although they tried to check on her, it was impossible to be with the woman day and night to see whether she fed the twins.

I feared the outcome of these events, but I was reluctant to intervene. During my stay in the village, I had made no distinctions between pagan and Christian Iba. I had never interfered with their customs and had tried always to maintain an objective position as an anthropologist. But this case was different. I couldn't do much, but I did go to the mother's hut and visit with her. And I held the babies, one of whom looked very sick. They touched me closely, being a twin myself and knowing what was probably going to happen to them. I didn't try to reason with the mother or argue with her. Instead, I just tried to show that I wasn't afraid of her because she had given birth to twins, nor was I afraid of the twins.

I left the village a couple of weeks later, and I suspect that the babies died.

## 1.3 – THE EFFICACY OF FAITH HEALING

### PART ONE

The Toba Indians have developed their own grass-roots, revivalistic religion. Many aspects of it are Pentecostal in origin, including speaking in tongues and certain group aspects of their church services. The Toba believe that illness can be cured by faith healing, which also occurs in church. During my first visit with the Toba, they seldom went to the clinic for medical help.

My first experience with Toba faith healing occurred after I had been in the field about six weeks. I had attended a local church service—which is the main activity in any Toba community, providing the arena where much of the social action takes place. After the service, several participants approached me and asked if I would accompany them to the home of an elderly member of the community who was dying.

The old man lay in a typical Toba house, constructed of mud walls with a grass roof. It offered little protection against the cold, damp air or the strong wind sweeping across the southern plains. Outside there was a light rain. I later learned that a doctor at the local clinic had diagnosed the old man's illness as an advanced case of tuberculosis. The doctor was surprised that the man had survived as long as he had. He had not been given any treatment because the doctor felt he was too far gone. The clinic staff also felt that if they gave the old man medication and he died the Indians would blame the medication and refuse further treatment.

The friends of the dying man brought him out into the rain so that we could all pray for him. We laid our hands on the man—this is part of the faith healing ceremony—and we all prayed. This lasted for fifteen or twenty minutes, if not more.

And the longer it continued, the more disturbed I became over seeing this old man subjected to the cold, damp air. He was emaciated and was coughing up a great deal of phlegm. He looked very close to death.

After the prayers, the old man and the others looked at me, and the local leader asked the man, "Are you healed?" Usually the response in such ceremonies is either a "yes" or a "no." If it is "yes," they stop praying; if it is "no," they pray again. But this time the old man simply looked at me and it was clear that I was expected to say something.

I asked him, "Have you eaten recently?"

---

Contributed by Dr. Elmer S. Miller, Temple University.

He replied, "I haven't eaten in a week."

"Why don't you take something to eat?"

"I can't eat anything."

"What about soup? What about broth?"

"I don't have any. I don't have any chickens. I don't have any food at the moment except some wild beans."

So I suggested that we take up a collection and contributed ten pesos to start it off. We collected twenty pesos in all, which was used to buy the old man a chicken.

I left the community the next day. When I returned for a visit about four months later, I saw the old man attending the local church services. He was clearly healthy and active, and he claimed that I had cured him. A few years later I made a third visit to the community. The old man was still there, still saying that I had healed him.

I didn't know quite how to respond to this. The news had traveled around that I had healed the man. When people commented on it I would not reply. What could I say?

## PART TWO

Several years later I was visiting a remote area by jeep with one of the local leaders. The road was very rough, and we had to ford a number of streams and rivers. Finally, we arrived at a house where a woman lay in severe pain. Her side was swollen, and she was feverish and perspiring heavily. She appeared to have all the symptoms of appendicitis. The only thing she wanted me to do was to take her to the local church service about seven or eight miles away. As the trip involved some rough terrain, I was reluctant to move her. I was afraid that the bouncing of the jeep might cause further damage, or even death. I was not afraid that I would be blamed if she were to die en route, but I was unsure how to handle such a situation. So, instead, I offered to take the jeep and bring back a local doctor. But no one considered this alternative. I finally realized that the only thing I could do was to acquiesce to her request.

The local church service began at eight that evening. These services can take a long time—the good ones lasting five or six hours. This particular service took about four and a half hours, and a great deal of time was spent talking about faith healing and the healing powers of prayer and the gospel. There were a number of local leaders at the service, and they prayed for the woman throughout the service. At least one hour was spent laying hands on the woman while praying.

At first, she was moaning from the pain. But toward the end of the ceremony she began to calm down and seemed to be more comfortable; she claimed that she was somewhat relieved. After the ceremony was over, the others asked her if she was healed, and she said she was. Then they asked me, and I suggested that now that she was healed we could take her to a local doctor just to check her over. But they disagreed, saying that if she was healed, why should she go to a doctor? And so I drove her back home.

I did not expect that the woman would survive. However, about six months later, when I returned to the community, I found her alive and healthy.

## 1.4–PROVIDING A STORAGE PLACE FOR WEAPONS

While I was in the field, I purchased weapons for a museum in the United States. I bought bows and arrows, spears, and anything else the people would sell me. One reason that they were anxious to sell their weapons was that about a year before at the instigation of the missionaries they had burned many of their weapons. This seemed a more profitable way of disposing of them. After I had been in the field about five or six months, there was another weapon burning, inspired by the missionaries, in the hope that this would cause an influenza epidemic to go away.

I also stored weapons in my hut. For the most part, the owners were politically important men who were friends of mine as well as good informants. They wanted the missionaries to think they had burned their weapons and were intent on becoming peace-loving Christians. Thus, they did not want to have spears and bows and arrows in their huts, where the missionaries could see them. On the other hand, these men wanted their weapons available in case they were needed in a hurry. So they would thrust them into the thatch of my house, knowing I would not tell the missionaries that they were stored there. On occasion these men would come to my house and say that they had to have their spears to chase a witch or because there was going to be a fight that night. In some cases, they simply retrieved their weapons from the thatch of my house. However, if the weapons were stored inside, I would let them in, and they would take their spears and then bring them back the next morning, saying, "We don't need them. Can we leave them with you again for a while?" Thus, these weapons were never my property; I was simply storing them for the owners.

There were often wars in neighboring valleys, although usually not in the valley where I lived. Sometimes when a war was being fought, people would say to me, "We are going to watch the fighting. Maybe we will get involved and maybe we won't; but we want to have our weapons with us. We have burned all our weapons or sold them to you, and we cannot go and watch the fighting without weapons. So would you please loan us the weapons that you bought from us or would you sell them back to us?" In all these cases, I refused to loan or sell them their weapons.

## 1.5 – USING A DISGUISED ROLE

I was studying Hassidic Jews to see to what extent their conscious attempts at cultural persistence were working. They were trying to recreate the Eastern European *shtetl* community in America and were going about it in a very methodical way. They had bought a tract of land and all the houses on it so that nobody would be allowed into the community who didn't follow the old traditions and the cultural rules set forth by the *Rebbe,* the leader of the community. I thought this was a very interesting situation. Here were a group of people who understood their culture, felt it was valuable, and tried to establish an environment to protect and prolong their cultural tradition.

After receiving a grant to do my research, and having found a place to live not too far from the community, I discovered that these people were having trouble getting incorporated as a village. They wanted legal incorporation so that they would have control over local affairs. By the time I came to study them they were tired of all the publicity their struggle had received, and they didn't want any strangers around.

So I went to some people who knew them very well and said to one of them, "What do you think would happen if I went to the leader of the community and said, 'Look, I want to study the way of life of the *shtetl* in America, and I would like to stay around here for a summer or two and write about your thoughts and ideas and behaviors and so on'?"

He said that he believed the leader would definitely throw me out if I did this.

So my problem was this: Should I ask the leader and risk his refusal? Or should I simply hang around without asking him?

After thinking about it for a long time, I realized I just didn't want to take the chance of being asked to leave. I had too much time and money invested in this project. I had spent a lot of time writing up a grant proposal and thinking out the theoretical issues involved and the kinds of ideas raised. It was just too much work to throw away.

So I started going to the religious services three times a day, since anyone can come into the temple. When people asked me what I was doing there, I answered that, as a Jew, I was interested in the Hassidic movement and in the *Rebbe.* Since this was a resort area not far from the city where I taught, I also said, "Well, I have the summer off; I teach during the year. And this is a nice area."

However, what I really ended up doing was giving them the impression that I might want to join their community. This particular sect of Hassidim didn't try to make converts, but of course they would have been very happy if someone decided to join them. I implied that if I could really decide that their way of life was right for me, and if I could get a job in the area, I would probably settle there. This wasn't too far from the truth. I was very interested in the sect, and I thought if I could get a job, I could do a long-range study of the community.

This approach to field work is very difficult, not only for moral reasons but for pragmatic ones. One of the most valuable field techniques is to get people actively involved with your work. When they know what you're trying to do, they'll come and give you leads about interesting things going on in the community. You can hire people as special informants, and sometimes find somebody to be a full-time assistant. You can do questionnaire work from house to house. You can do a lot of things freely, such as taking notes in front of people. But when you've disguised your identity, you also have to disguise your field work activities.

By the end of the first summer, I was sure that if I had told the *Rebbe* who I was, he would have let me study the community. The people knew me; they knew I wasn't any bother, and I seemed like a nice guy. I gave them rides into the city, and if they needed some help here or there, I was always available. But by that time, I was too embarrassed about it to ask the *Rebbe*. I just didn't feel like going up and telling him that I had come there under false pretenses, that I was really an anthropologist. I didn't have the guts to go through with it.

So I came back the second summer. I had a lot more work to do, and I figured I wasn't doing anybody any harm there, so there was no reason why I shouldn't carry on. And it's true—I didn't do anybody any harm, but it was still a difficult situation. Maybe one of the reasons that this research hasn't been fully published is that I still feel kind of funny about my role in the community, and I don't know exactly what to do about it.

But the funny thing is, as I was getting ready to leave at the end of the second summer, one guy I was friendly with said, "I never could quite understand what you do for a living."

And I said, "Well, I teach in a university."

"What do you teach?"

"Well," I said, "you really wouldn't understand, I don't think."

"Tell me about it," he replied.

"I study people in different parts of the world; how they live, their histories, their traditions."

"Oh," he said, "you're an anthropologist. Well, I tell you, I have a great place for you to study."

"Yes?" I asked, "Where is it?"

"Here, right here!"

## 1.6 – IMPOSITION OF THE ANTHROPOLOGIST ON THE COMMUNITY

During the seventeen months that I lived in a nomadic Eskimo camp of about thirty people, I discovered how many difficulties the presence of a foreigner—such as an anthropologist—can create in a tiny group of people. The outsider is always underfoot and can never be ignored.

Although in my case relations were often pleasant, there was one period of three months when things reached such a pass that I was ostracized. Three years after leaving this group, I wanted to return for eight months to gather additional data on the subject I had been studying and to do more intensive linguistic work. But after my first experience, I had become convinced that an anthropologist has no right to impose himself on people who find him uncongenial, even if they allow him to come. I knew that it would be difficult for the Eskimo to refuse my request to return; both courtesy and fear of the powerful white man urge compliance with almost any request made by a white person, and I hesitated to make a request that they might not feel free to refuse. Furthermore, I was not at all sure of their current feelings about me.

I had several conflicting memories of the Eskimo's attitude toward me. As I was leaving, my adoptive parents asked whether I planned to come back again. I said I might, and asked how they would feel if I did. The misunderstanding that had led to my original ostracism had long since been repaired, and my "father" had told me that he considered me a member of his family again. Nevertheless, when I raised the question, he looked as if he thought my return would be a very poor idea—until my "mother" assured him I didn't mean right away. Thereupon his face cleared, and he said he was sure somebody would adopt me, if not he himself, then one of the other men—he named a man he disliked. My "parents" said further that they would prefer to have a woman come rather than a man, because women are weak and therefore not a threat to the Eskimo.

Then there was the evening I spent camped on the sea ice route to the community where I was to take leave of the Eskimo. I had just told the four men who accompanied me what I was planning to pay them for transporting my gear to this community. One of the men said, "It will be all right if you come again, because you are kind; only next time don't bring any gear except a tea kettle and, if you are very rich, some cigarettes."

---

Contributed by Dr. Jean L. Briggs, Memorial University of Newfoundland.

On one occasion I overheard my "mother" telling a neighbor that they would not be sad when I left. But there were also the letters I received from my Eskimo parents after I had left. They said, "We didn't think we'd miss you, but we did.

To resolve my problem, I decided to go to the nearest community, 150 miles from my original field location, where I would find relatives of the people I had originally lived with. Since these people spoke the same dialect, I could gather reasonably adequate data from them. However, when I arrived at this community, I discovered that my former "parents" were temporarily living there. They treated me in the most friendly manner and readopted me. Rumor also reached me that they had said it would be a pity if I did not accompany them when they went back to their nomadic life. So I asked whether I might go with them, and, of course, they said yes.

The outcome was a cheerful one. After I had been with them for a month or so, my "father" asked me whether I was happier with them than I had been before. I said that I was. He replied, "So are we." On several occasions, my "mother" told me that my company was pleasanter than it had been before and that this time they didn't mind teaching me.

## RELATED READINGS

Briggs Jean L. 1970a. *Never in anger: portrait of an Eskimo family*. Cambridge: Harvard University Press.

———. 1970b Kapluna daughter. In *Women in the field: anthropological experiences,* ed. Peggy Golde. Chicago: Aldine.

## 1.7—FIREARMS IN THE FIELD

When I went to live with the Limpo I took with me a pistol that somebody in my family thought I, as a woman alone in the field, should have for protection. Another reason I had a pistol was that the government of the country insisted that I have some sort of firearm, and if I hadn't arrived in the country with it, they would have insisted that I buy one. Actually, it was not very efficient—just a little .32 caliber handgun. And I was not a particularly good marksman, even though I had learned to use guns as a child growing up in the country. But a shotgun would have been more useful if I was really going to need a gun for any reason.

The Limpo liked my pistol. It was a novelty to them since they hadn't seen very many guns. They were always getting me to come and kill their pigs with it. Also, the gun proved useful when I was going on a trek. The Limpo were sometimes unwilling to trek long distances because they were afraid to cross warfare boundaries. If I wanted to get people to go with me as guides or carriers, they would only go if I took the gun with me. Although I had no intention of ever using it, it nevertheless reassured them if we were going into strange country. So the only time I ever used it in the field was for shooting pigs, carrying it into strange country, and when Tinani went amok.

Tinani's first contact with Europeans had been a traumatic encounter. When he broke his arm, the missionaries sent him out to the coast by airplane for treatment and, partly because he was so terrified, he went berserk. He couldn't understand where he was being sent or why, and there was no one with whom he could talk. The pilot, who didn't know what to do with him, tied him up and left him in a shed at the airstrip to await the doctor's arrival.

Tinani later became a guide for some European explorers, traveling much more extensively than the average inhabitant of the valley in which I worked. One day, after having been away for a year or so, Tinani returned to the valley with two of these explorers. Because of his position as a guide to Europeans, he thought he was a big man, and he wanted to celebrate. He gave several large feasts for the people there, and hundreds of people were constantly crowding around the house where he was staying.

One day some equipment at the mission station was stolen. The missionaries thought that Tinani had perhaps taken the equipment. But it was never really settled, because Tinani suddenly came running across the station grounds acting in a crazy fashion which followed the approved Limpo manner. The missionaries tried to calm him down—first verbally and then with drugs. They gave him a couple of shots of morphine, and he gradually quieted down and fell asleep. They gave me some morphine tablets in case he should act up again.

During one period in the next couple of days I gave him about six of these morphine tablets, and they seemed to have no permanent effect on his behavior. He ranted and raved and carried on in the expected pattern for those whom the Limpo class as crazy. During this period he tried to come into my house where, he said, I had weapons that belonged to him. I had stored a number of spears and clubs belonging to the local Limpo, who wanted to convince the missionaries that they had given up warfare. Tinani was sure that some of these belonged to him. For almost a week he tried to get into my house; on one occasion he became very violent.

At about this time, the European explorers left the country, which upset Tinani very much. He went berserk as the airplane took off. There were times the Limpo tried to restrain him. However, they are afraid of people who act as Tinani did, and do not actively attempt to restrain such individuals unless it appears that they are going to kill someone.

Finally, one Sunday morning the situation with Tinani came to a head. A number of people were standing outside my house, while I was inside doing some work. Suddenly, I heard them shout that Tinani had arrived to burn down my house. I went out, and Tinani was just getting the torch from my cook house, which was about twenty yards away. He turned and was coming down the hill toward my house with this flaming torch in his hand. I shouted at him to stop, but it didn't seem to do any good. So I went back into my house and got my pistol from under the bed. I went out with it in my hand, intending to shoot in the air over Tinani's head to scare him. But, unfortunately, Tinani was probably the one Limpo who was familiar with guns, due to his travels with the European explorers. I fired one shot in the air. Instead of running away, Tinani dropped the torch, moved toward me, and tried to grab the gun. Fortunately, I was able to get the safety on so it would not fire as we struggled for it. Some other Limpo came running up and pulled him off me, and as they did so I dropped the gun. One of the Limpo picked it up and gave it back to me, and I ran into the house with it. Tinani picked up the torch, relit it, and again approached my house. I grabbed a big stick and charged him with it. This proved to be effective, for he ran off down the path while I hit at him with the stick.

Tinani never made another attempt to burn my house, although he did burn down a Limpo house in another village. But the Limpo did not really care; they are not as personally involved with their houses as I was. In the end, I was very sorry that I had threatened him with the gun; it was a foolish and dangerous thing to have done. I am just lucky that nothing serious happened as a result.

# 1.8 – HOW DOES A FOREIGN RESEARCHER INTERFERE TO STOP ILLEGAL ACTIVITIES

While I was working as a member of a research team on an African settlement scheme, a difficult problem arose. An international agency was supplying the settlers with rations, so that they could survive the first year before a harvest was obtained. It soon became obvious that these rations were ending up outside the settlement. At first I suspected that the settlers were selling them and using their own food from the previous year; but later it became evident that the food was being sold in quantity by members of the administrative staff. It was never clear whether the manager took an active part in these transactions or merely looked the other way as they occurred. But there was no doubt that his accountant was directly involved in the black market.

My feeling at first was that this was their country and it was not part of my role to interfere. However, I was finally approached one evening by a deputation of settlers who had either been told there were no rations or had been abused by the accountant. They begged me to do something.

I was planning to go to the capital the next day. When I arrived, I consulted with the coordinator of the research team. Following his suggestion, I went to see one of the senior African staff in the ministry and told him what was going on. Rather than cause a scandal which might implicate the manager, the ministry summoned the accountant to the capital, ostensibly to attend a training course. He was reprimanded and transferred to another settlement scheme. This put an end to the black market.

---

Contributed by Dr. James L. Brain, State University of New York College, New Paltz.

## 1.9 – TO TAKE A WIFE

Shortly after arriving at Budo, Leigh Foster was invited to stay with the village headman. The headman's house, like most others in the village, consisted of a simple veranda, a small section where the hearth was located, and a large, unpartitioned, central room where the family ate and slept. The household consisted of the headman, his wife, their unmarried children, and the headman's married daughters along with their husbands and children. Each of the conjugal families had a section against the wall where they slept at night. This uxorilocal extended family participated in a common household economy and ate together from the food prepared at the hearth. Leigh, along with the others, slept in this unpartitioned central room and contributed to the household economy by paying the headman each week for his board.

Foster's research seemed to be going well, and he was developing friendly relationships in the village, although the community thought it odd that a man of his age had no wife. Finally, the headman's wife and the mother of Foster's field assistant offered to find Foster a "wife" to tend to his domestic needs while he continued his research. The headman and his wife made it perfectly clear that they did not expect Foster to have any responsibility for the girl once he had left the village. The marriage could be annulled provided he paid an adequate compensation to tide the girl over until she could find another husband.

Foster refused this offer, although he did find the girls in the village attractive. Later on during his research, he learned that this sort of relationship was not unknown in Budo. When the country had been under colonial rule, European government personnel had sometimes made such arrangements with local village girls; indeed, a former magistrate had taken one of the headman's daughters as his "wife." Furthermore, the villagers welcomed these arrangements because of the potential offspring of such couples. Light-skinned individuals were considered attractive and accorded high status.

After Foster had been in the village about six months, the headman's wife again offered to find him an acceptable wife. Foster was in a quandary. Certainly such a relationship would help him in his field work, not only by freeing him of certain chores but also by enabling him to become more intimately acquainted with village marriage customs. However, he had an understanding with a girl at home whom he planned to marry. On the other hand, the villagers considered his unmarried status as unnatural and this offer was genuine and fully acceptable according to their own standards. Moreover, a girl frequently mentioned, and teasingly referred to as "his wife," had made him a sleeping garment and performed other tasks generally associated with a wifely status. Certainly, he would never have to mention this relationship to anyone, or mention it in his field notes; probably no one outside of Budo would ever know. Yet, he did not quite know how to answer the headman's offer.

# 1.10 – A PROBLEM OF POLITICAL IDENTIFICATION AND CO-OPTION

My research on processes of cultural-ecological change in a circum-Caribbean colony led to far more problems of political identification and co-option than I had anticipated. What I had first regarded as a straightforward investigation into the effects of a new cash crop on traditional subsistence patterns became a complex analysis of local and national political networks, the structure of political decision-making, and regional factional conflicts. I found it impossible to remain aloof from these political processes, as my position as outside investigator became in itself a potential political tool for a number of parties. This situation proved to be a difficult one to handle successfully while in the field. Moreover, my contacts with the country have continued since leaving the field, and I find that these problems are by no means resolved or eliminated.

## BACKGROUND

The administrative district in which I was working, which I shall refer to as "Cocal," had been settled about a century earlier by mestizo and Indian immigrants escaping social disturbances in an adjacent republic. These immigrants brought with them an agricultural economy and a Latin American culture and social system. As a result, the region developed a mixed economy of sugar-cane haciendas and subsistence agriculture.

The Indians served pricipally as laborers on the sugar-cane haciendas; but they also practiced part-time, shifting cultivation. Thus, they did not constitute a satisfactory full-time labor force. Local investors had established a central sugar factory in 1935, and independent Indian sugar-cane producers began to rival the entrenched mestizos. During the 1950's, the factory was sold to foreign interests, and a plantation-factory combine began to develop.

When I arrived in the country, the government had launched a massive program to increase sugar production, which was primarily focused on the Cocal region. The government anticipated and publicized a problem of continued expansion.

By the late 1960's, remarkable changes had occurred in the society of Cocal. There were about one thousand independent sugar-cane producers, most of whom produced on a very small scale. These small producers remained partially dependent upon subsistence cultivation. There were also several independent large-scale cane producers. About one-third of the cane delivered to the central factory was produced by an international corporation that had recently bought out the entire plantation-factory combine. Finally, a new factory had been built in the district to the south of Cocal in accordance with government plans to expand the sugar industry. This factory was deeply resented by cane producers in Cocal, especially when it became apparent that they would not be allowed to deliver their cane to the new factory. They felt that there was sufficient production potential for another factory in Cocal itself; as it was, further expansion in Cocal was now virtually blocked.

My original intention was to study the impact of the rapid growth of both large and small sugar-cane production on the traditional cultural ecology of shifting subsistence cultivation. The crucial issue was the future survival of peasant cane producers in the face of plantation growth and government policy which had contributed to a condition of ecological inviability. Plantation growth encouraged by the government had resulted in a land shortage while encouraging only seasonal employment. Sugar-cane production, also encouraged by the government, created a land shortage for shifting cultivation, resulting in a severe decrease in food production without providing a sufficient cash income to offset this.

It soon became clear to me that the reasons for the ecological changes which I was documenting had to be sought, at least in part, in the processes of political development and decision making that underlay this changing economic picture. It was for this reason that I began to immerse myself in the recent political history of Cocal. In so doing, I discovered that I had unwittingly become a part of that political process and that I had to face the responsibilities of my self-imposed involvement.

There was open political conflict within the association of cane producers, among rural political leaders, between foreign factory-plantation interests and various local sectors, and so on. There were numerous mass demonstrations, political rallies for cane farmers, and opposing delegations to the capital city with petitions for the premier and ministers of government. Foremost among these conflicts were the very issues that I was concerned with: shrinking lands for subsistence cultivation, underemployment of a rapidly proletarianizing rural population, accusations of favoritism in the distribution of cane delivery quotas and agricultural loans among small cane producers, and accusations of political self-enrichment on the part of some of those who administered the development.

## THE PROBLEM OF POLITICAL CO-OPTION

My wife and I had chosen to live in Cocal Town, the administrative seat of the district. The town's population of some six thousand had once been primarily mestizo in composition, but the rapid growth of the sugar industry had brought with it a large number of people from other parts of the country. As a result, Cocal Town had become one of the more ethnically cosmopolitan settlements in the colony. In view of the broad scope of my research, the central location of the town in such a small district, and the availability of documents and government personnel, a rented house in the town seemed the ideal living solution for us. Our house was extremely modest by the standards of the town; our only luxury was a jeep, which was essential for investigating the rural areas of the district.

## 1.10 – A Problem of Political Identification and Co-option

My first months in Cocal Town were spent in relative ignorance of the political dynamics that surrounded me. The situation was remarkably complex, and informants seldom presented me with consistent accounts. Even in reply to what I thought were the most straightforward questions of fact, I often received defensive, evasive replies. As time went on, I discovered that certain individuals had been lying to me. It appeared that the more deeply a person was involved in the political structure of the industry, the less likely he was to present me with an honest portrayal of activities. Those who did not distort reality simply evaded it, or they phrased it so cryptically as to render it meaningless to an outsider.

There appeared to be only one way out of this maze. I began to search for recent documents dealing with the development of small-scale production. I reasoned that official records and correspondence would at least offer a clearer, if not totally reliable, record of recent events. For reasons still unclear to me, I was given access to certain files of official correspondence and to large amounts of private correspondence. In addition, I read virtually every newspaper and local newsletter published over the past ten years.

Rather suddenly, the pieces began to fall together. I began to understand the political processes which my interviews with informants had so completely failed to penetrate. Most important, I could begin to explain the conflicting evidence (and often the rationale behind it) that I had been receiving. I sympathized with the Indians and other small producers; for they were victims of a political and economic situation far beyond their control, and the large-scale interests were devoted to maintaining their secondary status.

My new knowledge and understanding had unforeseen results. I discovered that I could now discuss current political issues with a certain degree of expertise that was reinforced by "inside" knowledge. No longer the ignorant questioner, I became an active discussant. I found welcome opportunities to air my own developing political analyses with the parties concerned. Although I carefully avoided taking a stand, I soon found myself surrounded by parties anxious to either co-opt me or to identify me politically with their enemies. To some I was an outside expert— potentially dangerous perhaps, but also potentially useful if the results of my study should be published. To others I became, to a degree, a political scapegoat; they questioned both my associations and my political motives.

I was visited frequently by individuals of all factions. I often entertained rural Indians, some of whom expected me to use my "influence" to obtain larger cane delivery licenses. I also associated with plantation personnel, large farmers, and civil servants in the Agricultural Department. It would be somewhat of an exaggeration to say that each of these parties wanted to "use" me by influencing the final outcome of my study. However, it was clear that some did have such ends in mind. Thus, while investigating a politically sensitive subject, my own role became politically sensitive as well. I tried to avoid major confrontations by maintaining a close relationship with as many opposing parties as possible, but this was a difficult task which resulted in a severe emotional strain.

Several examples will serve to demonstrate the uncomfortable situation in which I found myself.

**Example One.** One day I was visited at home by a delegation of small cane producers. The village which they represented boasted some of the district's largest cane producers. However, a recent government-guaranteed loan had enabled many subsistence producers and agricultural laborers in this village and in others to begin their own cane production.

The leader of the delegation asked me to support publicly the small farmers' ongoing fight for a larger share of the production quota. They felt that I held considerable influence with government officials as an outside expert. Given my obvious concern for the small producer (I had visited nearly three hundred peasant households by that time), they assumed I would be willing to represent their interests to public officials. I admitted to being sympathetic with the plight of Cocal's small producers but emphasized that I possessed no political influence. In addition, I stressed that taking such a political stand would interfere with my research.

The visitors were clearly disillusioned and somewhat annoyed with my reply. All that I could do was to indicate that my future publications might serve as political stimuli. This did not satisfy the delegation, however; they were obviously concerned with immediate problems and solutions. Because of this encounter, my relationships with the small farmers of that village were strained throughout the rest of my stay.

**Example Two.** Guillermo Williams was one of the largest cane producers in the district. On several occasions I had sought him out as an informant. Subsequently, he paid several visits to my house. At the time, he was an elected leader in the association of cane farmers and was leading a battle against delivering an extra amount of cane for increased production quotas that season. His stand made good economic sense, at least to the extent that the extra production might have reduced the final prices paid for sugar cane. However, many small producers and their supporters favored the increase on the grounds that it might ultimately result in larger delivery quotas for all small cane producers.

Williams sought my support in his fight. He knew that I had discussed the issue with numerous small producers and suspected me of openly opposing his position. I assured him that my public position was neutral and that it was necessary that I remain uninvolved in such issues. At that point, I had made no public statements indicating bias toward any parties in the dispute. My increasing association with radical leaders among small producers, however, had led Guillermo—a large producer—to assume that I opposed his conservative stance.

Ironically, this situation was partially resolved when Williams and one of the radical leaders of the small producers joined forces in response to another issue. The new conflict involved an attempt by a recently deposed leader in the association of cane farmers to make a political comeback with the support of the district's small cane producers. Williams and the radical leader, opposed on virtually every other issue, issued a joint attack on their mutual enemy. It may well have been such complex overlapping of Cocal's political arenas that made it possible for me to continue to operate in spite of the strains placed on my social identity.

**Example Three.** I had been entertained on numerous occasions during the first half of our year in Cocal by professional personnel from the factory-plantation combine. These were mostly elite townspeople who apparently viewed my acquaintance as a significant status factor. Not surprisingly, nearly all of them strongly supported the plantation and the large producers. In many cases, they viewed the small rural producers with disdain; any political action designed to improve the economic situation of the small producers was seen as a threat to large-scale production. They were extremely suspicious of supposed Communist influences among the rural people.

As my contact with the small producers increased, and my open discussion with all parties became more coherent and outspoken, my relationship with this important urban sector rapidly began to deteriorate. My contact with them decreased considerably (except for one family), and my social position in the town became more tenuous.

This situation was made even more difficult by my increased contact with Juan Cob, an important Indian peasant leader in an adjacent village. He had been a favorite of the national government during the period of rapid expansion of small sugar-cane holdings. He had been an elected legislator and rural labor leader until his position became too radical to be supported by a government trying to accommodate a plantation economy. Thus had begun a bitter political dispute that was by no means over following his defeat by a government-supported candidate in a primary election.

My contacts with Juan Cob, who became an indispensable informant, caused great concern among my Cocal informants and acquaintances. Many people who considered him to be an extremely dangerous radical, possibly a Communist, warned me to be careful. Some were beginning to suspect my motives. My interests were becoming increasingly unacceptable politically as the emphasis of my research focused more clearly on the political and economic factors that had led to what I regarded as an ecological crisis among small cane producers. My contention that Cob provided me with valuable, objective information by means of which I could evaluate and revise my analysis had little effect in dampening suspicions that I was myself a potentially dangerous radical.

A further action on my part undermined my relationship with Cocal's "establishment." It was my open opposition to the racist behavior of the elite. We were invited to several all-white gatherings. Following these, I made it clearer that I felt that my participation in such affairs conflicted with my relationship with other groups.

**Example Four.** I discovered one of my first political informants, Pablo Lopez, had been less than candid in our early conversations. He played an important role in the association of cane farmers from its inception, and was a favorite among many small cane producers. However, it later became apparent that he had been involved in dishonest electioneering and generally questionable activities in the association.

My position was simply an embarrassing one in this case. I had put considerable trust in his initial overtures and he was now aware of my increased wisdom. I was not anxious to become associated with his activities, especially as he was attempting to make a political comeback during our stay in Cocal. My solution was to avoid extensive contact with Lopez for the remainder of the research period.

This situation produced some extremely unpleasant side effects, one of which I shall mention here. I had been working intensively with Mateo Rivero, an informant from Juan Cob's village. Rivero had formerly worked as a field foreman for Lopez, himself a sizeable cane farmer; but he professed to be at complete odds with Lopez's political activities. In fact, he openly supported the radical politics of Juan Cob, who had recently issued a manifesto demanding redistribution of all cane delivery quotas. Rivero suddenly shifted his support to Lopez, who was trying to regain control of the cane farmer's association. The plan was to place Rivero at the head of the association's elected management committee and to reinstate Lopez as appointed administrative manager of the association.

Rivero was well aware of my strained relationship with Lopez and the reasons behind it. He attempted to justify his actions by claiming that his eventual plan was to rid the association entirely of Lopez's control and to establish himself as the champion of the small producers' cause. As a bizarre climax to this episode, Rivero, obviously drunk, paid me a visit, while I was suffering from an acute attack of malaria. In a teary confession, he professed to be torn with feelings of guilt about the whole affair and expressed the hope that we were still friends. As it was, he and his supporters lost decisively in the ensuing election for representatives to the association. Rivero and I seldom saw one another after his visit.

**Example Five.** About a month before I left the country, I moved to the capital city in order to carry out archival research on the early history of Cocal. I was somewhat surprised to discover that my field work had already generated considerable interest in certain circles in the city. Economic and political events in Cocal regularly made national news, especially since factional delegations from Cocal frequently visited government officials in the capital.

During my stay in the capital, it became widely known that the implications of my research findings were not at all complimentary to recent government involvement in the economic development of the Cocal region. Actually, I had said very little –and only in response to questions posed to me. What I had said was that sugar-cane cultivation among small producers had, for the most part, failed to offest the losses they subsequently suffered in subsistence production; and lack of consistent government support of small-scale production could only serve to worsen the already poor economic situation in rural Cocal. The implications of this conclusion, of course, were that I viewed the government's vocal "support" of small-scale farming solely as vote-getting politics in the face of a policy that actually supported the factory-plantation combine.

Sometime after my arrival I was asked to grant an interview to a reporter from a newspaper which was mildly critical of the government and strongly supportive of local business. Reluctantly, I agreed. What I told the interviewer was so dry, technical, and complex that I had to grant a second lengthy interview in order to clarify my analysis. The article made the front page with large headlines to the effect that I predicted a major economic disaster for the Cocal region. This was an exaggeration of my position, but the article was otherwise reasonably accurate.

Following publication of the newspaper article, I was asked to give a lecture concerning my research to a group of young people who met regularly to discuss issues of national concern. These meetings were widely known to foster points of view opposed to the government. However, since they received the moral sanction of the local campus of a regional university, I felt justified in presenting a lecture given from the point of view of an anthropologist concerned objectively with the processes of development. Again, the subject matter was relatively dry and technical; I avoided any direct criticism of government policy. However, the ensuing discussion focused on the implications of my research findings for future policy. The several civil servants who attended the lecture sat in stony-faced silence. Even worse, Pablo Lopez, now at odds with the government, attended the lecture and enthusiastically supported my conclusions, pointing out their meaning for government policy. I had not expected him to be there at all, much less to put me in the embarassing position of being classed as his ally in an antigovernment cause.

Within two days following the lecture, I received a call from the government ministry concerned with agriculture. I was asked to meet with the ministry's permanent secretary, with whom I had had earlier friendly dealings. He politely asked me to recapitulate and enlarge upon my public statements and assured me that the government was indeed concerned. He also requested a copy of the dissertation I planned to write. In parting, he gave me a copy of a rarely seen report on the country's agricultural problems written some twelve years earlier. This was my last official dealing with the government before my departure from the country; it was hardly what I had expected. It appeared that I was being pacified, when I fully expected to be chastised.

## RESOLUTIONS AND CONCLUSIONS

While in the country I had to make certain decisions regarding my role as anthropologist. The decision that so deeply affected my experience as a researcher was the degree to which I was willing to discuss openly my research activities and findings; my decision was to be quite open, within certain limits of reasonable propriety. To be this open was to invite results that I welcomed (information feedback, the checking of hypotheses, the stimulation of new ideas) as well as results that often made life uncomfortable (attempted political co-option, false political identification, and unpleasant or embarrassing personal confrontations).

I faced further conflicts as I wrote up my material after leaving the country. Should I publish potentially inflammatory statements concerning individuals and the government, or should I attempt to keep my analysis sufficiently abstract to avoid recounting events that might be regarded as damaging to individuals or institutions? I decided to include specific case studies and detailed descriptions of events as necessary documentation. What I had to say concerning individuals was almost entirely public knowledge. I said nothing in direct criticism of the government, although the implications of a number of my statements could be interpreted as critical of government policy. I regarded my major task as that of writing an analysis that could be evaluated by other social scientists concerned with problems of agricultural development. I also felt obligated to make this analysis intelligible to the participants themselves.

I sent copies of the completed dissertation to interested government officials and to the national library. This was the only interpretive record of the political background to an impending disaster in the sugar-cane industry. One copy was subsequently used as evidence in a government-sponsored investigation into the future of the sugar industry.

Since I left, the situation there has changed. Numerous small farmers have given up their cane deliveries in the face of deep indebtedness, lessening fertility of soils they cannot afford to improve, and disastrous attacks by froghoppers. There have been several costly strikes by field and factory workers. The plantation is in the process of attempting to sell some of its fields to local producers; rumors of an eventual pullout of the plantation-factory combine were for a time rampant. Yet foreign buyers had increased their import quotas for the colony's sugar, and the industry's future was not entirely hopeless.

I have returned three times to the country, and I have sensed no serious disaffection toward me on the part of the government nor on the part of informants with whom I had worked. I carefully emphasized that I planned no follow-up studies of the problem. I requested, but was not allowed to study, the results of a government-sponsored investigation; I was told that the material was still regarded as classified. Since that time a revision of the original study has been published in monograph form and sent to individuals both in and out of government circles.

My behavior toward the subjects of my research was thus rather bold from the time that I was in the field until the publication of the results of my research. Despite the fact that life in the field was at times difficult, there is little indication that any permanent damage resulted. In attempting to account for this positive state of events, I have come to two principal conclusions. First, the political identifications with which I was tagged in Cocal were ephemeral, distinct from national cleavages of a more permanent sort that might have placed me in a truly uncompromising position. Second, my ultimately antigovernment public stand was not regarded in political terms by those concerned.

The political issues that affected me were, for the most part, short-lived. Likewise, the factions associated with them were constantly shifting. Often my own political dilemmas were solved by a regrouping of forces that cancelled out the conflicting interests that claimed me. In no case did factions form along national party lines. In fact, while I was in Cocal, the opposition party showed no interest in taking advantage of the political conflicts there. These facts made my role no easier while I was in the field. However, they seem to explain why my fears of continued disaffection in Cocal have not been borne out.

As for my relations with the local representative government, two things are relevant. The political foundations of the present parliamentary government were based on an outspoken anticolonialism. Although the present owners of the factory-plantation combine represent colonial corporate interests, and although these interests are generally regarded as having strongly influenced recent government policy toward agricultural development, the present independence-minded government is by no means happy with this situation. The government, in fact, seems to have regarded the combine as an undesirable but unavoidable means for economic growth. If my writing implied that the government was being victimized by colonial economic interests, the choice was made to interpret my position as anticolonial, not antigovernment. Therefore, in the last analysis, it was probably most convenient to regard me as a nonpolitical critic in terms of national affairs. In any event, it was politically opportune for the government to ignore me at the time. To recognize me would have been to call needless attention to a problem that, in their eyes, was best kept quiet.

Finally, it must be remembered that the country in question was still in a colonial status, faced with conflicting goals and charters for national identity. During a visit there several years later I felt that the situation was rapidly changing. Research was being more carefully evaluated before clearance was granted. Young nationalists were apparently playing a more important role in government affairs, despite the fact that an independence date had still not been set. My own position is thus still unresolved. If I wish to carry out further research in Cocal, I may find a different research situation, one in which I cannot assume the same role as I did while originally performing my research there.

## 1.11 – MEDIATION OF A CONFLICT

**BACKGROUND**

The village in which I was doing research was a coastal settlement of fishermen and occasional wage laborers. The community was founded by immigrants from across a nearby political frontier, whose ties to their adopted country were still tenuous during the time I lived with them. In the past, prominent political leaders in the agricultural and trading settlements along the coast had claimed control over such communities and regarded those who lived in them as their political clients. Clientage was basically a symbiotic relationship; in return for trading privileges, the "patron" and his followers offered their clients political protection. While the fishing communities relied on these ties as a source of essential goods, including agricultural produce, there were constraints built into the relationship. If the patron abused his position by attempting to dominate or exploit the sea people beyond their wishes, they could simply take their boats and move elsewhere to seek new, more compliant "protection."

The village in which I lived was located close to the regional administrative center. The villagers believed that by virtue of this proximity to the district commissioner they had, in effect, put themselves under his personal protection. Although the commissioner was European, the relationship was seen largely in terms of traditional patronage. This view was shared by the neighboring shore people and was locally a source of some friction. Whenever I visited inland settlements, a question I came to expect was: "Why is it that you whites always favor the sea people?" While I failed to see any evidence that they, in fact, received preferential treatment, the feeling clearly existed, shared by both the villagers and their neighbors, that the community enjoyed a "special" relationship with the district commissioner.

**THE GROWING CONFLICT**

Midway through my field work, the village headman returned home one afternoon from the District Office with five official envelopes addressed to young men in the community. He asked me to translate the contents for him, which I did. Each envelope contained a notice directing the addressee to appear for a medical examination prior to possible induction into military service. The addressees were to be taken by boat to a large port city a day's journey away where the examinations were to take place.

The news was electrifying and resulted in an all-night meeting at the headman's house with the families involved. All who attended were adamantly opposed to the five men's induction. Their reasons seemed, for the most part, quite sensible. One of the supposedly young men was, in fact, a middle-aged villager with a wife and children. The others knew only a smattering of the national language and none could read or write.

The next day the headman, together with the parents of the five young men, went to the District Office to plead for a recall of the notices. They returned later in the day to report that they had had no success.

A second meeting was held without any clear agreement emerging as to what should be done next. Throughout the following two weeks, the villagers became increasingly pessimistic and talked of little else than the likelihood of these five men being taken away and never seen again.

Up to this point I had refrained from actively intervening, although I had offered some suggestions as to how the villagers might best present their case to the native chief. As the days passed, it became increasingly difficult to remain uninvolved, particularly since the villagers believed I had influence with the government, and especially with the European district commissioner. To make matters more difficult, one of the five young men who had received a draft notice was the brother of my principal field assistant and another was his cousin.

In any case, events quickly came to a head and eliminated all possibility of my noninvolvement. My assistant's brother, Pandi, and his cousin left the village at night and sailed to a neighboring country without first obtaining the required permission from the immigration authorities, which, under the circumstances, would have almost certainly been impossible to obtain. When the two men tried to return to their village, they were arrested and put in jail. According to rumors circulating the following morning, members of a rival village faction had informed on them. On hearing the news, Pandi's mother, a highly emotional woman under normal conditions, became hysterical and had to be cared for by her sisters.

Most of the families in the village began to make preparations to abandon the community. There was even some talk that residents of nearby shore villages, where similar notices had been received, were planning to assassinate the district commissioner. At this point, nonintervention seemed impossible, both in terms of personal conscience and from the point of view of doing any further field work. The village itself was on the verge of dissolving.

I therefore paid a visit to the district commissioner, who told me that a decision had already been made to release the two men from jail. However, the district commissioner insisted that he had no power to rescind the draft notices, although he had called for clarification and was now awaiting a reply from the national government. He agreed that the matter had been mishandled and that the official presentation of the notices, without any prior warning, had only increased the villagers' anxiety. For my part, I tried to make him aware of the strength of the villagers' opposition.

After my return from the District Office, I told the village headman and others of my visit with the district commissioner and reported the general content of our conversation. As a result, pressures for the immediate abandonment of the village were eased. Tensions were further relieved by the release of Pandi and his cousin. Two days later the headman was called to the District Office, together with the headmen of other villages in the region where similar draft notices had been sent. The headmen were told that the plan to conscript draftees had been abandoned and that the notices should be forgotten.

Village life then returned to normal and there was no further talk of leaving, although the villagers' confidence in the government, and in their own future, was seriously shaken.

My intervention had little, if any, effect on what actually happened; that is, on the final rescinding of the draft notices. Nor did most of the villagers regard my visit to the District Office as more than a contributing factor. I had, perhaps, succeeded in impressing the district commissioner with the extent of hostility generated by the draft call and also with the impracticality of calling up village men who lack any conception of military service.

Nevertheless, I believe that under the circumstances I had little choice but to assume the role of an intermediary between the government and the people I was studying, however modest this role may actually have been. Had I not done so, it is almost certain that my relations with the villagers would have become untenable. Indeed, the community itself would almost certainly have disappeared or been greatly reduced. More important, I felt at the time that by informing the district commissioner of the villagers' reaction to the draft notices, it might be possible to avoid a situation which would almost certainly be harmful to both the villagers and the government.

As a field worker, and as a guest who, in this case, had received considerable assistance from the government, I felt that it was neither my right to criticize the government's actions nor my role to mobilize or even actively encourage the villagers' opposition. The government was, in fact, fighting a border war at the time and had a genuine need to raise an army.

By intervening I sought only to make the district commissioner more fully aware of the effects the government's actions were having on those involved and how the latter perceived these actions. Doing so, I felt, was not incompatible with my responsibilities as an anthropologist. In this case, I was lucky, insofar as the outcome was successful. It might easily have been otherwise.

**RELATED READINGS**

Appell, G.N. 1966. The structure of district administration, anti-administration activity and political instability. *Human Organization* 25:312-320.

―――. 1973. *Basic issues in the dilemmas and ethical conflicts in anthropological inquiry*. Module 19. New York: MSS Modular Publications.

## 1.12—BREAKING A TABOO

During the eleven months I lived in the village I stayed in the house of the village headman. Several months after my arrival I began working with a spirit medium named Garani, who lived in the house immediately behind that of the headman. With his help, I was trying to work out the annual cycle of fishing activities. The villagers believed that Garani possessed considerable knowledge of when and where migratory fish could be expected to appear; they sometimes consulted him before setting out on fishing expeditions.

One morning our conversation turned to spirits and I asked Garani about a large rock that stood at one edge of the lagoon with two small flags on top of it. He told me that this was the home of a spirit who can often be seen from a distance, especially at night, but who is invisible when standing nearby—a fact which makes him particularly dangerous. The spirit appears as a man with huge eyes and long hair falling to his shoulders; he glows bright red from the waist up. Sometimes the spirit assumes the form of a turtle or skate and swims to the village, occasionally causing people to become sick.

Garani explained that shortly before I arrived this spirit had caused the illness of a woman who lived in a rather exposed house near the rock. Garani and several other mediums had put up the flags as offerings to the spirit in order to cure her.

After Garani told me about this event, I walked out to the rock during low tide, when most of the lagoon floor was exposed, and photographed it. I felt perfectly normal when I started out, but as I returned I began to feel increasingly ill. By the time I got back, I was feeling so sick that I asked one of the young men in the village to help me get to the nearest town, which was about two miles away, where there was a clinic.

The dresser at the clinic was alarmed and incorrectly diagnosed my illness as spinal meningitis. He radioed the nearest hospital and the doctor there sent a helicopter to pick me up.

After spending a week in the hospital, recovering from what proved to be a rather severe case of dengue fever, I returned to the village to find my position in the community greatly altered. I had ceased to be regarded as an odd, rather peripheral outsider with a curious interest in the village. The villagers interpreted my dramatic departure by helicopter as a sign that I was someone of great importance with influence in the local government. I was now seen as a valuable resource to be used to the advantage of the village. Furthermore, the fact that I returned at all was interpreted as tangible proof of my personal loyalty to and genuine interest in the community. Most villagers later confessed that they had never expected to see me again, if I recovered. After my return, they accepted my intrusion into their affairs much more willingly than before.

## 1.13 – THE PERCEIVED ADVANTAGES OF BEING STUDIED BY AN ANTHROPOLOGIST

I studied two land settlement schemes in Papua New Guinea, which were established in 1962, especially for the benefit of indigenous veterans of the Second World War. In such schemes, individual Papuans and New Guineans were allocated blocks of land on leasehold for commercial farming.

In the course of my work, it became apparent that the indigenous settlers were very critical of the way Australia had administered their country. In their view, social and economic development would have proceeded at a much faster rate if another country had organized resettlement. I was told that before the Second World War Australia had been criticized by other countries for her treatment of Papuans and New Guineans. All settlers agreed, however, that after the war conditions improved greatly. Still, they felt, progress was too slow. Most stressed, for example, the long delay before they received their blocks of land which, in their view, had been promised them because of their service during the war. This delay was sometimes attributed to the unwillingness of senior administrative officials to give Papuans and New Guineans an opportunity to advance. The settlers also thought that the Australian administration had required further stimulus to put more effort into helping Papuans and New Guineans. According to some settlers, one of the persons to prod the administration had been Queen Elizabeth. Two other settlers told me that conditions had improved after the Duke of Edinburgh had visited New Guinea in 1956, because he disapproved of the conditions under which the indigenous population had to live and had told the Queen what he'd seen.

The settlers' criticism of the administration also concerned several organizational aspects of the resettlement schemes. For example, the loans the settlers had received to help finance the development of their blocks did not provide funds for the employment of laborers. Consequently, the settlers themselves had had to clear the primary forest which covered most of their blocks. They felt discriminated against because they knew that Australian ex-servicemen in Papua New Guinea had received much larger blocks of land and much larger loans allowing them to employ laborers. Another source of dissatisfaction was that the Australians had received their loans in lump sums of money, while the indigenous ex-servicemen had received only a small part in cash and the remainder in warrants for the purchase of

---

Contributed by Dr. Anton Ploeg, Utrecht University

tools, seedlings, construction materials, and so on. Furthermore, various facilities, which the settlers felt had been promised to them, were lacking, including a primary school, a medical aid post, and good road connections.

The settlers had made several attempts to convince the administration to change those aspects of the resettlement scheme which they considered unsatisfactory. They had approached local administration personnel, visited top officials, and consulted the association of ex-servicemen, a politically influential institution. However, these efforts had been largely unsuccessful. In the view of the settlers, the main obstacle was influencing officials in Port Moresby, the capital of Papua New Guinea; they felt frustrated by their inability to make these officials change their resettlement policies.

When I arrived in the field in 1968, the settlers saw me as a sympathetic visitor, eager to listen to what they had to say, and, very importantly, based in Port Moresby. They hoped that I could help them effect changes in settlement conditions. I was repeatedly asked whether and how I would be able to help them, and on one occasion was warned to give my report to reliable officials, lest it be shelved.

After I had finished my first field trip, the administration started making several improvements. A causeway was built across the river bordering one of the settlements, thereby providing the missing link in the road connection with the main town nearby. The construction of internal roads was started, and the Department of Agriculture began to establish an extension station on the block which had been set aside for a community center. Supervision of the two settlements was also reorganized so that only one agricultural officer would deal with the two settlements, which were now included in the local government council area. The new agricultural officer reorganized and supervised a community store. Moreover, the holders of the blocks which were fully developed and well maintained were told that they were shortly to receive cattle and to fence in their blocks. Finally, the Department of Education announced their decision to establish a local primary school at the beginning of the coming year.

The settlers assumed that these developments resulted from my submitting a favorable report on their block development. They believed that I had thus succeeded in shaming the administration and compelling it to take action.

I heard about this reasoning when I returned to carry out additional field work. I was very concerned that the settlers credited me with what was solely the work of the administration officials. This would encourage their misconceptions about the administration's efforts to promote development. Second, officials were likely to blame the settlers, or me, or both, for the misunderstandings. However, I made only a few attempts to correct the settlers' view of my role—all apparently unsuccessful. Now I regret that I did not make a more vigorous effort. The problem was that had I consistently denied any responsibility for the recent improvements, the settlers might have refused to believe me; on the other hand, they might have begun to reassess the administration's attempts at development.

## 1.14 PROBLEMS AND CONSEQUENCES OF ACTIVELY HELPING THE HOST COMMUNITY

One of the current issues in anthropological field work is to what degree a field worker has the responsibility of helping the host community when it faces critical problems. This case outlines my experience. Involved are questions of both professionalism and ethical awareness; of whether these are contradictory or compatible stances; and how we explain our field-worker role to fellow anthropologists and to informants. In the case described here, the assumption was made that professional conduct in the field—data collection, rapport, confidentiality—need not be compromised by active commitment to the amelioration of a serious social and political problem. The outcome of the field experience modified if not challenged that assumption. As field workers, the desire to be helpful and fair may not be enough to get us through our field experiences unscathed.

I arrived in the Virgin Islands in January 1969 to study a large number of British West Indian labor migrants and the various associations they formed to serve their interests. At that time, nearly one third of the population of the Virgin Islands was made up of these labor migrants and their families, classified as "bonded aliens" by the United States immigration authorities.

British West Indian aliens had flooded into the Virgin Islands over the previous ten years in response to the booming tourist trade and the labor demands of a new oil refinery and aluminum plant. This immigrant labor population has continued to grow, despite active prejudice against it by Virgin Islanders and the Virgin Islands government. Typically, this bias has shown up most forcefully in education—for a number of years the children of British West Indian aliens have not been allowed to attend the already crowded government schools except in token numbers. Alien children who have gone to school have usually attended expensive private schools run by religious organizations. But most have simply roamed over the island until caught and deported by immigration authorities for defying the law that all children must be in school. The resulting scattering of family members over several islands, as well as the government's reluctance to accept large numbers of alien children into their own schools, laid the groundwork for considerable discontent among the British West Indians in the American Virgin Islands.

This discontent was not organized until the fall of 1968 when, at the invitation of the Virgin Islands government, a number of Vista volunteers arrived for the

---

Contributed by Dr. James W. Green, University of Washington

purpose of running day-care centers for preschool children, including aliens. White, aggressive, idealistic college students for the most part, these volunteers instead began to organize the British West Indian aliens, promoting a school which would accept alien children without restrictions, and which could be operated less expensively than the church schools. The Vista volunteers also sought out individual British West Indians who might be interested in leading a self-help movement to make certain demands of the government in behalf of all aliens. They sought more public housing, greater job security, easing of immigration restrictions, and—what was to become the battle cry of the movement—"free, compulsory, universal education."

At the same time, a private social science consulting firm under contract from the Office of Economic Opportunity was supporting a black community organizer working on another of the Virgin Islands, as part of a larger study of the alien problem. The organizer contacted the Vista volunteers in order to coordinate the timing and objectives of the two alien self-help organizations.

Stories of the growing alien movement appeared in the newspapers, along with criticism of local government policy toward the aliens, particularly in the area of education. The somewhat embarrassed Virgin Islands government asked the Vista people to abandon their plans both to establish an alien school and to promote an alien movement to run it. The request was refused and, consequently, some of the volunteers returned to the States, some were fired, and some decided to fight back. The latter group chose as their unofficial spokesman a Vista volunteer in his late 40's, a professional writer with a charasmatic style of leadership. He became headmaster of the new school and picked a small group of aliens to make up his school board. A building located in the middle of the island was made available by a sympathetic priest of the Catholic church, and in the winter of 1968-69 the school for aliens opened.

The school was immediately surrounded by controversy, as was its headmaster, who by now had been fired from Vista, presumably at the request of the local government. He publicly expressed his intention to challenge the government on the sensitive alien issue, and made numerous inflammatory statements to the island newspapers and in public meetings and was soon one of the island's most renowned personalities. Having recruited British West Indian teachers to work at the school for very little pay, he soon filled his four classrooms with over 150 alien children, all paying a small tuition. His demand that the government provide buses and free lunches was refused.

In public meetings the headmaster alluded to the racist mentality of the government, a particularly volatile point since he was white and most Virgin Islanders as well as British West Indians are black. He constantly harrangued the commissioner of education, a key political appointee, on the major legal problem: all schools in the Virgin Islands must be certified by the Department of Education in order to operate. Certification was being denied the alien school for a number of reasons, some known only in government circles. This constituted a serious political issue because the immigration authorities were legally required to deport children not enrolled in a certified school. Lacking certification, the right of 150 children to stay on the island with their families was in jeopardy, as were the "illegal" jobs

## 1.14 – Problems and Consequences of Helping Host Community

held by the school's teachers. Some members of the school board feared their own deportation as a political repercussion of the headmaster's statements and their involvement with his organization.

The most famous event of this stormy period in the life of the school and the fledgling alien self-help movement occurred when the commissioner of education, now cast as a villain in many of the media, stated that he would personally enter the school and take it over rather than grant certification to its present headmaster. The headmaster replied in the press that if such a takeover were attempted he would meet the commissioner at the entrance of the school with a machete. He further implied that he would be backed up by armed aliens.

There were two consequences of this event. First, the commissioner of education was removed from his post and given a noncontroversial, relatively obscure job in another government office. Second, the alien self-help movement was split into two factions. The smaller and weaker group supported the headmaster, while the larger faction privately considered ways to ease him out of the school and gain certification through cooperative rather than hostile relations with the government.

While the headmaster continued to run the school until the end of the spring term, the two factions became increasingly hostile to one another. To keep this conflict apart from the operation of the school, the headmaster asked the aliens to form a separate self-help organization, with a name and legal charter, for the purpose of expanding the alien movements on the island. Meanwhile, he would continue to run the school with a school board separate from, but including members of, the self-help organization. By the end of the school term, however, relations among the headmaster, his weak and divided school board, and the growing self-help group were so difficult that during an explosive school board meeting he was asked to quit his post and leave the island, a request which included thinly veiled physical threats. It was alleged at this time that he had been irresponsible in handling school funds, that his campaign against the government had hurt the alien cause, and that he himself had created the factions on the school board.

I had arrived on the island about three months before the headmaster's requested departure. I had visited the school, became acquainted with some of the alien leaders of the self-help movement and the school board, and was generally on good terms with the headmaster and with the leaders of both factions. Following his dismissal, the headmaster came to me, afraid to leave the fate of the school in the hands of the divided school board. He requested that I take his place as a neutral individual among those contending for control of the school and the self-help movement. His proposal was also presented to the members of both factions, who were unanimously in favor of the arrangement. Their reasoning, I later discovered, was not that a "deal" was being made—my becoming headmaster in exchange for the departure of the former Vista volunteer. Rather, they wanted a white United States citizen as head of the school because they felt that such an individual would be less vulnerable to threats from the Virgin Islands government than would a British West Indian alien. They also needed someone who could fill the post without pay.

As I had received a grant for my doctoral research and was already beginning to investigate the alien problem, I agreed to take the job on a volunteer basis over the summer and into the fall. My reasons for accepting the offer were varied. I felt that the aliens were being done an injustice by the Virgin Islands government not unlike the treatment often given blacks by white school boards. My British West Indian informants had been extremely cooperative in responding to my requests for assistance. Although many of them were not connected with the school, I felt I could reciprocate, however indirectly, by agreeing to act as interim headmaster. Finally, I knew the position would greatly increase my exposure to the alien community. Because the aliens were dispersed over the island, this was one of the few opportunities to contact many of them at once.

In taking this job, I stipulated two conditions. First, I would be allowed to do survey and interview work among the children and other aliens connected with the school; and second, the two factions would join forces and give me united support in the job. To both of these conditions they agreed, although I suspect that unity was probably beyond them because of the bitterness of their feelings for one another. However, I wanted to make it clear that I would not involve myself in their factional struggles, either on the school board or in the self-help movement. I refused to continue the earlier headmaster's campaign against the government and explained that my only public role would be to solicit funds for the school and attempt to maintain the informal agreement established between the first headmaster and the immigration authorities to refrain from deporting the school's students, pending final word on certification from the Department of Education. I announced my intention to take the school out of island politics, to improve the educational quality of its curriculum, to raise the teachers' pay, and to work for rapid certification.

The local political significance of this new tactic was considerable. The school was a great embarassment to the government locally; word of the alien situation was reaching congressional committees, partly through the controversy created by the school's first headmaster. Furthermore, the islands were only a year away from the first election in which they would choose their own governor, formerly a presidential appointee. There was much popular talk and self-congratulation on the "political maturity" which would be displayed by the electorate. Any adverse publicity created considerable nervousness in almost all departments of government. Thus, the new arrangement for operating the alien school must have relieved many Virgin Islanders.

From the beginning, I attempted to maintain a neutral role among the alien factions, both to protect my right to conduct interviews and do survey work and because I had a genuine interest in the educational quality of the school. But neutrality was difficult for a number of reasons. The decision-making powers of the school board had never been adequately clarified, despite considerable attention given by the members to constitutionality, parliamentary procedures, and norms of legitimacy in bureaucratically based actions. The school board was equally divided between the two factions, and the self-help movement was controlled completely by the larger group. Relations between the factions continued to be hostile.

## 1.14 – Problems and Consequences of Helping Host Community

The first crisis of the summer came with the takeover of the school by the leaders of the self-help movement, on a mandate from the parents. This occurred at a meeting which some members of the school board claimed was called illegally. Nevertheless, the action by the self-help leadership was decisive, and the weaker of the two factions—the one which had supported the first headmaster in his days of glory—was never again to play a significant role in the operation of the school, the school board, or the self-help movement. My position was made difficult because the president of the school board was the leader of the weaker faction, and both sides expected my support.

Following the vote to abolish the old school board, I declared that I would support the will of the parents and cooperate with the leaders of the self-help movement who now controlled the school. I retained my personal friendship with the members of the disbanded weaker faction. However, I began experiencing difficulties with the self-help leaders. It was clear they wanted me to continue my role overseeing the day-to-day operation of the school. But they also distrusted me, since from the start, I had not openly supported their faction—or any other. Word reached me that they were also bothered by the apparent prestige I enjoyed among the parents of the students, a prestige they were in part denied because of the authoritative style of their leadership and their reputation for factional dispute. Furthermore, they were West Indian leaders in a society where leadership is expected only from whites, and blacks in a position of power are regarded with the utmost suspicion.

The racial element in my role as headmaster was rarely mentioned, but it was clearly important. West Indians tend to distrust one another, believing they will receive better treatment from whites than from fellow blacks. On more then one occasion, I was told by parents that they would not send their children to the school if it had a black headmaster because of the possible "skylarking" with the tuition money.

I slowly became aware of the importance of my role as figurehead, implicitly sanctioning the statements made by the leader of the self-help movement, who was now also president of the school board. In several speeches to parents urging support for the school and the self-help movement, he observed that blacks were sure to start cheating each other once the white man was gone. The comment brought loudly affirmative remarks from the audience. He stated that as aliens and as Britishers they ought to pull themselves together like the blacks in the States were doing and follow their elected leader. He was clearly seeking personal support in these speeches, support he felt he could not obtain without the backing of a white face at the school. These feelings must have made it difficult for him to consider a West Indian headmaster for the fall term, which I had been suggesting to him throughout the summer.

In order to avoid the mistakes of the earlier headmaster, I scrupulously submitted financial records of the school to the self-help leaders. I checked with them on all decisions, no matter how trivial, so that they would be aware of every move I was making. I attempted to be completely candid in my role, so that there could be no grounds for suspicion. However, I made the mistake of continuing my personal friendship with some members of the defeated faction, individuals who were also excellent informants on matters other than those connected with the school. The president of the self-help movement never challenged my right to conduct a survey, perhaps because I had indicated I would share the results with him. He planned to use these findings in preparing a statement on the alien problem for an upcoming government hearing. We both appeared as witnesses at that hearing, as did other members of the self-help movement.

On the surface, relations between the movement leaders and myself were friendly, although internal feuding within the movement persisted. These conflicts were the result of numerous difficulties, including problems with the Department of Immigration; the failure of the movement to attract members over the summer; frequent threats by the teachers to quit because of low pay; the insecurity of the movement's leadership positions; constant bickering because of historical rivalries among residents of different islands; and the blunt and sometimes abrasive presence of the president of the self-help organization.

The summer term was quiet as far as the school was concerned, and my interviewing and survey work proceeded with the support of the movement leaders. What was becoming increasingly apparent to me, however, was the continuous turmoil over small matters of authority among various members of the executive committee of the movement, the hostile arguing over the legitimacy of the acts and pronouncements of each individual in his role as an organization officer, and particularly the gravitation of power to the domineering and authoritative president—an opportunistic man with strong personal political ambitions. There was tremendous interpersonal hostility among the committee members, particularly when titles and prerogatives within the organization were being considered. Increasingly, their activities consisted of lining up personal support on one small issue after another. This was accomplished outside the regular meetings through interpersonal gossip networks and in what were sometimes called "bush meetings," or secretive gatherings of a clique to plan an action.

This type of activity, which became more frequent and vicious as the summer progressed, further isolated the leadership of the movement from the general alien community, while at the same time consolidating power around one or two individuals, particularly the organization's president. The struggle became more desperate after I was asked by the leadership to write a request to the Office of Economic Opportunity (O.E.O.) for operating funds for the school. This I did, requesting $40,000 for the coming school year. Frequently delayed, these funds became available several days before I was denounced by the president at the parents' meeting.

Finally in late 1969 at a parents' meeting for the school a confrontation between the movement leader and myself took place, which at the time I was unprepared for but which now seems to have been almost inevitable. My relations with the members of the board had been cordial and cooperative up to that time. Yet to my surprise, and to the surprise of many attending the meeting, the president of the self-help group announced that it had been discovered that I had been leaking information on conditions in the school to important religious and political figures on the island. He also accused me of spreading rumors that the self-help movement was weak and faction-ridden and of coming to the island to advocate the overthrow of the territorial government. He added that my purpose in running the school for

## 1.14–Problems and Consequences of Helping Host Community

his group had been to embarrass the government in the eyes of the United States Congress and to embarrass the British West Indian aliens in the eyes of the Virgin Islands government.

After listing these charges against me, the president asked me to defend myself before the group of several hundred parents, although he did not ask for my resignation.

I am now aware that an essential purpose of the gossip network was to keep the leaders of the movement informed of my activities and statements. Apparently they feared that I might try to assume the powerful and threatening role of my predecessor by removing the self-help leaders from positions in which they could take credit for running the school. Perhaps my deliberate attempts to remain detached from their internal disputes contributed to this interpretation of my motives. I later learned that some of them—especially the president—actually believed I was plotting to take over the school once the $40,000 was received from O.E.O., and that I was going to replace them with the disbanded faction which had supported the earlier headmaster.

The self-help movement leaders also knew that I was friendly with several influential priests on the island, including a white United States citizen and an alien. I had discussed the problems of the school and the internal troubles of the movement with both of these men. At one point, I had asked the alien priest to act as mediator in the more serious disagreements among the leadership, a role he performed sincerely but ineptly. It was these contacts which prompted the charge that I had been revealing information to outsiders about the state of the school and the alien organization.

My discussions with members of the defeated faction were carried out for purposes of collecting information on interisland migration and various aspects of West Indian culture. But any association with these individuals was apparently preceived as hostile by the movement leaders for several reasons. One was their increasing concern with secrecy within the movement and within the school; I knew a lot but could not be directly controlled. Another reason was the delayed approval of the O.E.O. funds, which bolstered their belief that I was sabotaging the movement and waiting for the old faction to reorganize.

Furthermore, my role as a field worker made no sense to them, despite my attempts at explanation. What seemed most understandable was that I was writing a book, for a dissertation meant nothing to them, about the problems of the aliens. The leaders accepted that, but I doubt that they fully understood what it meant. My expressed interest in "customs" and "how you do things here" was not taken seriously since the aliens consciously devalued their own culture and didn't understand, in any case, how I could make my living doing that.

Finally, and perhaps most important, the aggressive president of the self-help group was rapidly emerging in the eyes of the Virgin Islands government as spokesman for the nearly 20,000 aliens on his particular island. While his movement dwindled over the summer to a handful of close friends, he spent increasing amounts of time before government hearings and in federal and territorial government offices, speaking authoritatively on the desires of all aliens on the island and the growing power and size of his movement. He was rapidly becoming a well-known figure in government circles and, as one of the few aliens to speak up on the problems of aliens, he appeared to represent a large base of alien support. The government apparently accepted his claims for the large size of his movement, and his frequent contacts with O.E.O. personnel and the leaders of island social work agencies gave credence to his claims. He probably felt that I was a personal threat to his position as a semi-official spokesman. What power I had was based on my personal popularity as headmaster, my effectiveness in dealing with the immigration officers, and the fact that I was white and a United States citizen. His influence was based almost exclusively on his considerable skill as an "operator" who could convince a number of government agencies, including the crucial Department of Education, that he represented a mass following of aliens potentially politically hostile to the sensitive government.

The president's respect for the power of my position was reflected in his refusal to ask for my resignation, a maneuver which was consistent with the factional process in West Indian culture. He attempted to remove me the same way countless others in the movement had been removed from positions they had held, through a long, drawn-out process in which charges are leveled, vigorous refutations made, personal insults exchanged, and new, temporary alliances made until one side tires of the contest and gives up in a show of disgust. The president of the organization had so far never lost one of these ritualized struggles because he had never given up.

I had two alternatives at the meeting. I could play a typical West Indian performance of challenge and counterchallenge until one of us quit. Or I could refuse to participate in the ritual by dropping out of the confrontation immediately. It was clear that I had the backing of the parents for a number of reasons. I was a white citizen; I had done my job well and kept the school open during an unsettled summer. Also, the leader of the movement was not personally popular except in his own clique, where he also had problems keeping people in line.

I chose not to participate in the fight. I made a short speech, contesting each point and reaffirming my faith in the school and in the leaders of the self-help group who operated it. I concluded by urging the parents to join the self-help movement and to support the man who had just denounced me. I then sat down to the only applause I had ever heard in a public meeting of that organization and to the warm congratulations of many parents following the meeting.

I still had faith in my somewhat simple white liberalism of the time. In urging the parents to support the organization which had just denounced me, I hoped they would back this particular group of leaders, especially the organization's president, for, despite all his calculating manipulations, I sincerely believed that he offered the only hope for effective collective action. I have since changed my mind; it now seems to me that he could never have organized the alien community, given his *modus operandi*.

Ironically, I may have inadvertently contributed to the leader's problem. By refusing to condemn the man who denounced me, I undercut his position that I was hostile to him, the school, and the alien movement. Avoiding participation in the West Indian faction ritual, I probably confounded his expectations of

## 1.14—Problems and Consequences of Helping Host Community

how I would react and thereby embarrassed him before his potential supporters.

I also withdrew because I could not run the school indefinitely. My time in the field was limited. Nor did I want to encourage the continued dependence of this group of West Indians on white leadership, since I believed (mistakenly) they might rally to their own leaders if they had to. My main concern, however, was in the appropriateness of fighting to maintain my position in the school when I knew that in six months I would have to leave the island.

After quitting my post at the school, I attended to other aspects of my field work, associating with aliens who had never been involved with the school and who were interested in me as a fishing, drinking, gambling, and conversational companion. I rarely saw any of the members of the self-help movement again, except briefly in public places. I never returned to the school, nor was my letter of resignation acknowledged.

I later learned that in private meetings of the leaders of the movement there was talk of reprisals, but nothing specific was agreed upon. The man who had forced me out discussed with his cohorts the necessity of barring me from the school grounds, although I had already made the decision not to return. He claimed he could stop the publication of whatever I might write about the aliens and that he could prevent my getting an academic degree. But these threats were always vague; their articulation was apparently sufficient to satisfy him and others that I would somehow be "taken care of" at a later time. At this point, the movement leaders were preoccupied with the problems of handling the O.E.O. funds, particularly given the West Indians' distrust of their own leaders' ability to manage money honestly and effectively.

Within three months of my departure from the school I learned from friends that my participation in the movement had been largely forgotten and that the ongoing crises among the leaders absorbed much of their time. Indeed, their hostilities and problems were exacerbated by their new financial responsibilities. Whereas my failure to communicate to them my role as field worker certainly contributed to my departure from their school, the more serious difficulties lay with their problems in creating a collective self-help movement in a society marked my interpersonal hostility, fierce individualism, and constant suspicion, as well as the problem of physical survival common to the rural poor everywhere.

From such a turbulent experience, motives are impossible to sift out and the apparent sequence of events, of "what really happened," just barely so. Clearly, my presence kept 150 children in school for a summer and kept the immigration officials away from the door. Relations between the territorial government and the self-appointed leaders of the alien movement were allowed to mellow slightly. First steps toward certification of the school were achieved although they were timid and hesitant.

Yet substantive gains for the self-help movement were slight if not lacking. Paid membership declined. Parental distrust of alien leaders grew. Day-to-day burdens of managing the school fell to the already underpaid alien teachers. The receipt of $40,000 by men earning $50 per week and predisposed to suspect the worst of one another must have created tremendous anxieties. At least two officers of the self-help leadership quit when the money came, loudly proclaiming that whatever might happen with it they didn't intend to go to jail when the federal government would demand an accounting. The internal crisis within the movement continued, and the government apparently found relief in the absorption of the alien leader in their own troubles.

At this writing, four years later, the school continues. Its financial foundation remains shaky, but it has received government certification. The fear of deportation has thus been lessened in many of the island's British West Indian households.

My field work among the aliens was not terminated by this struggle, but my research on the self-help movement was clearly ended by it. Fortunately, I had been working for some time on three other fronts: the male subculture connected with bars and street corners in a small town; a rural crossroads store which was a local social center; and archival materials in the island library. After resigning from the school, I devoted all my time to these projects. One evening an alien informant, who was also a close friend and had never been connected with the school, sympathized with me over drinks, asking with a sigh if I had finally learned my lesson about staying out of West Indian politics.

I still cannot answer his question. The experience has confirmed for me that no simplistic formula, based on liberal humanitarianism or any other creed, can provide an easy guide for deciding what is best. Clearly, the desire to do right is not enough. Those who think they shock the anthropological establishment with pronouncements about the necessity of throwing their weight with all and any oppressed peoples are equally innocent of field reality. Yet as anthropologists we have an obligation to those people whose customs we study and whose cooperation we rely on as investment capital in personal career building. How should the obligation be met?

Briefly, we can begin by acknowledging that most of whatever we do in field situations will have little effect on others beyond our circle of informants and acquaintances. Some anthropologists, of course, have acted in ways which have had profound impact on colleagues and informants. Cases exist of forced returns to home base, curtailing of research projects, reprisals against host communities, and the closing off of whole countries to further research. These things happen frequently enough to demonstrate the destructive effect of the irresponsible acts of some. But for most, we should be humbled by appreciating how powerless and inconsequential our best efforts really are. It is only megalomania which causes some to think the future of whole societies hangs on the success of their field experience. What is really in the balance is the future of careers and egos. It has been argued that anthropologists give voice in the counsels of the great to the aspirations of those both voiceless and powerless. We should be so fortunate!

We also have an obligation to the specific individuals who have given us assistance. Help in finding a job, a genuine and sympathetic ear, shared drink and food have been the best I could offer informants. Why should I not treat them as friends, since that is what many become? Giving rides into town or helping pull fish pots are not dramatic forms of intervention and aid. Their effect on the host community can't really be known. But by returning what individual informants are willing to share in the way of interest and candor, the relationship becomes more balanced between giving and taking.

If a lesson was learned, as my West Indian friend would prefer, it was not whether or not to stay out of island politics. It was that any unfamiliar social world is difficult and complex, and simply to state it that way is as banal as it is true. It is impossible to say whether or not, facing similar circumstances, I would involve myself again. In either case, however, I would certainly be more cautious in choosing and developing a role. What now remains as the value of my field work to myself is the candor and warmth of informants who were also friends. It is a modest gain to point to but, just like the public clash of factions and interests, it is profoundly real.

## 1.15—A PROBLEM OF INVOLVEMENT

One of my graduate students had returned from the field for a few months to consult library sources and make a preliminary analysis of his data. And now he was about to return to the field to continue his research. He came to me for some advice.

He had been contacted, he told me, by one of the new organizations dealing with the rights of indigenous peoples, and he asked me what I knew about their organization and what I thought his reply to their inquiry should be.

His field work was among a group of hoe agriculturalists in a region that had not been visited by anthropologists before, although there were a number of mission stations located there. His research was proving to be interesting but modest in terms of its contribution to the body of anthropological knowledge or theory. The main problem in the field situation was that the indigenous people were having their land taken from them by the government and commercial concerns for the development of commercial crops. This student believed that the practice would continue until many of the people he was studying became landless peasants. He maintained that there was little he could do about this, as everyone in the government was making money illegally from the scheme.

His immediate problem was whether to reply to the inquiry from the organization dealing with the rights of indigenous peoples. Unfortunately, I could tell him little except that I thought it was a useful group and that any information that he could provide them concerning the plight of these people could possibly be of some benefit. They had asked him whether, on the basis of his special knowledge of the area, there were any problems that should be investigated. He finally decided not to reply to the inquiry as he was uncertain whether the organization would use his information with descretion. He was afraid that if his name was linked with the organization the government would prevent him from returning to finish his field work.

## 1.16 – A CHALLENGE TO ANTHROPOLOGICAL INQUIRY ON AN INDIAN RESERVE

When my dissertation research ended in 1967, I had spent a total of over fourteen months on the Messalon Indian Reserve. I had received full cooperation from the people during that time. However, in 1968 I began to suspect there was a growing reluctance to my continuing research which required living on the reserve again.

After completing my thesis, I had sent portions of it to informants to check for accuracy and wording prior to its final typing, and had incorporated their suggested changes. One of the finished copies of my thesis was sent to the Band Council and another to the local hospital. A third copy was given to the agency office, and I loaned my own copy to many informants to read, telling many others of the location of available copies.

In both my thesis research and my present work on voluntary associations (starting in 1968), I have been concerned with the nonconservative Indian faction on the reserve. My closest contacts have been with a group whom I have termed the "elite." These individuals interact in the context of church work and voluntary associations and are primarily employed by the federal government. They are middle-class activists who contribute to their community through leadership in the local organizations which are not affiliated with the Band Council.

The Messalon Band Council in its role as boundary maintainer is repeatedly approached by agencies of all types for permission to conduct land-use studies, housing surveys, research on multiproblem families, etc. The council and most of the people have become saturated with such requests and the council is hesitant to support further research. Furthermore, charges of economic exploitation, personal status aggrandizement, and indifference to Indian causes have been repeatedly leveled against anthropologists. As a result, securing permission to reside on the reserve has become increasingly difficult. Other forms of closure to social inquiry have also occurred. And most of the Indians believe that the publishing of books makes you rich. Acknowledging that one has bettered his position economically or otherwise, although not directly through the sale of books, does not appear to alleviate the problem.

In applying for permission this time to reside on the reserve I also applied for permission for my research assistant, a graduate sociology student. A letter requesting that my application be brought before the council was sent, and it

Contributed by Dr. Sally M. Weaver, University of Waterloo.

included a copy of my research proposal as I had submitted it to the Canada Council. A layman's interpretation of the proposal, in fact the press "blurb" required, was given in the letter itself.

When I appeared before the council to request residence for myself and my research assistant, the members were listening to a presentation of a book published on Messalon Indian history. The author stressed that this was the first book about the Messalon Indians that was written "from your point of view." He emphasized the significant contribution of the Messalon Indians to the maintenance of Canada as a British possession and requested that the council endorse the book for use in the reserve schools and those of the province as a whole. He proceeded to read rave reviews of the book, which further appeared to validate his claims of the value of partiality.

The council responded most favorably to this presentation. As one member put it, "This might be the true picture of our history!" Furthermore, the desire of "getting Indian history into the textbooks" and eliminating the "savage" image strongly appealed to the council, as it does to most of the Messalon Indians.

I was next on the agenda. In making my request for residence on the reserve, I again explained the purpose of my prospective research: to record the history of certain voluntary associations, a topic chosen because of the lack of governmental intervention and the evidence of exceptionally viable leadership within the community.

Two council members asked exactly how much money I would make from publishing my thesis. I replied that I would earn nothing from the sale of the book—if it sold—but that publishing the book would mean that my work had been partially accepted by the academic community. They also asked if my assistant would earn a degree as a result of the proposed work. My answer was that she would not.

One council member remarked that the "book" was so thick she hadn't had time to read it and implied that for this reason she could not grant me permission to reside on the reserve. Another member asked how I knew that what I was writing "was the truth." He said that many people differ in their views of the same event and asked how I could sort out different versions and choose the "true" one. I replied that my main goal was to present the range of varied opinions on an event and that I was not intending to judge who was "right" or "wrong."

Finally, two other council members spoke strongly in my favor. One suggested that if more studies were produced showing "both sides of the story" the press might be less inclined to present a negative image of the Indian to the public. Another said that such research helped the community learn its own history. The council finally voted in my favor eight to four.

The summer of 1968 passed smoothly. I interviewed the council members informally, and some apologized for the treatment I had received during the meeting.

In April of 1969 I again requested permission for four months' temporary residence, with my assistant, to complete my research on voluntary associations.

A week before I made this request, I spent an evening with one of the council members, the only one at that time to have read the thesis which I had provided almost two years before. He was disturbed about some of the things I had written, and wished to discuss them.

First, he felt that my use of the word "myth" to refer to some of the oral traditions implied "it's not the truth." I replied that it is difficult to determine the truth of such traditions, but offered to change to word to "legend," of which he approved.

Second, he felt that I degraded the conservative component of the reserve. In my introduction I had stated that much professional attention had been directed to conservative culture patterns, but that the subject of this study was to be the nonconservative patterns. He claimed that I had stated that the council ignored the interests of the conservative people because they do not participate in elections. What I had actually stated was that the conservatives had given me several examples of what they considered ill treatment from the council—in the areas of road maintenance and housing. He considered this impolitic and I agreed to alter the wording as best I could to eliminate the touchy issue.

Finally, the "class issue" bothered him. Part of my thesis involved three categories which the Indians used to make status evaluations. I presented their own terms for these groups, their criteria for defining the categories, etc. The council member wanted to know if the class structure on the reserve was any different from that used by whites off the reserve. I replied that in my opinion it was no different, since the same kind of criteria were used off the reserve by whites to categorize their own people.

When the council met a week later, I was presented with strong statements of economic exploitation and the nonutility of my research. Although many Messalon Indians accept the usefulness of recording past and present traditions, some feel that more practical studies, such as the documentation of land alienation, would be of greater utility to them. One council member informed me that a Mr. Smith, who had been on the reserve years ago, had never presented his work to the council. The member who had read my thesis came to my defense, as did others who felt that "if it wasn't going to hurt, why not." The vote again passed in my favor—seven to four (one member was absent).

Two months later, I approached the council on another matter. By this time, two other members had read parts of the thesis. One objected to the inclusion of "all that history" for no particular reason, as far as he could see. Another member objected to the term "elite," stating "We are all equal out here." I explained that the status differentiation rested not only on power in the community but on economic conditions. I pointed out that, as political leaders, the council members had been dealing with welfare cases that very morning which were similar to those in white communities. These economic differences were not unique to Indians. I further explained that the term "elite" was a technical term, and I concluded that it would be impossible to withdraw it from my work.

One of my reasons for approaching the council was to request permission to borrow a picture they owned of a former outstanding community leader so that I could have it copied for my book. My request was met by a tied vote—one which the chief councillor broke in my favor because he felt that the picture "should go in your book."

My second request that day was to ask the council if they would pose for a picture to be included in the publication. The council agreed, with the exception of one member, who refused on the grounds that she didn't have anything against me personally, but since she thought "too many people are in here now" doing research, she could not compromise her stand for the sake of the photo.

I later learned that what she objected to were the actions of anthropologists in the north who apparently came into the medical center where she was temporarily working and "took over."

A month later, the same member reported hearing from the assistant Indian agent that a 'wandering anthropologist" was loose on the reserve. The assistant agent had discovered that this individual did not have permission from the council to reside on the reserve and that he did not have a grant to do research. I later learned that the researcher in question was from the Department of Education, and his work had been sanctioned by the Messalon Indian superintendent of schools, who was himself a member of the Messalon tribe.

That the elite, who strongly supported my work, did not come to my defense during this time is readily explainable. During the past six years there have been frequent conflicts between the council and the elite over the council's reluctance to sanction elite-sponsored community projects. The elite feel that these projects "should be the council's job" but since this has not been the case, they, the elite, will see that these projects are implemented, in spite of council opposition. The elite find deference to the council unrewarding, and in some cases undeserved. Thus, any elite influence in the council is very fragile, and in most cases is nonexistent.

Thus, although anthropologists have gained rapport with individuals sufficient to undertake reliable work, the surfeit of anthropologists and other researchers is beginning to undermine Indian attitudes toward our roles as researchers and the kind of work we undertake. Our motives, particularly humanitarian ones, are also being challenged. For example, at a recent seminar an Indian speaker challenged anthropologists and "other 'ologists" to prove that they wished to conduct research for reasons other than "to add more letters to the end of their names." He suggested they direct their efforts to action "for" the Indian.

Given the atmosphere of fear and anxiety on the reserve in the last two years, it is not surprising that white researchers are now facing opposition. Furthermore, it cannot be assumed that the resulting problems of entry will remain confined to a single reserve community.

## SECTION 2
## RELATIONS AND RESPONSIBILITIES TO RESPONDENTS AND INFORMANTS

**INTRODUCTION**

The cases in this section deal with various facets of the relationship between the field worker and his or her informants and the presentation of self in this relationship. As such, this section and Section 1, "Relations and Responsibilities to Host Community," are clearly related, covering many of the same ethical issues and dilemmas.

There is one major lacuna in this section, however. None of the cases presents the informant's view of this role relationship. Yet one hears rumors of various abuses: an anthropologist banking the proceeds from a book he helped an informant publish; a married anthropologist promising his informant that he will marry her if she returns to the United States with him; etc.

The field worker frequently discovers that those individuals who first offer to act as informants in the host community are either emotionally unstable or opportunistic. I learned this early in my own field work. My first informant told the villagers that I carried a gun in my pocket and that they should watch out for me—I had no gun in the field. He also warned members of the village to keep away from me so that he could maintain me as his exclusive property; he did not last long.

As field work proceeds and the investigator has the opportunity to get to know the people in the host community, more reliable informants can be selected. Relations with such individuals frequently evolve into close friendships. Casagrande (1960) presents a series of portraits by anthropologists of this type of informant. With respect to the relationship between anthropologist and key informant, he notes, "In final analysis it is unique among the various forms of human association" (Casagrande 1960, p. xi). Golde (1970) also includes articles that are relevant to this issue.

It has been my own experience that one of the great psychic costs of field work is the inability to maintain friendships with one's informants because of subsequent geographical distance or other contingencies that now arise in the modern world. For in many ways I find myself emotionally closer to those few informants who participated in my work than I do with friends in my own country.

However, it should be emphasized that the development of friendships across cultural barriers is not easy; it requires an extraordinary amount of patience and understanding on both sides. The processes that are involved in building such a relationship, the methods used to test its fiber, the problems of inherent mistrust and status inequality, and factors that lead to the breakdown of the relationship are all insightfully delineated by Edgerton (1965).

## RELATED CASE MATERIALS IN OTHER SECTIONS

*Section One: Relations and Responsibilities to Host Community:* Firearms in the Field; To Take a Wife; Problems and Consequences of Actively Helping the Host Community.

*Section Five: Relations with Other Social Scientists and Responsibilities to the Profession:* Mind Assault.

*Section Seven: Publication: Responsibilities and Liabilities:* Competition with One's Informants.

## 2.1 – PARTICIPATION IN ILLEGAL ACTIVITIES

For the first few days of field work in Mountaintown, I had a hard time locating where the men were during the day. Finally, several days after I arrived, the woman at whose house I was boarding introduced me to her son-in-law, John. He took me out to the higher pastures where the crews were working at that time of year. It was a Friday, and I accompanied him while he paid his crews. I knew virtually nothing about the running of sheep and cattle operations. Consequently, all my questions were very basic, the answers were mysterious to me, and the terminology was unfamiliar.

We ate lunch with one of the crews and sat around and talked for a couple of hours. John and his friends then went off to do some work, and they sent me into town to get some beer, which was about the only useful thing I could do. As I drove John's truck down into town, about twenty miles away, I noticed that it was extremely difficult to shift from first to second gear. Instead you had to go from first to third fiddling with the clutch. But I managed it somehow, reached the town, and picked up the beer. We drank and talked most of the afternoon.

We returned to Mountaintown for dinner, and afterwards we ended up at a bar in the next town, which was several miles away. In addition to John and myself, John's father-in-law, Ed (the husband of the woman with whom I was boarding), joined us. By about nine o'clock in the evening we were all feeling pretty happy. We had been drinking what I thought was a tremendous amount of beer, but since I was new to the culture, the people, and their patterns of socializing, I really didn't know what was considered heavy drinking. I did notice that Ed, who had not been with us during the day, must have been drinking beforehand, because he had some trouble walking and talking.

We remained in the bar about two hours, and Ed continued to drink rather heavily. Finally, he said that he had to go home; his wife disapproved of his drinking. At that point it really didn't matter, but he felt that he had to leave, so he asked John to take us all home.

John said, "Just take my truck and I'll get a ride with someone else." Apparently Ed didn't bother him again, but went outside, got into the truck, and drove off.

I became a little concerned in overhearing the conversation. I was worried that John's father-in-law was so drunk that either he wasn't going to make it home or he wouldn't be able to operate the gearshift in the truck. I mentioned the shifting problem to John, but he didn't reply.

I suppose I could have offered to drive Ed home, but at the time I did not think of it. I had been drinking much more than I was accustomed to, although I felt sober. There is something about the field-work experience that keeps you sober long past your normal inebriation point. Anyway, I was functioning and thinking quite well—but I didn't think of that alternative.

About half an hour after Ed had left the bar—we were still there drinking and socializing—he came back. He told John that he had burned out the engine of the truck and ruined it. Ed was not making a lot of sense—he was still pretty drunk—and John just ignored him. But it occurred to me that Ed probably hadn't been able to get the truck into second gear and had driven it faster and faster in first until he had probably broken a rod. However, John brushed him off and said it wasn't true. He thought his father-in-law had never gone anywhere but had fallen asleep in the truck for a half hour or so. Ed went over to the bar, got another drink, and then disappeared.

Around one o'clock in the morning the bar began to close, so we had one final drink and left. John couldn't find the truck anywhere. Then he remembered what his father-in-law had told him about it, so he arranged for a ride home with a couple of friends in their pickup truck.

Billy and Sam weren't close friends, and I never saw them socializing with John during the rest of my stay in Mountaintown. But they said that they would give us a ride. The four of us got into the pickup truck and drove several miles up the road, where we came across John's truck sitting in the middle of the road. The headlights were off, and there was a huge pool of oil in the road underneath the engine. Everyone got out, and at this point John remembered what his father-in-law had told him about ruining the engine. He didn't show any signs of being upset, perhaps because he'd been drinking heavily. Again, I had been in town only three days and hadn't yet learned to pick out any clues to the way people demonstrated their feelings.

We all looked at the engine; the others crawled under the truck and poked around. The three of them finally agreed that the engine had been ruined. I wasn't sure how they arrived at this decision. But the consensus was that the engine would have to be replaced and would cost about $1,200. At this point, John was clearly upset. He didn't think he could possibly afford that much money. Yet the truck was his only means of transportation; he needed it every day to get to work.

After it had been determined that the engine would have to be replaced but that John could not afford a new one, the three men decided they would have to get the insurance company to pay for it. Billy asked John if he had insurance; he nodded yes. The three of them decided they would have to figure out a way to make it look like the truck had accidentally caught fire.

I was silent during this discussion. No one asked my opinion, but they seemed to want my agreement that it was a terrible situation and that John couldn't possibly afford to replace the engine. And I agreed with them on these counts.

They decided to tow the truck up the road to a deserted stretch where they could arrange it to look like an accident. John and Sam got into John's truck, I climbed in with Billy, and we towed the truck up the road to an area where it would be safe to burn it.

## 2.1—Participation in Illegal Activities

When we'd placed the truck, we spent about ten minutes deciding how the scene was to be set up. John had a large can of gasoline in the back of the truck, which would have made quite an explosion if it had caught fire, so we removed it. We also took several expensive tools out of the cab. The men tried to figure out how much they would have to leave to make it appear as though it had been an accident and how much they could salvage, because they knew John would not get paid for the contents of the cab. We spread some gasoline around the inside of the cab. It was decided that John's story would be that he was driving along and flames started coming up through the floor boards into the cab. So he turned off his engine, jumped out, and tried to throw out as many of the tools as he could.

I was beginning to feel somewhat uneasy at this point. I tried not to do anything, although I realized that simply by being there I was choosing to participate to some extent. The question of choice is a tricky one. I suppose that when I left the bar I could have started walking down the road, avoiding a situation which I had some inkling about. However, my decision to accompany the three men was largely influenced by the fact that I was new in town. After three days it was exciting to feel a part of a social group. The entire day had been very productive in terms of establishing contacts and initiating field work. I was worried about how long it would take me to be accepted in the town and to find good informants. My time in the field was limited, and I didn't want to jeopardize any opportunities while there. I distinctly remember thinking about this as the others were throwing things out of the truck cab and we were looking up and down the road to see if anyone was approaching.

I remember taking only a couple of things out of the cab. I really didn't get too involved for the simple reason that I didn't know what to take out and what not to, and I didn't have the confidence to act out the scenario. It was more for that reason than any sort of legal or moral reason that I didn't participate more fully.

While they were arranging the scene, the three men decided I was not to be involved in the accident. The story was that John had been driving alone in the truck and I was coming up the road with Sam and Billy in their pickup. We were all returning from the bar when we came across John, whose truck had just caught fire. He was in the midst of throwing things out, so we stopped to help him.

Then there was the problem of how to notify the fire department. It was decided that Billy would take the pickup, drive to the nearest pay phone, and call the fire department. We must have become quite sober by this time, since our calculations were more careful now. We tried to figure out how long it would take for Billy to make the call and the fire truck to arrive, so that we would know exactly what to be doing at any given moment—in case people came by before the fire truck arrived. At this point, I did contribute to the planning by estimating that it would take about ten minutes to get to the booth and make the call. Although this wasn't a crucial part of the operation, I felt I was becoming a captive of the developing situation.

When the fire truck arrived, followed by six or seven cars—everyone in Mountaintown liked to go to a fire—the four of us were shoveling dirt from the side of the road onto the truck, which was by then blazing quite dramatically. The fire was put out and everyone stood around. There were a lot of people there whom I hadn't yet seen in the three days I had been in town; many of them didn't know who I was either. I didn't talk to them at the scene of the fire, but they all knew I was there. This is an interesting point, because the description of the incident subsequently presented to the insurance company involved three men, excluding me. The town accepted this. In a sense, they were protecting me and themselves, as well.

On the way back to my house—by then we were all sober—John started to think about what he had done and what the consequences might be. There were two things I particularly remember talking about. One was that Ed should not be told what we had done. John predicted that his father-in-law wouldn't remember anything about the evening after nine o'clock because he had been so drunk. If Ed claimed that he was the one who had driven the truck and burned it, we would deny it. John said that he would talk with his father-in-law in the morning to make sure he didn't remember anything about the latter part of the evening.

The second thing I recall talking about was my role in the incident. John said, "Do you agree to this story that we have put together about the three of you driving along and coming upon me?"

I said, "Yes."

He asked if the insurance agent were to ask me whether this story was correct, would I say yes. I said that I would. But it was at this point that I really began to wonder what I should be doing about the situation. I had never imagined being so involved after only three days in Mountaintown, let alone having to resolve this predicament.

---

Several days after the burning, I learned that John had bought a used truck. He had calculated what he would get from the insurance company, and using that as a guarantee for payment, he had purchased another truck.

During the rest of my field work, until I was preparing to leave, my involvement in the events of that night was never discussed. As a matter of fact, the event itself was never discussed except for two minor occasions. The day after the burning, someone remarked casually to me, "What a terrible thing happened to John last night!"

And I replied, "Yah, I guess so."

Even though I saw Ed frequently during the rest of my stay, I never mentioned the incident to him nor he to me. But I did hear later from another son-in-law that he did not think that the burning really happened as was alleged. I expressed some surprise, and he gave me the "real" story, which he had heard from Ed. I was not connected with it. Ed apparently had agreed to go along with the story John told him about the burning, but did not believe it.

A couple of weeks before I was to leave, John asked me if I wanted to go have a beer with him. We stopped along the road, and he said that he wanted to talk with me about the truck burning. This was the first time that he had mentioned the incident to me since it had happened. He said that at that time they really did not know very much about me, so they tried to keep me out of it. He didn't say for

## 2.1—Participation in Illegal Activities

whose sake, but it was obvious that it was for the sake of both of us. But now the insurance company was giving him a lot of trouble; they didn't believe his story. Since the incident, he said, he and the others had gotten to know me and like me, but he was worried that the insurance company was going to take him to court. He wanted to know whether I would come back and help him if this happened.

This request really caught me off guard, for the second time in my field work. I had hoped that the incident would be forgotten, because I had occasionally felt uneasy about my role that evening and about having compromised my own beliefs, to a certain extent. John's request raised the whole question again. More specifically, it also raised the possibility that I might have to tell the insurance investigator a fabricated story and, worse, go to court and commit perjury. John was still sticking to the original story that he was alone in the truck when it caught fire. The only difference now was that he wanted to add a third person—me—to the pickup which came up the road as the truck was burning.

I asked him if he really thought that this would make his case stronger. He believed it would because I was an outsider and would lend credibility to the story. The investigator had claimed that John's friends were sticking up for him. If I were to support his story, it would bolster his claim.

I remember thinking very clearly about my own motives and interests in this situation. To forestall having to answer John's request, I started talking about whether the investigator had the legal right to bring the case to court. Then I tried to find out more about the aftermath of the burning to determine how likely it was that John would actually have to call on me.

According to John, the burned truck had been taken to the local truck dealer from whom he subsequently purchased the used truck and where the insurance agent had inspected the burned vehicle. In the dealer's office, the insurance agent challenged John about his story. The agent said that he had found gasoline spots on the floor of the cab and this indicated arson. Furthermore, the tools and other equipment had been taken from the cab. At this point, John apparently lost his temper and started yelling at the agent. After the dealer calmed him down, John told the agent that he worked with gasoline-powered equipment and that, as a result, he always had gasoline on his clothes, oily rags in the cab, and gasoline stains on the cab floor. Later, the dealer warned John that he had really riled the insurance agent and would have to be careful, as it seemed to him that the agent was going to go after John with a vengeance.

After John told me about this encounter with the insurance agent, I began to calculate on the likelihood of my being called upon, and I started hedging on my support. He had been somewhat distant with me after the burning incident. When I had questioned him about his operation, he had been evasive—much more so than other operators. I didn't know whether to attribute this response to his personality or to the nature of his operation, which was a rather "fly-by-night" affair. His high initial investment was based almost entirely on credit and his permits for range use were short-term. These factors made his operation more risky than most of the others. In any case, as an informant he had been of little value.

John repeated his question of whether I would come back and help him if he needed me. He volunteered to pay for my expenses if I would come back and testify for him.

I was interested in studying John's operation; he was one of the more marginal—and more colorful—operators in town. On one level, I thought of suggesting some sort of reciprocity; that is, if I could do something for him, would he do something for me? At the same time, I was trying to calculate how likely it was that I would have to testify for him. I figured that if there wasn't much chance that I would have to make good my obligation, it would be worth the risk of saying I would come back if this would make him more willing to talk about his operation. What I found surprising—and somewhat disconcerting—about my reactions to John's request for my support was that I was as concerned about the effect my decision might have on my own data gathering as I was about the legal and ethical aspects.

During my stay in the field, I had developed some very strong attachments to many of the people, and not just because they were my informants—some of my best friends were some of my worst informants. I came to care about these people; about what might happen to them as a result of outside forces; and about what they could do to protect themselves and their way of life. These feelings obviously complicated my motivations. However, I will never know exactly to what extent I sacrificed my moral views for my own professional and research interests or for the sake of developing friendships with several of the people.

I had come to realize that the truck burning incident was not unusual in Mountaintown. People occasionally burned their houses, their cars, or their rangeland—this was one of their methods of dealing with outside agencies over which they had few formal or legal means of control. Of course, they recognized, just as I did, that this type of behavior was defined as illegal by the larger society. However, their attitude toward such behavior was different from what mine had originally been. Thus, during the conversation with John, when I was trying to make a decision about assisting him, I tended to rationalize the truck burning as part of a process used over the last half century by the people of Mountaintown to deal with an ever increasing threat to their livelihood and well-being by encroaching outside agencies and corporations. They had few formal or legal means of recourse. As a result, they had developed these illegal methods to bring some sort of control over the situation.

Of course, it was not easy to excuse the burning. I was working in a setting in which I was a citizen of the same society as the "natives." I was committed to a particular legal system, and was acutely aware of my obligations as a citizen. I did not find it as easy to explain away illegal behavior in my own country as I might have in a foreign country, because I felt a more personal commitment to the legal system in question.

Finally, there was the matter of choice. How much choice did I have in participating in the original event and how much choice did I now have, faced with John's request? Originally, I had thought that the anthropologist had little choice in such illegal situations. During my time in the field, I continued to regard the event of the truck burning as offering few, if any, alternatives. But, to an extent, I had been naive. When Ed first told John that the engine was ruined, it occurred to me that he might be right; but later, when we drove up the road to look for the truck, I didn't anticipate the actual consequences of finding it ruined. At the time, I was interested in finding transportation home. I didn't know anyone else to request a ride with, and walking was an unappealing alternative. Once we came upon the truck, I couldn't avoid observing what was going on. They had to do something quickly; they couldn't take me home and then come back because another car might come along and see the mess in the road. So in a sense things happened, but I had failed to anticipate their ramifications, and thus was caught up in the ensuing events and in the scenario that was constructed.

However, in regard to John's request to change the story and involve me in it, I had considerably more choice. It was so near the end of my stay that I could have easily postponed giving him an answer until I had left Mountaintown and returned to my university at which distance I could write him a letter saying that I didn't want to be a part of the story.

In fact, I initially tried to evade his request by arguing that even if I did agree, I would not be any good at it. I pointed out that I had never been in a situation like this before, involving arson, fraudulent claims, and perjury. Furthermore, the insurance agent was probably a shrewd person, with which John agreed. I continued that I probably couldn't stand up to the questioning in court, and I might hurt his case rather than help it. He admitted this was a possibility but thought I could handle it. I was much less confident of my ability. I hadn't been very competent in helping to set up the burning scene; I had never been in court before, nor had I ever been required to answer such questioning honestly, let alone dishonestly. I was concerned both about hurting John's case and about revealing the fact that I was committing perjury. I wondered, too, about what effect such a predicament would have on my relations with the rest of the community. John replied that he knew the dangers involved but he still felt he needed my support. He was beginning to sound somewhat desperate. This made me even more nervous because I reasoned that if he needed me that badly, the case couldn't be too far from court!

By the end of our conversation that afternoon, I had tentatively agreed to his request. However, I insisted that I would have to have more time to think about the situation. I wanted to help him as much as I could, but I wasn't really sure I could handle the courtroom situation. I added that I didn't want to hurt him or me.

In my two remaining weeks in Mountaintown, John and I did not discuss the case again. I was content to let my deliberately ambiguous agreement stand; apparently, John was also satisfied to leave the matter alone. However, he continued to be an uncooperative informant. Since leaving Mountaintown, I have received no further word from John.

## 2.2 – A CASE OF PRIVILEGED COMMUNICATION

Roger Thompson had recently spent eighteen months in Melanesia with the Grand Lake people. When he was invited to contribute a chapter to a colleague's book on myth, Roger decided to discuss one of the Grand Lake myths about the origin of certain magical powers. The story would illustrate a point that he wished to make about the authority of the shaman in the lives of the people.

After carefully translating the myth, Roger reviewed his field notes to check a few details. As he was turning the pages in his notebook, he discovered that two of them were stuck together. When he separated them, he found that the second page, which had been concealed by the first, contained a few short notes describing how he had come to record the myth, the details of which he had forgotten. According to his notes, he had persuaded the leading shaman in the village to recount the myth provided that Roger promised never to reveal it to anyone else. Suddenly Roger wondered whether he was violating a confidence by contributing a discussion of this myth to his colleague's book.

## 2.3 – A MEDICAL EMERGENCY

While I was living with a group of Eskimo in a village 150 miles from the nearest hospital, an old woman suddenly became ill. Her symptoms included a swollen and painful abdomen, fainting, frothing at the mouth, and severe pain in the vicinity of the heart. My do-it-yourself medical guide gave me no help. The woman's family was prepared to sit with her and wait for the illness to run its course. One Eskimo man said to me, "I think she'll burst; people do sometimes." But I found it difficult to sit by and do nothing as the Eskimo did.

Several men, including the old woman's son, were leaving that same day to go and trade in the community where medical aid was available. I suggested to the woman's husband that he send a message about his wife's illness, so that the priest who served as a medical aide could either send medicine or a plane to take the woman to the hospital. her husband asked the sick woman whether she wished such a message to be sent. She said no; she did not wish to go to the hospital— where she had already been several times. At this point, I didn't know what to do. If I respected the woman's wishes and did nothing, I might be responsible for her death. However, if I ignored her answer and sent the message myself, I would be asserting my will over hers and going against the strong value which the Eskimo place on personal autonomy in decisions of life and death. Finally, I decided not to send the message.
message.

In two weeks or so the woman was well. Later I happened to meet a doctor who had been acquainted with her case when she was in the hospital on a previous occasion with the same symptoms. He said that, as fas as he could tell, her illness was psychosomatic. He had not been able to find anything physically wrong with her.

---

Contributed by Dr. Jean L. Briggs, Memorial University of Newfoundland.

## 2.4 – THE ETHICAL PROBLEMS OF DOING FIELD WORK IN A SETTING OF INTENSE SOCIOPOLITICAL CONFLICT

Like the nation of which it is a part, Mona, an urban subdistrict, is beset by a fierce political polarization between adherents of the church-supported Christian party and those of the rival Communist party. The church once reigned supreme in the nation. However, it has recently suffered massive defections to the Communist party, despite such strong countermeasures as the excommunication of Communist party followers. Although officials of the church claim to take no part in politics, they also claim the right to protect the interests of the church against its enemies, namely the Communist party, and do everything possible to defeat them. The Christian party is thus formally independent from the church, but in fact greatly dependent on its support. The Communist party has sought to discredit the church and the Christian party by charging that they represent the interests of a few wealthy capitalists against the interests of the masses. The Communist party, however, avoids direct attacks on the church religion, so as not to alienate potential Communist members who have a church background. The church's position, however, is clear: one cannot be both a member of the church and a supporter of the Communist party; the two are mutually exclusive.

Because religious and political allegiances are so intertwined in Mona, the community is not only split into two mutually hostile camps around election time, it is also in a constant state of social tension. Attendance at church services is interpreted as allegiance to the Christian party and opposition to the Communist party. Similarly, attendance at a Communist fund-raising affair is taken as a rejection of the church. The Communist party adherents have their own social centers in the community, where their leisure hours are spent, while the church adherents have their own social gathering points. A Communist party youth group was organized to challenge the church's monopoly on youth socialization. This serves to further divide the community, with youths as well as adults presumed to fall into the one camp or the other.

The goal of my field work in Mona was to examine the formal and informal organization of political power. To do such a study, I needed the cooperation of members and leaders of both the church and the Communist party. Needless to say, the issues which I wished to investigate were extremely sensitive ones. Given the great importance attached by the people to the political struggle, they could hardly be expected to welcome an investigation into the way in which their own party wielded power. Thus there was some question as to whether the proposed field work could be carried out at all, for it could not be undertaken unless the researcher was treated by both sides as a friend rather than a foe, a social contradiction given the mutually exclusive sociopolitical allegiances.

Furthermore, there is little if any precedent in Mona for the role of impartial observer which I wished to assume. This is not to say that the people are entirely unfamiliar with the work of social scientists. Rather, they make the same assumption about social scientists that they do about anyone else—the individual must be a partisan of one side or the other. The most important identifying mark of the social scientist, indeed asked by the people, is whether he is a church or a Communist party adherent. If he is a church adherent, it is assumed he will study the corruption of the Communist party and the salutary role of the Christian party; and if he is a Communist social scientist, vice versa. Thus, any claim of objectivity is seen as a mask which permits the social scientist to do reconnaissance work in enemy territory.

These suspicions are in part offset by the desire of the people to present their side of the story so that the outside observer is not brainwashed by the opposition. In other words, everyone whose loyalties are not completely crystalized is a target of proselytization, a potential supporter. For this reason, the fact that the anthropologist is seen talking with the leaders of one side may be cause for leaders of the other side to want to talk to him, to rescue him from a misfounded political allegiance. Thus, I discovered that an effective way to elicit information was to ask an individual whether something told me by a member of the opposed party was in fact true. For example, when I mentioned to the Communist leader in Mona that a church partisan had told me that the local Communist officials were paid, the Communist leader issued a long denial, supplementing it with a wealth of information on the various Communist officials in Mona. Of course, the problem in dealing with this type of advocacy is that all information received by the anthropologist is suspect. However, once both sides of an issue are fully ascertained, it can generally be determined where the truth lies. In any case, this is only different in degree from most anthropological field work. The biases of informants must always be taken into account in evaluating information.

Both parties were especially eager to provide me with information after they discovered that I planned to write a book telling the Americans about life in Mona. Something of a dialectic was at work. On the one hand, the competing groups did not want to reveal any secrets; on the other hand, they were eager to have their own partisan views publicized. Thus, not only was my research in Mona immersed in the competitive environment, it actually became one of the prizes contested for.

The difficulties of carrying out field work in this setting are considerable. Despite my claims of objectivity, the people were constantly trying to determine where my loyalties actually lay. I could either lie or tell the truth and risk alienating one or both groups. For example, one evening I was driven home after a Communist party meeting by a Communist activist. He asked me whom I would vote for if I could vote in the local elections. At first I tried to avoid answering by saying I did not know enough about all the parties to be sure. But he kept insisting on an answer, becoming more suspicious the more I stalled. Finally, I answered in the following way: "I guess that if I were a local worker I would probably vote for the Communist party." I was merely stating a sociological proposition, since the majority of workers in Mona voted for the Communists. Actually, I was not then at all sure that I would not vote for a third party, a splinter group of the Communist party. To voice adherence to this group, however, would have stigmatized me with both the Communist and the Christian parties. If asked the same question by a Christian party member, I would have answered differently in order to protect my relations with the church people. In either case I would answer dishonestly in order to protect my research interests.

Field work is fraught with such half-truths, and in doing research in a situation of sociopolitical polarization, a systematic pattern of half-truths inevitably arises. One presents oneself as one thing to one group and as another to the second group. This requires both undercommuniation and overcommunication. The field worker undercommunicates to group X those views he holds which are relatively favorable to the competitor, group Y, and he overcommunicates those views he holds which are relatively favorable to group X. The suspicion by the local people that the outsider may not be a student or a social scientist but a spy ironically only serves to further the researcher's reliance on half-truths and image manipulation, and thus creates something very much like the spy role for the field worker. Playing up to group X in order to gather better and more information is at the heart of the research role. Entailed in this too, like the spy, is the necessity of segregating social contacts with the two sides, talking with one side at a time so that the right face can be put forward.

As an example, I used overcommunication when I was introduced to the head of the Communist party in Mona. I knew that I must win his confidence and friendship in order to continue with my research. I also knew that, as an American, I might be highly suspect. Therefore, I hastened to explain my role to him. I told him that I wanted to study Mona because of their Communist government, something unknown to the people of the United States. I said that there was much blind anti-Communism in the United States, and I hoped through writing about the Communist party in his country to show Americans the error of their views. Likewise, in discussing such issues as the Vietnam War, imperialism, American capitalism, and the working class, I was able to convey to the Communist leaders that I was sympathetic to many of their stands on major issues. In short, I was overcommunicating the areas of agreement with them and largely avoiding areas of disagreement. I was neglecting, also, to fully explain to them the critical nature of social analysis.

Undercommunication is the other side of the coin, also frequently practiced in field work. The investigator rarely tells one side what he or she has learned from the other side on certain matters. For example, though I had heard the details of a political battle waged the year before against a church group by the Communists in Mona, I undercommunicated the extent of my knowledge to the participants so as to check up on their stories. Furthermore, though I regularly read the newspaper of the Communist splinter group, I never would be seen in public with the paper for fear of the reaction of the Communist party supporters to my reading of this taboo publication.

The field worker also may undercommunicate the extent of his relations with the competing group. For example, when leaving the Communist party local headquarters to see the priest at the nearby church, I was circumspect in my reasons for departure. By leaving one side to visit the other immediately after discussing sensitive political matters, I risked accusations of acting as an informant.

This kind of undercommunication for the purpose of separating arenas so that one can play different roles cannot always be maintained. There were numerous incidents when such a separation of roles failed me.

Such an incident occured at the second Christian party meeting which I attended. Ths meeting was part of the election campaign and a Christian party congressman was the guest speaker. I was sitting in the back row of the small room. In the middle of the speech, one of the female leaders of the Communist youth group entered the room. All eyes turned to the girl—both her parents were renowned Communists in Mona—as she approached me and said in a loud voice, "Oh, you must have come here to count how many people go to these Christian party meetings." I quickly responded, "No. I came to see what the Christian party people have to say." I hoped that this would sooth the audience without antagonizing the girl. She then made a point of dramatically kissing both my wife and me before walking out the door and slamming it shut. All the while the Christian party congressman, no more than twenty feet from us, continued to speak. Already wishing I could vanish from the face of the earth, my wound was to be further opened. The other Communist youths who had accompanied the girl began revving their car engines outside and screeched away with their horns blaring. Meanwhile, all I could do was sit there, sweating it out, speculating on my chances of maintaining good working relations with the Christian party.

An example of conflicting arenas inadvertently juxtaposed occurred on election day when I had stationed myself at the Communist party section headquarters, located across the street from the polling place. All the local Communist party leaders and several members stood outside as votes began to come in from across the street and were posted on a large board. I volunteered to compute the percentages so that they could be posted quickly on the board. As I stepped into the street to get the latest results from the polling place, a car stopped beside me. It was the local priest, one of my most valuable informants. Standing only a few feet from the Communist leaders, I was acutely aware of their stares as the priest engaged me in conversation on the elections. There was little I could do. I could not abruptly terminate the conversation and risk offending the priest, yet my chat with him was probably undermining my relations with the Communists.

It should be apparent, then, that while the field worker may try to separate arenas in dealing with a highly polarized social environment, no such absolute separation is possible. The researcher must therefore prepare for the eventuality of a breakdown of his dual presentation of self so as to minimize its potential damage. I think the reason why such incidents as these—and there were several of them—did not produce disastrous consequences for my research is that I kept my undercommunication within certain limits. Although I played down the extent of my relations with the opposite side, I always tried to mention the fact that I did want to speak with both sides. I also tried to explain my role as an objective observer. While this was never fully accepted, it provided me with an explanation to fall back on when caught between the two arenas.

Another ethical problem is the conflict between the anthropologist's professional goals and his moral standards. All too often the moral duty of the field worker to his host community is oversimplified by identifying it only with the role of proponent of his community's interests to higher political authorities. This, of course, is an important role. However, it ignores what anthropologists should be the last to ignore, namely the heterogeneity of the local social organization and political interests. In an environment of social polarization, this moral duty of the anthropologist is less easily satisfied, and the effects of taking this moral stance on field work, not automatically salutary.

The problem for the anthropologist is that professionally he is rewarded only for what he produces out of his field work and not for how he resolves conflicts in his own moral standards in the field. Acting according to one's conscience entails possible isolation from part of the community. But if the field work is to be successful, the anthropologist must collect information from all sides of the dispute. Traditionally, anthropologists have shied away from this ethical problem by embracing a relativist position. This rationale, however, is of little use where such extreme polarization exists and there is little moral unanimity. Let me give three examples of this problem.

I was attending a members only meeting of the Mona Communist party during an election campaign. The head of the local section launched a diatribe against a new priest in Mona, accusing him of actively engaging in political work for the Christian party. I was friendly with the priest and knew that the charges were untrue. The priest was in fact sympathetic to left-wing causes and bitterly opposed to the Christian party, regarding the church's support of it as a religious disgrace. Although I knew these accusations were false, I did not dispute the charge. I felt that to do so would ruin my hard-earned and vital rapport with the Communist party in Mona, barring me from further attendance at these important public meetings.

The same priest began a tutoring program at his newly founded church for the children in the poorest part of Mona. These children were having great difficulties in the public schools, many of them dropping out before the minimum legal age and many failing year after year. They were ridiculed by their classmates for their ignorance and were ultimately consigned to the most menial and exploited occupations. My wife, recognizing the urgent need for such a tutorial program and the dearth of qualified teachers, volunteered to assist in the tutoring.

Although her participation provided a valuable opportunity for studying the establishment of the new church, I was apprehensive about my wife's public identification with it. I knew that the program would provide crucial help for disadvantaged children in Mona, but I was worried that my wife's participation would antagonize my Communist informants and threaten my relations with the Communist leaders. I discussed this with my wife, but she decided to go ahead and participate in the priest's program.

To minimize the negative effects of my wife's involvement with the new church, I seized on two local conceptions of women to dissociate myself from any expression of adherence to the church. First, there is the traditional characterization of women as "weak" in matters of religion and they are regarded as particularly susceptible to the priest's appeals. As a result, women in Mona can attend church without being categorized as anti-Communist. Second, people in Mona assume that all American women have asserted their independence by breaking away from the authority of their husbands. American women are seen as uncontrollable. Thus, I was able in part to turn the issue around, receiving sympathy for my lack of influence over my wife. This presentation was aided by the fact that my wife also gave private tutoring lessons to one of the leaders of the Communist group in Mona. In short, she tried to play the role of the unpoliticized American woman, just trying to help the youths of Mona in any way that she could.

However, my wife's association with the new church did provoke a few tense moments. One of these occurred at a Communist demonstration when a Communist activist cornered her and asked whether it was true that she was teaching at the church. When my wife admitted that she was, the activist became angry, claiming that such "progressive" priests merely served to lure unsuspecting people into the clutches of the reactionary church. I refused to get into the argument, saying that my wife had the right to do whatever she saw fit. In this case, I was emphasizing my wife's role as an independent American woman.

Finally, I was in Mona when I learned of the decision by the Nixon government to increase the bombing of North Vietnam and to begin mining Haiphong Harbor. As an American citizen opposed to the United States war, I wanted to protest these acts. A mass demonstration was being planned in the city of which Mona is a part, sponsored by the Communist party and various other organizations protesting the escalation of the war. I decided that I could not sit by while the slaughter continued, and I organized a contingent of Americans against the war to participate in this demonstration.

I made this decision with some trepidation, for the Vietnam war was hotly contested between the Communist party and the Christian party. The Christian party, which controlled the national government, had always backed the anti-Communist foreign policy of the United States, while the Communist party obviously opposed it. The more unpopular the war became, the more the Communist party used this issue to attack the Christian party. Any public identification on my part with the antiwar forces might antagonize the church leaders in Mona. From the point of view of maintaining productive relations with them, I should have avoided public involvement in the antiwar demonstration. I might have tried to salve my conscience by attending the rally as a spectator. Instead, I decided to become involved as an organizer of the demonstration. This involved making speeches in public, where I could easily have been seen by the church leaders.

In fact, I encountered no pronounced ill effects from this activity for two reasons. First, these events took place relatively late in my field work; I had already become quite friendly with and fairly well known by the church people. Second, the two sides were so severely polarized that the Christian party people would never attend an antiwar rally, nor would they be likely to discuss the event with

Communists who had attended. However, had I undertaken this political activity earlier in my field work, or had my role in the demonstrations become better known among the church people of Mona, my work with them would have been seriously limited. I do not know if my decision to become involved in the demonstration would have been different had the escalation of the war occurred earlier in my field work.

the people were so friendly and trusting toward a stranger. Not only did I request their cooperation and aid, but I came with questions about extremely sensitive topics—the church, the Communist party, and political struggle. As a participant observer, I was at their mercy, completely dependent on their good will. Although my role as researcher required constant awareness of the image I was projecting and assessment of the audience I was addressing, my personal relations were on the whole extremely friendly. That this was the case is a constant source of amazement to me, though without this friendliness and trust my year in the field would have surely been a frustrating and unproductive one.

## 2.5 – DISEASE AND DEATH: RESEARCH IN THE UGURU DISTRICT

Roger Pierce had just finished building his field station and was awaiting the arrival of his wife and two children. His older child was two and his younger only six months. Roger was somewhat concerned about exposing them to the various diseases which prevailed in the village. He had built his field house so that he could isolate his children from direct contact with informants, if necessary.

Of particular concern to Roger was the high incidence of tuberculosis. He had noticed that the village headman had a very bad case of glandular tuberculosis, with open, draining sores on his neck. When Roger had first arrived in the community, the headman had asked if Roger thought he could be helped at the district hospital in Uguru, about ninety miles away. Roger had replied that he thought the doctor there might be able to do something for him. While Roger was building his field house, the headman visited him a number of times and inquired further about the hospital. During these discussions, Roger tried neither to encourage nor discourage the headman from going to the hospital. He repeatedly made the point that the headman should make the decision for himself. However, Roger did offer to take the headman into Uguru, if he decided to go to the hospital for treatment, since Roger regularly drove there for supplies. He also said he would be glad to accompany the headman to the hospital and see that he was admitted.

As Roger was completing his field house, the headman told him he had made up his mind to go to the hospital in a month or so. Roger wondered about the long wait, but someone explained to him that there were certain taboos that had to be satisfied first. Also, Roger discovered that the headman's wife and sisters were quite distraught over the headman's trip to the hospital and were trying to discourage him from his plan.

About a month later, Roger heard that his wife and family had arrived in Uguru, and he notified the headman that he was planning to drive up the next day. The headman said that he would go with him and enter the hospital.

At the hospital, the doctor told Roger that the headman would have to stay for several weeks. Roger explained this to the headman and left him there, promising to visit every now and then to see if he wanted anything. Roger then picked up his family and returned to the village to continue his field work.

About three weeks later, another village member, Nasingu, came to Roger and said that he, too, would like to go to the hospital, but he had no money. He explained that his "body was full of water" and that he had had the condition for some time. However, it had become so bad that he was unable to work in the fields, and he wanted to see if the doctor at the hospital could cure him. Nasingu asked Roger to loan him $15 to help cover his expenses. After some consideration, Roger agreed to loan him the money and take him to the hospital the next time he went to Uguru.

Several weeks after Nasingu entered the hospital, the headman returned to the village in much better health. The doctor had given him a large supply of pills, with instructions to take them daily. About a week later, news arrived at the village that Nasingu had died. Nasingu's wife became hysterical, and it was clear that a number of other villagers were extremely disturbed.

Roger later learned that the night following the news of Nasingu's death there was a meeting at Nasingu's house of all his close kin. The next morning the headman told Roger that Nasingu's wife was considering suing him for contributing to Nasingu's death.

Roger was taken aback by this turn of events and was concerned about the possibility of having to pay a considerable fine in order to keep peace in the village. But he also felt that the suit had no basis in fact and only indicated the degree to which he had failed to be accepted in the village. Since Nasingu's death was clearly either the result of a disease which could not be cured or the responsibility of the hospital, Roger felt that the suit was only an excuse to relieve him—a rich American in the eyes of the villagers—of a considerable sum of money.

Roger questioned his chief helper and informant about the reason for the suit. He was told that the villagers believed hospital beds were unclean and extremely dangerous because people had died in them. They also believed that the spirits of these dead lingered around the beds and that anyone sleeping in the beds would be killed by these spirits.

Roger argued with the headman that it was not his fault that Nadingu had died, since it had been Nasingu's decision to go to the hospital, not Roger's. He had only helped Nasingu get there by loaning him money and giving him a ride into Uguru in order to avoid the expense of the trip. The headman agreed that the suit was unjust and tried to dissuade Nasingu's widow from pursuing it.

Investigation of Nasingu's death by the local police subsequently revealed that he had not died in the hospital, but had left of his own accord and against the doctor's wishes. On his way home on foot, and a short distance from the hospital, Nasingu had sat down under a tree and died.

Several days later, the widow came to Roger's field house and told him that she would drop her suit against him, but that she did not know where she was going to get the money to repay the loan he had made to Nasingu. Without her husband's help in the fields, she said, she was only able to raise enough food for her children and did not have any grain left over to repay the debt. After some thought, Roger said he was content to forget the loan since she had had so much trouble. The widow was obviously relieved.

Roger later learned that the circumstances of Nasingu's death precluded his burial in the village cemetery. For ritual reasons he had to be buried in the cemetery close to the place he died, and his funerary ceremonies were therefore required to be abbreviated. However, it was not clear to Roger how these consequences of his death outside the village had affected Nasingu's widow or influenced the advice given.

It was not until the end of his field work that Roger began to understand the full implications of his acts and concluded that he may not have acted responsibly in either the case of the headman or that of Nasingu. He discovered that the explanation for illness among the Uguru people was based on the belief that the world was filled with spirits which took vengeance whenever any of the local taboos were violated. In effect, illness was the penalty for an antisocial act. In the context of these beliefs, Roger began to view his actions as contributing to a weakening of social control. If the indigenous beliefs were threatened or destroyed, antisocial acts would increase as a result. His two acts of mercy—one of which ultimately failed—when weighed against his contribution toward the possible destruction of the local belief system, did not seem so merciful. In the long run, he may have contributed to considerably more suffering.

## 2.6 – CONFLICT IN THE ROLES OF FRIEND AND INFORMANT DURING THE FEEDBACK OF RESEARCH RESULTS

I had done field work in a community of whites and Indians at intervals for a period of seven years before I finished my dissertation. In it I dealt with the nature of the relations between these two ethnic groups and the resulting conflict and tensions between them. I thought I had captured rather well the insider's view of the structure of these relationships.

The summer after finishing my dissertation, I returned to the community to do additional research, fill in the lacunae in my work, and make revisions necessary for publication. I brought with me a couple of copies of my dissertation, having been convinced by the arguments for telling your informants what you are doing and giving them access to the results of your research. I planned to ask a couple of friends in the community to read the dissertation and give me their views about it.

Because parts of the work dealt with the problem of how the Indians are hassled by the police, I asked a friend, who is both an Indian and a policeman, to read it. But his loyalties were so divided, he could not handle the situation. He never talked to me again.

Another close friend was Frank Porter, a white man I had met the first summer. He had inherited a large farm, which he managed well. Although he had only a high school education, Frank was a sensitive man who read and thought a lot and who was concerned with the difficulties faced by the Indians. In fact, he was a bit of an outsider himself, in the sense that he was reflective about what was going on. He knew things were not as they should be and that somehow he was part of the problem.

Frank was very active in his church. He had had trouble at various times in his life—frequently involving relationships with Indians. This was of great interest to me since I was concerned with the nature of the relationship between Indians and whites. When I first met Frank, I told him about my research interests and my concern with the nature of the interethnic relationship. When we talked about his relationship with Indians, my understanding was that he knew that I was collecting data, but at the same time we also became friends.

In the course of our conversations, Frank told me some things in confidence about his relationships with various Indians, things that could have reflected badly on him. For example, he had gone through a period of heavy drinking. His drinking companions were often Indians. The white people in the community assumed that drinking with Indians involved several other illicit activities, such as sleeping with women, getting into drunken fights, and so on.

Frank finally became so disturbed about his future position in the community that he had decided to quit drinking and join Alcoholics Anonymous. At the time, he was drinking with an Indian man who was a close friend. At Frank's suggestion, both men went to Alcoholics Anonymous, and Frank quit drinking but his Indian friend never did. This became a sensitive issue in their friendship, and it has never been resolved.

he knew I was interested in the relations between Indians and whites. Second, I was an outsider and therefore a "safe" person to confide in. Finally, we were good friends, so he trusted me. These were things that he never told any other member of the community.

While in the field, I lived in a tent. Frank would come by late at night with a thermos of coffee, and we would sit and talk. Or we would run into one another in town and go off some place to talk. We were good friends, and I thought he was aware of what I was doing. These conversations were not formal interviews. I also told Frank things about myself, how I felt about Indian friends, about my life at home, and so forth.

When I came back the summer after finishing my dissertation, I wanted Frank to read it. First, I wanted to be sure that I had not said or implied anything about the community that was erroneous. Second, I naively thought that Frank and I could learn something from one another if we discussed the situation—from his point of view as an insider and from my point of view as an outsider. Also, because I admired this man and thought he was both sensitive and wise, I respected his opinions. I did not hope to ameliorate the relations between whites and Indians. I was only concerned about recording and interpreting this relatively tense situation as honestly as I could, and it seemed to me that one way to do that was to show my dissertation to Frank, discuss his response to it, and learn if he had any grievances.

Frank was eager to read the dissertation, since he hadn't seen anything I had written up to that point. He took off with it, and I did not see him for about two weeks. When I finally saw him in town, he was strangely distant. About a week later, he came by to drop off the dissertation. I was very excited when he came by, and I thought we were now going to sit down and discuss what I'd written. Frank obviously didn't want to talk about it. I asked him what he thought, but he didn't say anything. He was very distant. I offered him coffee, but he didn't want any. He honestly wanted to get the hell out. But finally, Frank began to talk about the dissertation. He was upset because I had included some stories that he had told me. I had used pseudonyms and had disguised the incidents in various ways. But he still recognized them and remembered things that he had told me five, six, and even seven years ago. Frank felt that I had betrayed a confidence. I argued, "But no one in the world will know that it is you that I am talking about." I don't think he was so much worried about anyone else finding out that he used to drink a lot—everyone in the community already knew that. But he felt that I had used him as an object.

Frank also said that it seemed to him that I had portrayed everything that was wrong as the fault of the white people. This was not my intention nor do I think it was an accurate interpretation of what I had written. But Frank was sensitive enough to feel a certain responsibility for and perhaps anguish over the conflict between whites and Indians. He felt that he wasn't doing enough. And he said to me in an exasperated tone, "Look, I am trying to keep my farm together and raise my children as good people. You know it's hard enough doing that, but you expect me to straighten out the whole world!"

I think this miscommunication was partly the result of my own naiveté. I had written something I thought was a reasonably accurate interpretation of the pattern of relationships between Indians and whites. And I assumed that Frank, who had been both informant and close friend, would find this interesting. I thought he shared my understanding that he and I were working on a number of different levels. On one level, we were friends. On another level, I was there with a job to do—I wanted to write about relations between Indians and white people. On a third level, Frank, as a somewhat disaffiliated member of the community, and I, as an outsider, were standing aside and discussing what we had mutually observed.

But Frank apparently did not see the various levels of our relationship. He felt betrayed, troubled, and guilty, and he wanted to have nothing more to do with me. He felt that I had made use of confidences that were shared between us as friends, treating him merely as a case.

Perhaps I could have presented the dissertation to Frank more carefully rather than just giving it to him to read on his own. I merely told him it was my dissertation I was revising for publication and that I wanted his opinion. What I might have done was to talk with him about it, going over each page together. Perhaps he would have been less insulted; perhaps not. As it stood, Frank absolutely refused to talk with me about the dissertation. But the most tragic thing was that I had lost a real friend. Ironically I thought I was doing the ethically correct thing by showing a key informant and friend the results of my work. But what I did, in effect, was destroy a valuable relationship which disturbs me very much.

Since then I have written Frank and sent him a set of photographs of his family and farm. I even tried to call him a couple of times. However, I learned later that he told another friend that he would never talk to an anthropologist again.

## 2.7—DEATH FROM A WOUND

During my second field session, a man was shot in his upper right thigh. I saw him a day or two after he was wounded and noted that the injury did not seem serious. There had been an intervillage fight and several people were wounded and were walking around with bullets in them. So it didn't strike me as something that I should follow up. However, when I saw this man six months later, I noticed that the bullet was still in the wound, which had become seriously infected. He was very weak and could hardly move. Obviously, he and his clan members were awaiting his death. He would stumble out of the hamlet to urinate and defecate and then stumble back and lie all day in his house. His hamlet was located high up a steep mountain side. I went up each day to give him injections of penicillin, but they didn't seem to help.

After several days, the doctor came to the nearby police post, and I asked him to look at the wounded man. Some of his clan members brought him down on a stretcher to the level ground so that the doctor could examine him. The doctor decided that the man was too weak to undergo surgery for removal of the bullet. The doctor told the clan members to take him to the hospital at the provincial capital—about ten to twelve hours away by boat—where the doctor would try to build up his strength before taking the bullet out. At first the clan members agreed to this, but at the last minute they changed their minds. They said that they did not trust the hospital, that he would just die there. He was going to die anyway, they said, and nothing could save him.

I tried to insist that they take him to the hospital, but was unsuccessful. They do not draw a line between life and death as Americans do; they already perceived him as having moved into the category of the dead. And for them death is not horrible, or frightening, as it is for us. They see it all the time and accept it as a normal part of their lives. Funerals are seen as desirable ceremonies. They provide the occasion for a ritual exchange of goods which promotes both the economic and the social system.

## 2.8—AN ACT OF COMPASSION

Cliff Elkins was returning to the main camp at Siku after a month of reconnaissance in the mountains. He was looking forward to good food, mail from home, and, above all, relaxation. He was also eager to learn what his co-worker, Roger Kemp, had accomplished during his absence. As Cliff walked through the village of Siku with his guide, he noticed that the people seemed unusually excited and agitated. He did not have long to wait to find out what had happened as Roger met him at the door of their field house and told him the following story.

"Siku's feud with Telim has flared up again. The people of Telim just destroyed three Siku fishing boats and killed an old man. The Siku people are demanding revenge. This morning, as they were talking about an ambush, a woman from the Telim people showed up in the village. She had run away from her husband, crossed the strait in a small canoe, and came here seeking the help of a relative. I was sitting here working on my field notes when I heard a commotion outside. I ran out and found a group of angry men encircling this woman, about to kill her. I reacted instinctively; I shoved my way into the middle of the crowd and pulled her out. She's in the back room now, and I'm going to take her down to the police station tomorrow."

Cliff did not know what to say. He was not yet familiar enough with Siku society to predict the people's response to this interference, but he knew there would be a strong reaction. He was irritated at Roger for acting so impulsively and presenting him with this new crisis at a time when he just wanted to relax, wash, change, and get a decent meal. Cliff did not conceal his annoyance.

"Why did you get involved in this? You know the missionaries say that this is just one way of committing suicide. The woman did not come to you for protection. It was an incredible gamble on her part, seeking protection from her kin. Why did you have to go and jeopardize our whole expedition?"

Roger replied, "For God's sake, man, don't tell me you'd sit by and watch them kill her! No one can be that cold-blooded. Don't you have any morals at all?"

Cliff coolly responded, "You don't have to put on the hero act with me, Roger. You're only kidding yourself if you think you've saved a life. These people are still going to kill someone to even the score. You may have saved this particular woman, but you've condemned another person to death. They're going to kill someone and you know it!"

Roger walked away. The next morning, after a tense goodbye, he started out on the two-day trip to the police station with the woman he had saved. Cliff spent the day resting and reading his mail. The following morning, as he began to type up his reconnaissance notes, he was interrupted by a yell from the beach. A group of men returning to the village were signaling that they had ambushed and killed a Telim villager.

## 2.9 – THE CONSEQUENCES OF INVESTIGATING A SENSITIVE SUBJECT

One of the administrators I met warned me to be very circumspect in my study of shamanism among the Eskimo. He said that the Eskimo are aware that whites frown on the practice, and he related to me the consequences of one investigation into shamanism. The anthropologist had been working in a highly missionized Eskimo community and had finally persuaded some Eskimo to sing shamanistic songs for him. Shortly thereafter, one man who had recently been converted to Christianity committed suicide as a result of his guilt over participating in an activity which was an important part of the native religion.

I wondered how I could approach the subject of shamanism among the group of Eskimo I intended to study without causing any harmful psychological effects.

---

Contributed by Dr. Jean L. Briggs, Memorial University of Newfoundland.

## 2.10 – INTERVENTION IN A CURING SESSION

I learned that my key informant's brother was going to be given a cure. My informant had gone into town to get in touch with a man skilled in black magic—an obeah man. The obeah man agreed to cure this boy at a tremendous cost to his family. The boy was afflicted with what we might call schizophrenia. Periodically, he would take off into the woods, and people wouldn't see him for a long time. They wondered how he survived. Sometimes he scared people; occasionally he threatened someone. It was difficult for me to learn much more than this about the boy, except that he was really a problem for his family and the entire community. I don't think it was because he had ever harmed anyone, but some people were worried about what he might do "when the demons got into him."

I got ahold of my informant after he came back from town and took him to my house. We sat there, talking and drinking for four or five hours, and I got my cook to prepare a good meal for both of us. The obeah man was expected to arrive in the village late that night.

I started talking to my informant about how ridiculous this undertaking was. He would have to pay about $300 for the cure, which was a fortune for him. He was only a peasant farmer, and it had taken a long time to save this amount of money. We argued back and forth.

I tried all kinds of tricky arguments. "What is going to happen when this obeah man comes here? Is he going to find your brother in the woods?"

"No," my assistant replied, "the obeah man said we had to get my brother and keep him here until he arrives."

I said, "What kind of obeah man is that? If he really understands all kinds of hidden things, he wouldn't have to get you to hold your brother here. He would find him. What does this man know anyway? He's not trained. In our society we call this mental illness, and if you give me a chance, I'll take you and your brother to the city. I know some people at a clinic there. It won't cost you very much. Your brother will get some psychiatric help. This will do a lot more for him than anything you can do here."

I knew what was going to happen to the boy, and I was arguing for humanitarian reasons. They were going to tie him up to a tree, flog him a little bit, and pour hot water and then cold water on him. An informant had told me about the curing session saying, "You're an anthropologist, and this is something you ought to see. You ought to bring a camera and see how we deal with people who have demons inside them. It would be a very interesting thing for you to write about in your book.

By late afternoon, and after a bottle of rum, I thought I'd convinced my informant to cancel the curing session. He told me he was going to get a taxi into town, find the obeah man, and tell him not to come.

I was feeling very relieved and pleased. I was really convinced that at certain times you have to abandon the role of anthropologist and just be human. You just can't stand by and let people suffer for no purpose. I said this to my cook, adding, "You see, if you really put your mind to it, science is going to win out over these superstitions."

And she said, "Well, I don't know; I'd rather wait and see."

The next day I ran into a friend who asked, "Did you get a chance to see the curing session last night?"

I replied, "What curing session?"

And he said, "Didn't you know that the obeah man was supposed to come last night and cure the crazy boy?"

"Did he come down?" I asked.

"Sure, a lot of people were there!"

"Did they do the regular things," I asked, "like tie him up, beat him, and throw hot and cold water on him?"

"Sure. He seemed a lot calmer afterwards."

As far as I know, the boy was just as crazy afterwards as he had been before the cure. But the treatment seems similar to shock therapy. In the mental hospital where I used to work, they'd grab someone, put him down on a bed, and put cold, wet sheets around him, which they continued wetting.

But I was doubly upset about this situation. I really didn't know whether I should have interfered as I did with the local culture. Not only did I try to stop the curing session, but I was unsuccessful. At least if I had succeeded, there would have been some consolation that the boy had been spared the physical torture of the session. But having failed, it bothered me that I also missed getting some good ethnographic information.

However, I wasn't sure that if my advice had been followed it would have been of any help to the boy either. His brother would have had to take him to the city once a week. It would have been a big bother for him to sit there all day. The boy would have seen a Western psychiatrist who no doubt would be unfamiliar with the villagers' culture. Even in the United States—where doctor and patient are members of the same society—the treatment of schizophrenia has not been very successful.

Probably the most important part of this whole incident was not the cure for the boy, but the fact that his family felt that they were doing the right thing. Also, the community felt that it was a community problem and that the family had made the right decision in trying to solve it. After the curing session, the boy's family was absolved from the problem and the community could say, "Well, they had the obeah man. There is nothing more that can be done. We tried to get rid of these demons. If the boy is still crazy, his demons are just too strong to be driven out."

## 2.11 – EMBARRASSING INFORMANTS

In the area where I worked, women had, until recently, been prohibited from entering the local pubs. However, a new law had been passed allowing women to enter the pubs, most of which responded to the change by setting up a separate section of tables for women accompanied by male escorts. In most pubs, this area was screened off from the men's section. But in one pub which I frequented, no effort had been made to screen the women's section. Instead, it occupied an area on one side of the room which had a rug on the floor under the tables. The floor of the men's section, on the other side of the room, was bare.

I was aware that Indians frequenting this pub were meeting with a subtle type of segregation and that certain unspoken rules operated to delimit the activity of the Indians in the pub. However, I was not sure exactly what these rules were or how strongly they were enforced. I was determined to test them out and also to find out how the Indians responded to these rules. As a start, I took my wife and an Indian friend into the pub one afternoon and led the way to a table in the women's section. The Indian and his wife were reluctant to sit in this section. They were obviously most embarrassed. I tried to reassure them and insisted that it was perfectly all right for us to sit there. However, shortly after we were seated, a waiter came up and said that all of us had to go sit in the men's section, even though this was in fact an illegal action on his part.

I did this to test the validity of an unwritten rule of segregation, but I wondered afterward whether I should have gone this far in embarrassing my informants to test my data.

## 2.12 – DEALING WITH THEFT

After I had been in the field for almost a year, I went out to the coast for a two-week vacation. Since I had been troubled by petty theft, I carefully locked my house before leaving, and my neighbors put taboo markers around it to keep spirits and thieves away. They assured me they would protect my belongings.

But when I came back, I found that the house had been broken into and a number of valuable shells and trade goods, including blankets and steel axes, had been taken. These things were not that valuable from my point of view—they were worth about $50 in all. However, for the Manu they were objects of wealth.

I tried to find out from my neighbors who had taken my belongings, but they claimed no knowledge of it. After a few weeks I learned that the thief was a young man named Marak, who had previously been employed at the mission station. He had worked for the missionaries for a long time, but they had finally let him go because they didn't need his help anymore. Marak never understood why he had lost his job; he assumed it was because the missionaries were angry with him for some reason.

About three weeks before the theft, I had given medical treatment to Ning, who had been wounded in a fight with Marak. Ning was the son of one of my very good informants as well as a friend of mine. Ning had provoked the fight by stealing Marak's wife. In retaliation, Marak shot and wounded him. Apparently, Marak resented the fact that I had given Ning medical aid. As far as I could figure out, there were no other motivations for his theft. He'd had trouble with Europeans in general, and he had also felt that I had sided with his enemy in this fight.

Once the neighboring Manu discovered that I knew who the thief was, they urged me to take my gun and go after Marak to get my belongings back. They insisted that it was the proper thing to do. But no one was willing to accompany me. In any case, I didn't want to follow their advice.

One day about a month after the theft, I met Marak as I was walking along a path. But he ran away before I had a chance to say anything to him. I didn't see him again.

Two months later, in October, I overheard a conversation among several of my friends and neighbors. They were joking about the fact that Marak had given them some of the loot he had stolen from me. They were laughing about this and saying what a good thing it was. I got the impression that they were planning to steal some more things from me. After hearing this, I was determined to do something about the theft, but I didn't know quite what it should be.

The next day there was a marriage payment ceremony during which valuable goods were to be distributed. I went to the ceremony and learned that as part of the distribution Marak was to be awarded some shell bands. He wasn't there to receive them, but his father received them for his son. After the distribution, I went up to Marak's father and said to him in Manu, "Look, you know and everyone knows your son stole many things from me! So it is only right that you give me your son's shell bands in restitution for the theft." Marak's father protested that he had never heard of this man Marak. It wasn't his son, and he disclaimed any knowledge of him. Thinking how the Manu would react to this obvious lie, I tried to grab the shell bands and started a fist and foot fight with Marak's father. He yelled for help, but no one offered it. We struggled for a while until he finally gave up the shell bands.

Afterward, I was remorseful at my loss of temper. I felt that I had acted appropriately in the sense that this was the way the Manu would have handled it. Nevertheless, I felt that I had taken unfair advantage of the man, and I was sorry about that. Even as a woman I am taller than most Manu men, and I had on hobnail boots when I kicked Marak's father in the shins.

As we went home, my friends and neighbors assured me that I had done the right thing; they described the incident to everybody we met along the trail, saying what a great warrior I was and showing them the shell bands. But I was worried that Marak might take revenge by burning down my house. It is this kind of incident which can lead to war among the Manu.

Marak never did retaliate. However, the stories about the fight between Marak's father and me became more and more elaborate and wild as the days passed.

In December I attended a pig feast. Marak's father made a special point of giving me a big piece of pork and embracing me. The following spring Marak approached me through a middle man and asked whether I would be willing to take two pigs as the rest of the payment for the goods he had stolen from me. I agreed to accept them. After Marak brought me the pigs we became friends. One of the pigs died two days later—of poison, I believe.

## 2.13 – DEALING WITH THREATS OF AGGRESSION

I was doing field work in an American dependency shortly after the Korean War. It was largely a white community, with only a few blacks. In the neighborhood where I lived, about three miles outside of the town itself, there was only one black family, consisting of a mother, her married son, and her grandchild. This family lived across the road from us, and I developed a friendly relationship with the son and through him a friendship with his mother. I liked her, and I think she liked me.

A good deal of my work was carried on with the help of veterans. I discovered that a large number of men who had served in World War II and in the Korean War were living in the town, and I was able to establish rapport with them very quickly. After I had been there for some time and had spent a great deal of my time with the veterans, four or five of them became very close friends. I spent many of my days and nights with them.

I spent a lot of time socializing in a small shop a few hundred yards down the road from where I lived. In this store, apart from the fact that it was where you bought drinks, snacks, and other things, there was a small dance hall with a jukebox. This was a favorite hangout for many people, and the jukebox was played day and night. The men would stand around drinking a locally produced corn liquor. The pattern was to start drinking when you met your friends in the morning and continue throughout the day. But, as a rule, people did not get drunk.

On one particular occasion, after I had been in the field for over a year and had established several warm friendships, I was sitting in the dance hall talking to a group of people while we ate and drank. A veteran, with whom I was friendly but not close, came into the shop for a drink. He was a middle-class, petty entrepreneur involved in various kinds of activities. It was late in the afternoon, and he was already quite drunk. He had a drink at the counter, as I remember, and then brought another to the dance floor where the jukebox was playing. He sidled up to the table where a number of us were sitting and listened to our conversation for a while. Suddenly, without any warning, he started to assault me verbally. He claimed that I worked for the CIA and warned me that if I didn't leave the country I would get the kind of treatment given to Americans who were opposed to making the country independent.

This occurred during election time. It was a hot campaign. Many people were involved with the Liberation party, which subsequently did not do very well in the elections. But there was a great deal of sentiment for self-government on the part

## 2.13—Dealing with Threats of Aggression

of the young people and the veterans. My friends, in particular, were strong supporters of self-government. Many of the Liberation party members, among them my friends, were probably socialists at heart rather than liberationists, but the Socialist party had no legal status and so they allied themselves with the liberationists in order to vote. The man who charged me with CIA affiliation was probably a socialist supporting the Liberation party.

In any event, this particular veteran continued to abuse me. I noticed that my friends were shocked and had become very silent. They were embarrassed by the fact that this man was abusing a friend and a person of some status, and yet they did not know how to handle the situation.

Suddenly I observed that my friend, the black woman, who was physically very large and strong, had walked over to the door and picked up a wooden bar, a two-by-four about five feet long which was used to lock the doors of the store. She walked over to the man who was abusing me, holding the club with both hands behind her back. She nudged him and then faced him squarely. She told him to stop talking that way about me; they didn't like it and it was nonsense to accuse me of working for the CIA. He was insulting a guest and a close friend, and he had better stop it.

At first he didn't seem inclined to stop, so she brought the club around from behind her back and held it up to threaten him. She said that she would hit him over the head if he didn't stop it and get out. When he saw the club, he was intimidated. Then the other people came to life; some of the young men grabbed him and hustled him out the door to his car, and he drove off.

I had an experience similar to this with another drunken veteran in town. I had an old car that I used to get to town to do my shopping, and it was also the neighborhood ambulance and bus. One day I was driving several people back from town, when I saw a man walking toward us in the center of the street. He was obviously intoxicated. I stopped to ask him if he wanted a lift somewhere. But instead of answering me, he began to accuse me of being a CIA agent and a goddamn representative of the government. He called me all sorts of names and seemed about to pull me out of the car and beat me up. He was such a large man he could have broken me in half. He had a reputation for being a violent drinker and very tough. I was really frightened. But two of my friends who were in the car with me quickly got out and led him away. I saw the man a number of times after that, but nothing was ever said about the incident.

The sequel to these encounters is rather interesting. After the elections, in which the liberationists were badly defeated, their supporters were so frustrated by their poor showing that they decided the electoral process was no way to win what they wanted, namely independence and freedom. The veterans were leaders in much of this because they had been abused during the war. They had been organized into segregated units. The excuse offered by the government was that they had language problems which warranted such separation. Blacks were also segregated, and these veterans did not like being treated like the blacks. Thus, the defeat of the liberationists exacerbated the bitterness that many of the veterans already felt toward the government.

Sortly after the election, the local veterans invited the man temporarily in charge of the outlawed Socialist party to talk to them. His own son was in jail for refusing to submit to the draft, and the actual leader was also in jail. Because it had been outlawed, the party had rigorous requirements for membership. If you were a member, you had to denounce the United States; you had to destroy your draft card, if you had one, and refuse to serve in the armed forces. Thus, joining the party meant taking serious risks.

A secret meeting was planned to be held in the back of the store where the leader would speak. Some friends had told me that the man was coming, and I hoped to be able to attend the meeting and hear what he had to say. But I did not expect that they would let me come. They were risking enough at it was, and they might fear I would turn them in. Therefore, I decided to stay at home rather than try to attend the meeting.

About fifteen minutes before the meeting was to begin, one of my friends came running up the hill to my house and asked me whether I was coming to the meeting. I said, "I didn't think I could." And he replied, "You are to come to the meeting; we want you to come." So I accompanied him to the meeting feeling very pleased. In spite of the fact that on two occasions I had been accused of having CIA connections, my friends were willing to trust me in a critical situation of this kind.

# SECTION 3
# RELATIONS WITH HOST GOVERNMENT

**INTRODUCTION**

Relations between social scientists and host governments have seldom been easy. In recent years many of the new nations have actively discouraged or prohibited social science research for various reasons. As a result, the willingness to tolerate social inquiry has now come to be one measure of the degree to which a nation has an open society.

The problem of access to the field has not been helped by the involvement of United States government agencies, like the CIA, in the internal affairs of other countries. As a result, in many instances American social scientists are looked upon with suspicion. In other instances, they are viewed with envy due to their apparent access to funding. One country has now demanded that it share the overhead of any grant to an American researcher working there. In some countries, American researchers are not permitted entry unless they are affiliated with a local university or hire local undergraduate and graduate students in their research projects. Unfortunately, this latter contingency can at times interfere with the scientific goals of a project. In still other instances, governments view the cultures of their societies as nonrenewable resources. They refuse to let foreign researchers study these cultures in an attempt to save them for the time when they have their own social scientists.

All this suggests the obvious: foreign governments operate under a different cultural and moral system than that of the social scientist. Some of the major ethical dilemmas arise when the researcher runs full tilt into the coutours of the local system, as when "speed money" is required to facilitate a research project.

Not all these complex issues are covered in the case materials in this section, for in many instances it has been impossible to collect representative cases. Only the bare facts are available (see Beals 1969 for a discussion of some of these problems in foreign research). Also, I have been unable to collect any materials dealing with the host government's encounters with the anthropologist. There is, however, one article that does describe this perspective, albeit in a colonial situation. For this please consult Cochrane (1970).

## RELATED CASE MATERIALS IN OTHER SECTIONS

*Section 1: Relations and Responsibilities to Host Community:* How Does a Foreign Researcher Interfere to Stop Illegal Activities; A Problem in Political Identification and Co-option; Mediation of a Conflict; The Perceived Advantages of Being Studied by an Anthropologist.

*Section 2: Relations and Responsibilities to Respondents and Informants:* Participation in Illegal Activities.

*Section 4: Relations with Representatives of Outside Agencies and the Public with respect to the Host Community:* On the Horns of a Dilemma: A Problem of Intercession.

*Section 5: Relations with Other Social Scientists and Responsibilities to the Profession:* In the Field With an Intelligence Agent; Politics, Permits, and Professional Interests: The Rose Case.

*Section 6: Dilemmas in the Use and Misuse of Social Science Knowledge:* Misuse of the Anthropologist's Information.

*Section 7: Publication: Responsibilities and Liabilities:* An Attempt to Control the Contents of Publication; *Social Organization of Manu'a* (1930 and 1969), by Margaret Mead: Some Errata.

## 3.1  A REQUEST FOR INFORMANT NAMES BY A GOVERNMENT OFFICIAL

As a member of a small group of graduate students under the direction of a faculty advisor, I was engaged in field research during the summer. Prior to the actual field work, we wrote to the governing officials of the country in which we intended to conduct our research. We explained that, like other universities from the United States which were concerned with furthering anthropological research in the general area, our own university was interested in instituting a field training program for a group of its graduate students. We emphasized that, although the research might be used in developing Master's theses, the proposed project was strictly a part of the graduate academic training program. However, we went on to say that similar programs of other institutions such as ours had in the past produced area specialists and that our project might produce students who would conduct valuable research in the future. We felt it unwise and ethically wrong to commit ourselves to future research problems determined by interests other than our own, and therefore we never specified to whom such research "might be of interest."

As anthropologists, it seems to me that we should recognize an obligation toward the government of the people we study, if only by virtue of the fact that they allow us to conduct research in their country. However, those who are the object of our field work come first. Thus, at issue here is the degree to which an anthropologist should be responsible toward the government of those he studies. I see no simple solution to this question; indeed, I am not entirely unsympathetic toward those who would question my statement that anthropologists should accept some responsibility toward the government.

In stating that our project could lead to future research of interest, we committed ourselves to nothing specifically, yet we were willing to let government officials interpret our statement in whatever way they wished. On the other hand, we felt our statements *vis-à-vis* the aims of the summer research project were clear. We assumed that the problems we were prepared to research were too narrow to be of interest to government officials, and that, on the basis of a three-month field training program, there would be no problem with requests for our data from government officials. In short, we felt we accurately represented the nature of our project and foresaw no problems.

The government officials responded positively to our letter and expressed a willingness to cooperate with us during our stay. From the outset, they were helpful in numerous ways. They made maps and various kinds of data available, and accompanied us into the different regions we were considering for research. They were generally interested in our research. This was especially true of the director of agriculture, who asked our faculty advisor a number of times about the problems we were studying and what we would do with the data we collected. Our advisor indicated that students in the past had frequently written their Master's theses based on the data collected during summer field training. This official requested several times during the summer that copies of such theses be sent to him. While our advisor indicated we would comply with this request, we understood that the decision to send the government copies of our papers was ours alone to make. While we had no strong feelings one way or another about the ethics of sending copies of our papers to the director of agriculture, we did not feel we could flatly turn down his request in view of the interest and help he had extended.

Toward the middle of the summer, a personal feud erupted in the Department of Agriculture. The director of agriculture had arranged to have a civil servant in his department transferred out of the capital city to a remote region of the country. While we carefully avoided any involvement, we were nonetheless sympathetic with the transferred man, whom we believed was the object of a vengeful political decision.

Our understanding of the case was that the civil servant had privately criticized the country's prime minister. We believed that the prime minister had somehow learned about this and had asked the director of agriculture to get rid of the man. Because he was a civil servant, he could not be relieved of his position without a hearing, which would have required a series of charges supported by evidence. Thus, the director, whom we saw as "knuckling under" to the prime minister, decided to transfer him to this remote area. The civil servant protested that he could not legally be demoted unless he had specifically violated certain regulations. The official claimed the director's transfer order was tantamount to a demotion, and therefore illegal, since the post he was being transferred to was ranked lower than his current position.

During the last month or so of our stay, the civil servant remained in his office but the director refused to acknowledge him in his official capacity. We later learned that not long thereafter he gave up his battle and acceded to the director's transfer order.

The situation engendered a good deal of acrimony while we were in the field. We all carefully avoided becoming entangled, which was not easy since both the director and the civil servant took advantage of any opportunity our presence offered to express their opinions of one another.

Despite these and other political machinations, and my own reservations about the director of agriculture, our relations with the government officials remained amiable. As a result of their continued interest and cooperation, we felt obliged to cooperate in return. Thus, toward the end of our stay we decided to hold a meeting with the officials who had expressed interest in our research. This was to

## 3.1 A Request for Informant Names by a Government Official

serve two purposes. We wished to meet the expressed interests of the officials and return the courtesies extended to us by presenting verbal accounts of our research. Second, we hoped that comments by the officials would serve as a check on the conclusions we had reached. The oral summaries did stimulate interesting and useful discussions among the students and government officials. At the same time the government officials did not require answers that would have revealed information we did not wish to offer. I do not believe that the confidence of our informants was betrayed in these oral presentations or associated discussions. In general, the conference seemed a success. We felt that we had discharged our debt to the government officials by reviewing our research results with them.

During the meeting, I explained that my research was based in a small fishing and agricultural community where I was studying the structure of the informal male groups that gathered regularly at the various small shops in the village. I had found that the members of these groups were usually of the same social age, engaged in similar occupations, and supported the same political parties. Each of the groups regularly patronized a particular shop, and the owners of most of these shops could exert considerable influence over these groups of men by virtue of their ability to extend or withhold credit.

The director of agriculture apparently felt that he could make use of more specific data. About a week after the conference, he asked our faculty advisor for a list of names of the patrons in the village, the men who constituted their clientele, and their occupations. Our advisor indicated that such information was usually confidential but that the decision to supply it was mine to make.

When I discussed the situation with my advisor, he stressed the fact that he had told the director of agriculture that social anthropological research dealt with institutions, roles, and the structure of role behavior, and this kind of information would be made available to him. However, since social anthropological research does not deal with specific individuals, this type of data cannot be made available. My advisor assured me that since there had been no stipulation to provide the government with names of informants I should feel free to refuse the director's request.

Because of the dispute between the civil servant and the director of agriculture, I had come to question the director's integrity. I was therefore not confident that the data he requested would be useful for constructive purposes. Equally disturbing was the fact that the director had not made clear his reasons for requesting the data. As I did not see him after the conference, I was never in a position to ask why he wanted my data, and he had not given a clear reason to my advisor when he made the request for the data. Even assuming he was interested in introducing new and better agricultural techniques, I had no idea exactly what he wanted to change and if his wishes coincided with those of the people who worked the land. A shop owner who complied with the director could make things difficult for any man reluctant to comply.

There was also a political consideration. The director, who was a member of the political party in power, would certainly get the support of those proprietors backing his party, but he would probably be opposed by proprietors backing the opposition party. It was difficult to assess the effects of this aspect of the situation on the village as a whole, but clearly there would be conflicts arising from different political loyalties.

It was also evident that if the director did in fact have the best interests of the people in mind if he were interested in introducing changes that would improve the quality of life in the village—other channels were available for introducing these changes. And they could be presented in such a way that the villagers would be free to decide whether or not to accept them.

My overriding concern was that the requested data specified the locus of power in the village, the most influential individuals. Such information could easily be used for political ends and could harm the people I had studied and come to respect. It could be used to coerce, while the other channels visible to me left the decisions as to whether a change was to be accepted or rejected up to the farmer himself. Because of all these concerns and uncertainties, I decided to withhold the data from the director.

However, my problem did not end with this decision. If I simply refused to give the information to the director of agriculture, my actions could have seriously disrupted the work of another anthropologist who had just begun a long-term field study. Also at stake was the question of future work in the area by myself and other anthropologists. Thus, it seemed unwise to flatly reject the request.

Instead, I went to a shop owner who was an ardent supporter of the director's party. The clientele of this shop were fishermen—the former occupation of the shop owner himself. I asked this man if he would be willing to discuss with the director some of the problems of introducing new agricultural practices into the village. As I had suspected, the shop owner was delighted to do this because it would enhance his political status. Then I left a note at the office of the director of agriculture stating that I had contacted the shop owner who would gladly cooperate with him. Since the owner was influential only with the fishermen, not with the farmers, I decided that a meeting between the two men would not result in any real changes among the farmers.

## 3.2 – FIELD WORK IN A RESTRICTED REGION

Roger Cloutier was a foreign graduate student in the United States. He was a permanent resident of the country of Interalia, although not yet a citizen, and a member of a minority group in that country that was commercially successful. In the winter of 1965 he completed his course requirements and decided to return to Interalia for several months to visit his family. He also wanted to conduct research on the commercial activities of his group while at home to provide him with data for his dissertation. However, prior to returning, he learned that the government of Interalia had decided that no further foreign scientific research would be allowed until the potentially explosive political situation had subsided. As a result of this decision, several foreign researchers were refused visas and one biological study in progress had to be terminated. Cloutier in his application for reentry, however, only stated his desire to visit his family; research was not mentioned. He wondered what steps he should take on arriving in the country. Should he discuss the matter with the ministry concerned with the type of research he was planning to do? Or should he begin interviewing informants without any prior discussions with government officials? Should he at least reveal his plan to the resident in charge of the area so that he would know of Cloutier's movements and the reasons for the interviews? Or should he consider abandoning the project altogether?

Cloutier decided to conduct his research without notifying the government.

## 3.3 FIELD WORK IN A CLIMATE OF GOVERNMENTAL SUSPICION

Prior to leaving for the field, we applied for visas from the consulate of the country where we planned to work. We sent the consulate all the information on our project, including the fact that it was funded by the United States Department of Health, Education and Welfare. We received our visas, arrived in the country, and immediately registered at police headquarters as required. We had no difficulty in obtaining from the police renewable, one-year residential permits for the town where we would be based. We were told that such clearances would suffice for us to carry on our work unhindered. We also registered at the local American consulate. After spending six weeks in a major city studying the language spoken in the area of the proposed field site with the help of urbanized tribesmen, we departed for the region where we were to work.

At the regional headquarters, we asked the district commissioner for permission to proceed into the area where we intended to do our field work. This was a marginal mountainous region, inhabited by a group of people who had never been fully incorporated into the national political system of this ex-colonial nation. The district commissioner gave us permission to proceed, offered any assistance that we might need, and wished us good luck.

A week later we arrived at the town which was to be our base of operations and presented our credentials to the local magistrate and the officer in charge of police. Then we began to make preparations for our field work. We attempted to locate area representatives of the tribe we wanted to study, engage servants, and familiarize ourselves with the local social organization.

At the time, the country was in a period of severe upheaval due to widespread dissatisfaction with the incumbant regime. Continual student rioting had resulted in the universities being closed. Because of the politicized status of the universities, our association with the faculties there would have been suspect, so we were never able to obtain their support for our investigation. In the middle of our fieldwork, these civil disturbances culminated in the declaration of martial law, and the control of the government passed into the hands of the military.

The political insecurity was felt at all levels of government so that few civil servants would respond to our requests for fear that if the government fell the new government would use such actions as excuses for purging office holders. In remote regions such as the one in which we were working, the unease was particularly acute among the local officials, for even in calmer times such places were considered to be under only marginal control. The situation was exacerbated by the custom of bureaucratic graft. Each new government comes into power on the grounds of reform, and those caught taking graft are quickly removed from their posts. However, after a few years of such reforms, bureaucratic graft again rises to the same level as previously. The problem is most pronounced in regions which are isolated and therefore only minimally supervised by the central government. Thus, local officials in outlying regions were particularly anxious about their future and reluctant to jeopardize their positions through overt support of suspect foreigners.

Our position was particularly difficult because we had not been able to determine the main outlines of the network of corruption and graft. Some government officials were deeply involved; others were not. Those taking graft at this particular time of political unrest were suspicious of outsiders not integrated into the local network of graft. Thus, we did not know whether or not the difficulties we encountered were attempts to shake us down for substantial "gifts." If so, should we acquiesce to this widespread procedure? What would be the ramifications? Certainly if we were caught, we would be asked to leave.

We were also suspect because many of the civil servants we encountered did not comprehend our mission. Consequently, our movements became increasingly restricted and we were constantly watched, while our friends and informants were subject to questioning by the national police. Most of the government officials with whom we dealt assumed that anyone who wished to visit what they considered to be a disagreeable area must have a sinister purpose. The tribal people we were studying were seen as savages with whom the educated elite in the government did not associate.

Our field work was not facilitated by the fact that the government viewed the United States as an unfriendly power, based on the supposition that the United States was providing more economic aid to their enemies.

After two weeks in the field, the district commissioner informed the local magistrate that our movements were to be restricted to the town area until further notice. I went to the regional headquarters, which was a day's journey away, to find out from the district commissioner what had prompted this restriction. He assured me that it was only temporary and would probably be terminated shortly.

I returned to our base and in the meantime began to do some research in the town. I started mapping fields to find out about the system of land tenure in the region, and I also established contact with members of the tribe we wanted to study who were settled in and around the town. In doing this work, I would show the villagers these maps and explain them: here is so and so's garden; here is the river; and so on. I also tried to find out the economic status of various individuals, revenues produced by crops and cattle, and similar information.

In turn, the people often asked me what I was being paid. I realized that if I told them the truth it would make me about the second richest man in the entire region. So I responded with a figure which was actually half my grant. But this still made me one of the richest men in the area. The villagers were astounded at such a fantastic salary for someone who was just out to study customs, particularly since students in their country received almost no financial aid. Official suspicions were strengthened by this issue of salary: why was a mere student being paid so well to study people with so few and such disagreeable customs? Some suspected me of spying for the CIA.

I heard later that some of the landlords and officials were suspicious of my inquiries into land tenure. There were two possible reasons for this. First, there was the story going around that certain AID funds intended for agricultural development wound up in the wrong pockets. Second, the local land tax official, who was supposed to have a map of the area so that he could assess each individual's tax accurately, possessed no such map. When tax time came around, he would charge people for more land than they had. If they complained, he would tell them that if they wanted to be charged for the land they actually owned, they would have to pay him something on the side. Thus, an accurate map would not have been to his advantage.

A further complication arose as the result of the stratified, caste-like social structure of the region. Attempts to gain rapport with representatives of particular strata—in order to get a balanced picture of the total social structure—often made members of other strata suspicious.

In any event, I waited two weeks without hearing anything further from the district commissioner about our restriction to the town area. Then I sent him a letter, which was composed with the help of a civil servant from the tribe which we wanted to study. I wrote the district commissioner that it was necessary to resolve this matter quickly as our time in the country was short. And I requested that he send us his present instructions in writing in the event that it was necessary to bring the matter to the attention of higher authorities. If such instructions were not received within two weeks, we would assume that we had his permission to carry on our work unhindered.

We heard nothing until almost seven weeks later, when we received a letter from the district commissioner stating that unless permission for our research was granted by the Office of Internal Affairs of the Foreign Office our stay would have to be terminated.

I immediately wrote the governor of the region, explaining the circumstances, and stating that we had received no clarification on the issues involved from the local government officials. Furthermore, I made it plain that a trip to the capital of the country to meet these new requirements for our field project would have taken a month or more out of our very valuable field time.

Ten days later, we received a message from the district commissioner via the local magistrate that unless we obtained the proper permission we would have to leave the area forthwith. However, I told the local magistrate that no further action should be taken until he heard from the governor. Three weeks elapsed, then another letter arrived from the district commissioner, instructing us to leave the area.

It was now apparent that we would have to terminate our field work no matter what we did or did not do. In desperation, one evening we slipped into the mountains and, accompanied by a local mountaineer, spent a week with a number of different tribal groups in a "blitz" of data gathering. This adventure was terminated when we heard that the authorities were becoming increasingly anxious as to our whereabouts, and we feared that our hosts would be the ones to pay for any further defiance.

So we returned to the town, after spending a little over four months in the area, and left for the capital of the country. There we contacted the American consulate and learned that, in fact, we had not obtained the proper permission to do field work in the area. We were told that clearance for our project should have been obtained from the central government by the American consulate. However, they pointed out that even if we had followed these procedures, we would not have received permission. Thus, we should consider ourselves lucky to have accomplished the little field work which we we did.

We never did get the necessary permission for continuing our field work. After two months spent gathering supplementary data from urbanized tribesmen and doing library research, we left the country. Altogether we spent approximately nine months in the country, and just over four doing actual field work. However, despite the far from ideal nature of this field experience, and its brevity, enough data were ultimately salvaged to provide the basis for an updating of the ethnography of a little known region and people.

## 3.4—POLITICAL RAMIFICATIONS OF FIELD WORK AMONG THE KLEE

The Klee region where I worked was just beginning to be brought under the control of the central government. Police detachments were located around the countryside without adequate supervision and the police were taking advantage of the people. They helped themselves to crops and often chased women. I am not sure whether rape actually occurred, but certainly a good deal of harassment was involved. The police sergeant in charge of the detachment near our village came from a different and more acculturated tribe. He was particularly sadistic, often taking goats on the pretense of settling disputes, appropriating one or two as damages, and so on. Some of his actions appeared quasi-legal; others were blatant abuses of police power. Once, the sergeant forced a man to give him his daughter in marriage.

The Klee continually complained to me and asked me to intervene. In a couple of extreme cases I did write a few letters to government officials. But I was reluctant to interfere because of the anti-American attitude of the government.

The Klee people did not understand my relationship to the central government. They assumed that since I had wealth I must have tremendous power. Also I was white, and other white people in the area were influential, so I must be as well. I was unable to dissociate myself in their eyes from the missionaries and the other Europeans, and so they believed I had much more influence than I really did.

To make matters more difficult, some of the Klee would respond to police harassment by saying, "You can't do this! I belong to the American. I am one of the American's people!" This was probably the worst thing they could have said. When certain government officials heard about it, they asked me why the Klee were saying they were my people.

The situation worsened and came to a head over a misunderstanding of a Klee ceremony. As part of this ceremony, the men stage a mock attack on people in the village. Men working in the fields jump up, grab spears, and chase after nearby people. I once triggered such a mock attack. Several days later, some police hangers-on did the same. I believe in this instance it might have been a bit more threatening and not so clearly a mock attack in the minds of the people. For these hangers-on were considered sort of scabs. They worked as houseboys and informers for the police and were disliked by the local Klee. So I can imagine the villagers were more threatening to them though I do not believe they intended to kill them.

## 3.4—Political Ramifications of Field Work Among the Klee

The Klee pursued the police hangers-on with spears, and the hangers-on reported the incident to the police. They claimed that they had been driven off; yet, being Klee themselves, they should have known that it was only part of a ceremony. The police interpreted the incident as a real attack. They retaliated by burning down two villages. Although no one was killed, these were important villages with tremendous numbers of sacred objects in them. Furthermore, the police took Kimeno, an important man in the village, to the police post.

The Klee people came to me for help; they were afraid of further trouble from the police. I immediately knew that a mistake had been made. However, I was reluctant to intervene, although the people begged me to do so. For a couple of hours it was a standoff. I tried to explain that my intervention would be worse than doing nothing at all. But my decision to remain uninvolved became intolerable; these were my friends and informants asking for help in a situation which they did not understand. Finally, against my better judgement and telling the Klee that this would be worse for them, I went to the post to try and do something, if only to relieve my own feelings of guilt.

The man in charge at the police post was a sophisticated military man from the central government. He was questioning Kimeno when I arrived, and I went to a corner of the room and sat down. At that point, he began to beat and kick Kimeno. Kimeno sat passively on the ground while he was kicked in the face and teeth so that blood flowed; He was clubbed on the head and his loin cloth torn. I knew that I had caused the beating by arriving at that particular moment. I thought that it was intended to put me in my place as much as to put Kimeno in his.

I am sure that the police were more restrained in their dealings with the people in the village where I lived because of my presence. Kimeno did not come from this immediate area. But I was convinced when I left the field that my closest friends would be attacked next, and possibly more viciously than those in Kimeno's village. And why? Just because I—an American—had lived there. To the Klee, the United States was just another village far down the river. But to the central government I was a very real threat. They were afraid of the spread of American political power.

And so I left the field, knowing there was nothing I could do and very concerned that my presence there had probably made the situation worse for my closest friends, my best informants, and the people with whom I lived for two years. The villages would attract retaliation, and harsher methods would be used to demonstrate that this American business wasn't real and that they were in fact under the power of the new government.

A complicating factor in this for which I feel responsible is the manner in which I treated the Klee. They were a proud, independent group of people, and I was their first introduction to the outside world. I always paid for anything I wanted, such as food or labor. And I led them to believe that they could deal with all outsiders and government people as equals, that they would be treated with respect and could demand respect. And so I suspect the Klee reacted more strongly than they would have otherwise to police brutality and corruption because I had taught them to expect better treatment from outsiders.

It is ironic, but if I had abused them and treated them like "niggers," I would have prepared them for what they are now facing at the very bottom of the ladder in terms of power and economics as they are brought into the national political and economic system. I couldn't have done anything different, but my presence there was in many ways a great disservice to the Klee. A few monographs and articles seem a meager justification and are of no benefit to the Klee in their present difficulties.

## 3.5 THE ANTHROPOLOGIST AS A POLITICAL CATALYST

**INTRODUCTION**

The anthropologist, like any other visitor in a foreign country, is an outsider. But as a researcher, the anthropologist differs from other strangers. He uses people as informants to obtain data and others, in turn, use him for their own ends. Once the anthropologist begins to ask questions, no matter how apolitical his intentions, he begins to participate in the society—he becomes involved.

The following incidents illustrate how the anthropologist can be lured into a political, and sometimes embarrassing, situation. Hopefully, by reporting the problems associated with obvious cases of involvement, some of the more subtle forms of involvement will also become apparent.

**PART ONE. LANGUAGE AND THE QUESTION OF NATIONAL PRIORITIES**

When the public information officer learned that I was collecting local folk songs and folk tales, he asked if I would play some of my tapes and discuss them over the national radio. I agreed and taped an interview in which I discussed the similarities of local lore with that of neighboring countries, similarities in the languages, and the general academic opinion of the local patois. The portion which compared folk tales was deleted from the broadcast because the government was opposed to my emphasis on historical connections with certain neighboring countries. But my comments on the local patois as a language in its own right and not just a street dialect were broadcast. I had stressed the fact that the language was broadly condemned by the educated populace, especially teachers, most of whom were foreign. Native teachers usually emulated their foreign counterparts and even went so far as to forbid the use of the patois in the classroom. I deplored this practice and the attitude which prompted it, and suggested that it caused more harm than good, inhibiting the learning process. I advised that instead of treating the patois as mere slang, teachers should recognise its worth, deal with it as a language in the classroom, and teach the standard language as a foreign language, especially in the early grades.

After the broadcast, I learned from a senior clerk in the Ministry of Education that my comments were coolly received; but I didn't expect to hear any more about it. Later, during a social function, I talked with the minister of education. Included in the conversation were a Jesuit educator who was influential in local affairs, a local senator, and an Anglican minister who was a principal at one of the

Contributed by Dr. Norman D. Ashcroft, Adelphi University.

country's few high schools. Asked to clarify the remarks I'd made in the interview, I defended myself by saying that I didn't think the schools increased a child's learning potential by denouncing his speech habits. I suggested that with such an approach communication could, and often did, break down between student and teacher. It was not a matter of correcting bad grammar or speech, I argued, but rather of recognizing a cultural and linguistic heritage—one which, although oral rather than written—was just as rich as any Western tradition.

To support my case, I offered the following examples. I told of an incident which had occurred during one of my frequent trips to urban schools. A teacher slapped a child for speaking the patois in the classroom. Since the child did not understand why he was being punished, the teacher slowly explained—I believe partly for my benefit; but the child could not comprehend. Again, the teacher explained, and the child asked in good street dialect why he had been hit. In frustration, the teacher quickly replied in patois that he had been slapped for using the patois.

I also pointed out how foreign volunteer teachers were often the subject of jokes spoken in a dialect which they couldn't understand. The minister angrily insisted—I now think for the benefit of his foreign advisors—that in defending corrupt speech I was in fact defending and prolonging ignorance in his country. The Jesuit calmly attempted to explain to me that it was necessary for a small country to set national priorities; one is that children must be taught a literate language. I tried to point out that I wasn't advocating that literacy be discarded as an educational goal, but I was interrupted by the minister, who repeated that the patois must be rooted out, since no other country spoke it (which wasn't true) and it would be impossible to engage in diplomatic relations with Western countries using the patois. The Anglican minister added that the dialect was in fact the basis of poverty in the country and once such ignorance could be eliminated the country would be well on the road to becoming a God-fearing nation in which misery was a thing of the past.

I am now convinced that his hostility had less to do with my defense of common speech than with certain politically sensitive arrangements. Increasingly, over the past few years, the nation's educational system had become tied to the organized religions in the country. In fact, at some levels the churches completely dominated the schools. Many of the teachers and most, if not all, of the administrators were foreign. The schools were primarily funded by outside sources, and these sources inevitably were religious denominations. These foreigners had little use for the patois and did not consider it to have any linguistic status.

**PART TWO: PROVIDING INFORMATION AND ADVICE CAN ENTANGLE A RESEARCHER IN POLITICAL FEUDS**

The government proposed that the Jesuit high schools be allowed to grant an Associate of Arts degree, after the American pattern. Since the country's educational system had long been modeled after the European system, a debate arose in the country's senate. Two prominent senators asked my opinion on the meaning of the American A.A. degree and its status in the American educational system. Was the degree necessary for a student to get into a four-year college, as some Jesuits claimed? What exactly did the degree mean in terms of higher education in America? Would the degree mean much more than the normal credit given for two years of college?

I replied by noting the differences among the states; nevertheless, in no state did the A.A. degree necessarily offer a student any more than two years of college credit. Moreover, I believed that while junior and community colleges were broadening their educational scope, the use of a degree to give credit for two years of college work was on the decline. Finally, I suggested that the senators contact several other sources for more accurate information.

A few weeks later, I was invited to attend the senate debate over the bill. During the debate some of my earlier remarks to the two senators, and the references I had given them, were repeated, although my name was not mentioned. After a long and heated debate, the motion to grant legal status to the Jesuits' proposed A.A. degree was defeated. As I was leaving the senate building, the public information officer told me that the defeat was the result of my opinions, as related during the debate.

A week later, I was scheduled to make a courtesy call on the prime minister. The appointment was cancelled and changed three different times over the next three weeks. It never took place. Prior to the senate affair, I had received full cooperation from various governmental agencies, who understood and supported my research efforts. In particular, the postmaster general had been very helpful. I had requested the post office to supply me with the value of postal money orders sent from the United States as well as the number and listed value of parcel post packages. I had been promised this information and fortunately the promise was made in writing. Shortly after the senate affair, the postmaster general asked to be relieved of his commitment to provide me with the information. I refused, claiming that I needed it to complete my research. I reminded him of his past cooperation and of his written promise. Two weeks later, he explained that it was impossible to provide me with the information, since the post office did not keep such records. However, I had learned from a clerk that the requested information was already on his desk. Again, I reminded the postmaster of his promise. Two days later, I was called into his office, where he offered to give me the information provided I sign an agreement never to publish it in the country.

But this was not the end of the harassment. I had been working in the surveyor general's office, making copies of maps. Following the senate affair, I was informed that these maps were not open for public inspection. When I explained that I was conducting historical research and that I had already copied most of the maps I needed, the surveyor general said he would take the matter under advisement. In the next two months, I made several attempts to obtain the two remaining maps which I needed, but to no avail. One day I asked a friend to go to the surveyor's office to ask if the maps were available to the public. If so, she was to make a copy of each for me. She did so, with no objection from the office personnel.

A third incident following the senate affair concerned an exemption from certain taxes. Normally anyone doing agricultural research was exempted from vehicle taxes. When I first arrived in the country, my research was classified as agricultural. Several months later, when I applied for the exemption, I was informed I was eligible, and the decision would be given shortly. In the meantime, the senate debate took place. After a couple of months had passed and I still hadn't received notice of my exemption, I made inquiries and was informed by the same chief clerk that my request had been denied.

## PART THREE: RESEARCH OR PROPAGANDA?

Another researcher in the country had been studying the country's political history and had become intrigued with the role of the Catholic church in national politics. Because of my interest in education, we collaborated on an article concerning the development of the educational system. In an otherwise historical paper, we included some critical remarks concerning the roles of the government and the churches in education. The paper was accepted for publication in the United States but had not yet been published by the time both of us left the country. Only two or three other people in the country knew of the manuscript, but they hadn't read it. Nevertheless, the minister of education told my colleague that he had heard of the article and considered it inflammatory and a distortion of the country's history, not based on any fact. He suggested that the country did not need people like him and that, if he wished to remain, he had better begin to report accurately and fairly. At this point, we both thought of shipping our field notes out of the country.

## 3.6 – PRESENTING RESEARCH GOALS IN AN ACCEPTABLE LIGHT TO THE HOST GOVERNMENT

My doctoral research, funded by a United States agency, concerned the local politics in a remote area of a large, non-European nation. In my research proposal, I stated that I planned to investigate the use of kinship as a mechanism for organizing local-level politics. In addition, I emphasized in my proposal the fact that my work would provide ethnographic data on the area, virtually untouched by anthropological research.

Having received my research grant, I applied to the host country for permission to do field work there. However, in my application I did not use the same terminology I had used in my research proposal. I feared that an administrator would misinterpret my interest in local-level politics and deny my research request on the grounds that I might interfere in internal political affairs. The word "politics" frequently evokes concern over sensitive issues in emerging nations; many of these countries prohibit research in such sensitive areas. My fear was that an administrator in the host country would interpret the word "politics" in this sense, rather than in the more specific sense in which political anthropologists use it (i.e., determination and implementation of public goals and power relations within a local community). Therefore, in sending a condensed version of my fund application to the host government, I stated only that I was engaged in an ethnographic field study to record the customs of a disappearing society. I also stated that I would be studying the various cultural domains of kinship, economic relations, religious behavior, social organization, art, and language. I explicitly stated the source of my funding, and indicated that I was planning to cooperate with local scholars. However, I avoided any reference to my interest in local-level politics.

Although I received permission to carry out my research, I wondered whether I had misrepresented myself to the host government. Also, I was concerned about how the government would respond if they were to learn of the contents of my research proposal.

## SECTION 4

## RELATIONS WITH REPRESENTATIVES OF OUTSIDE AGENCIES AND THE PUBLIC WITH RESPECT TO THE HOST COMMUNITY

**INTRODUCTION**

The cases in this section represent only one side of the encounter between the social scientist and representatives of outside agencies with respect to the community being studied. There are other points of view that would illuminate the type of events described in these case materials, but such cases are difficult to come by. This problem is particularly salient with regard to missionaries. Based on the cases, it would seem that relations with missionaries are difficult for the anthropologist to handle well. As I was unable to collect any case materials expressing the missionary's perspective on such encounters, I have included E. Nida's article on the anthropologist as an exploiter of the missionary.

From the viewpoint of the host government, the role of anthropologist is frequently ill-defined and therefore misunderstood. As a result, encounters with representatives of government agencies are often tense for the anthropologist. This is particularly so since this role, lacking definition, is open to interpretation in terms of the fears and suspicions of the government representatives. For example, an American anthropologist was visited in the field by a representative of the American legation to the country, who asked a number of questions about the anthropologist's field research. When representatives of the government subsequently learned about this meeting, they interpreted the anthropological role as a cover for more devious activities.

One of the interesting aspects of the encounter between the social scientist and representatives of outside agencies is the fact that it frequently takes place at the social peripheries of the community being studied, in what might be called a social no man's land. Here two, or more, actors, not full members of the local social system, meet. Their roles are largely determined by their relations with others who are outside the arena of the encounter. As a result, the definition of their roles is far from clear to the participants. With few controls and no explicit boundaries to the performance, the roles are available for interpretation according to the inclinations and proclivities of the actors. As a result, the performance of these roles can become exaggerated and distorted.

The anthropologist can also be caught up in role distortion when he is encouraged to expand his role boundaries in response to positive feedback from the members of the local community who do not understand the anthropological role in the first place and wish to manipulate the role for their own advantage.

The task of the anthropologist is to discover the local meanings of events and the culturally based motivations of the members of his host community, and then interpret these to outsiders. But this further complicates the problem of role definition and distortion. In relations with representatives of outside agencies, he must deal with their personal prejudices *vis-a-vis* the members of his host community as well as their cultural assumptions that cloud their understanding of the action system of the local community. Since these interpretations of events and motivations may have little relation to the ongoing cultural reality of the host community, conflicts between the anthropologist's view and that of representatives of outside agencies are almost inevitable so that the actual anthropological role is seldom acknowledged.

## RELATED CASE MATERIALS IN OTHER SECTIONS

*Section 1: Relations and Responsibilities to Host Community:* Providing a Storage Place for Weapons; A Problem in Political Identification and Co-option.

*Section 2: Relations and Responsibilities to Respondents and Informants:* Participation in Illegal Activities.

*Section 3: Relations with Host Government:* Political Ramifications of Field Work Among the Klee.

*Section 6: Dilemmas in the Use and Misuse of Social Science Knowledge:* Misuse of the Anthropologist's Information; Differential Access to the Results of Anthropological Inquiry: A Dilemma in Professional Responsibility.

*Section 7: Publication: Responsibilities and Liabilities:* A Problem of Publishing on Identifiable Communities and Personalities.

## 4.1 – THE PRIEST, THE MAMAOANS, AND THE ROLE OF THE ANTHROPOLOGIST

Mamao is a small atoll approximately 20 miles in circumference, with only about 700 cultivable acres and one residential area of approximately 1,000 square yards. Heloise Morrison had just arrived in Mamao on a trading ship. Her preparatory work was over; she could say a few polite phrases in Mamaoan, and had made the necessary visits to administrators and ecclesiastical officials stationed some 400 miles away. These individuals were ultimately responsible for the secular and sacred affairs of the Mamaoans. Now she was eager to learn at first hand about this isolated, highly egalitarian society of 500 people.

A new priest had arrived on the same ship. He seemed pleasant enough, but they had little in common. Heloise was not a Catholic, and he was of a different nationality, although predominately European in background.

During the first two months of her stay, Heloise became acquainted with the villagers and made some progress in learning their language. The Mamaoans were hospitable and open toward her. And the priest had encouraged her to drop in for a chat any time. She felt obliged to pay him occasional social visits, although she found the chatting tedious and his attitude toward his flock condescending. He frequently spoke about the stupidity of the schoolchildren and the difficulty of dealing with the slow-thinking elders in their tedious deliberations. He also refused to sit on the floor with the villagers on festive occasions and dictated that a table should be provided for him at all feasts, although this had not been the practice of the previous priests.

By the end of the second month she was aggravated by the priest's attitude and recorded in her diary, "He likes to play God." His superior attitude galled her, and she felt that he was shirking his responsibilities as a teacher to indulge his passion for fishing. He was officially the head schoolteacher and should have been instructing the older children in English.

Her visits to the priest diminished accordingly. But because the Mamaoans were devout Catholics and appeared to defer to him in all matters, it seemed unwise to express her attitude toward him, especially since she was not a Catholic and the Mamaoans were defensive about their faith.

As the months passed, the priest spent less time at the school and more time fishing; worse, he began to meddle in local secular affairs. For example, ignoring the fact that the island doctor was responsible for the public health of the atoll residents and the local administrator oversaw contacts between Mamaoans and foreign vessels, the priest forbade the villagers to go out to visit Chinese and Korean fishing vessels. When he was disobeyed, he decreed that all articles obtained from the vessels should be burned and those who had visited them should be quarantined.

Heloise felt that the priest's interference produced tension in the village, although she thought that she might be projecting some of her own annoyances. In either case, she decided that for her own peace of mind she would avoid the priest altogether and continue to keep her opinions to herself. However, some Mamaoans began to express obliquely their own feelings, which corresponded to hers. They said that the men who went fishing with the priest were not fulfilling their responsibilities to their own families; that former priests had shown more concern and affection for the people; and that he was not teaching the schoolchildren as he was supposed to. Heloise was careful to respond with neutral comments, only asking about the other priests.

The situation grew worse as the priest's demands increased. While some people helped him for political reasons, hoping that he would support their ambitions, or because they were dependent on the mission for economic support, people generally acquiesced to his demands out of fear. In two instances the priest withheld communion from men who had refused to meet his demands and used other religious and social pressures against them. Also, many Mamaoans believed that the priest had the power to curse them.

At the beginning of Heloise's sixth month in Mamao, one of the elders with whom she regularly visited said that he had told the other elders that they should help Heloise as much as possible; that the work she was doing was good; and that she had no malicious intent. Heloise was a bit puzzled by this statement, but she thanked him for his help and concern since he did not seem inclined to elaborate. He did add, however, that the men who went fishing with the priest were foolish. They only got bones from the catch because the good meat was salted and dried and shipped to the priest's family. This shocked Heloise and she said so, since the villagers regularly gave fish from their own catches to the priest. And she learned some villagers argued that the priest should not be allowed to send his catch to his family on another island since fishing in their waters by outsiders was prohibited in order to conserve their resources.

A week later, the priest called a meeting of all the adult villagers and publicly chastised Heloise's friend, who had gone to him in private to explain that some of his behavior was contrary to the Mamaoans' ideas. People seemed to be confused and embarrassed by the confrontation. They did not talk to Heloise about it, so she did not ask. But she did go and visit her friend, the elder, who was eager to explain. He said, "The priest acts as if he is the king, but we believe that everyone is the same. He says that we are inferior and he is superior." He added that the priest's domain was the sacred and he had no business meddling in secular affairs even though the other elders, who were afraid of him, let him do so. He was also outraged by the priest's attire (short pants and no shirt), his encouragement of female visitors in the evening, his clique of fishing buddies, and his betrayal of confidences. Although some other friends commented to Heloise about the priest's behavior, and she could not help but be sympathetic, she continued not to initiate conversation on the subject herself.

## 4.1 – The Priest, The Mamaoans, and the Role of the Anthropologist

During the first couple of months of her field work, the young native doctor had been very helpful to Heloise. But for the past four months he had been somewhat distant, and she assumed that either he was busy with his work or he was somewhat miffed that she no longer needed help. However, shortly after the elder had complained to Heloise about the priest's behavior, the doctor told her that he did not like the way the church had changed, but he seemed reluctant to elaborate. Heloise did not pursue the matter, although she was aware of the conflict between the doctor and the priest. Once, when she had asked about a woman whom she hadn't seen for a couple of weeks, she had been told that the woman was sick but her husband would not take her to the hospital because of the priest's influence over him.

Several nights later, the doctor came to see Heloise. He explained that he had been hesitant to speak to Heloise because she was not a Catholic. But now he was so furious he had to talk to someone who would not repeat his remarks. He chose Heloise because she was an outsider. He poured out all his difficulties and frustrations in dealing with the priest; his list of grievances was considerably longer than that of the elder. Close to the top of the doctor's list was the priest's undermining of the cooperative society in order to force the villagers to buy imported items from him.

However, the doctor's major grievance concerned the priest's attempts to prevent the villagers from seeking medical help from the doctor. The priest had told them the doctor was bad. It had become so difficult, according to the doctor, that when one of the mission sisters fell ill, the other sisters were afraid to call the doctor because of the priest's attitude. However, they eventually did summon him one day when the priest was out fishing. The doctor further confided in Heloise that he had been forced to let the nurses run the hospital so that some medical aid would be available to the Mamaoans.

As the months passed, factions for and against the priest developed in the village. Heloise tried to remain neutral to keep up her contacts with all the villagers, but inevitably she was identified with the anti-priest faction. She supposed that her avoidance of the cleric and her friendship with many of his critics made this unavoidable, but there was another reason.

About a month before Heloise's departure, a friend told her with considerable embarrassment how in the early months of her stay the priest had repeatedly told the villagers assembled for six o'clock Mass, which Heloise did not regularly attend, that she was collecting information about them which was uncomplimentary. She was planning to write a book on the basis of this and make a lot of money. He had advised the people not to answer her questions but to respond, "I don't know." He told them that it was a sin to tell her about certain things and encouraged the elders to restrict her access to the village, which they had not done. As Heloise's friend explained, many of the people had believed the priest because priests are wise and knowledgeable and because they were afraid of him. Now most of them knew better and were embarrassed.

One incident occurred just before Heloise's departure in which the Mamaoans made it clear to the priest that he had completely overstepped the boundaries of his role. The old women of the village had reprimanded three younger women who regularly visited the priest to gossip with him. They were transgressing a village rule that prohibited women from calling at the priest's establishment after sundown. The priest responded by publicly chastising the old women. They insisted, however, that the rule was theirs to enforce. This incident provided the turning point for the village. The old women's refusal to acquiesce as the male elders had done spurred outright criticism of the priest. Eventually, complaints to the bishop by the leading members of the church resulted in the priest's dismissal.

Throughout this period of conflict, the villagers admired Heloise's patience—a great virtue in such a small, isolated society where one cannot escape from others. They confided in her because they knew that she had not repeated their confidences as the priest had done. And they respected her strength, for she did not succumb to the ill will of a person who had powerful connections with sacred powers. The priest had surely cursed her, but she had not fallen ill.

In retrospect, Heloise concluded that she had indeed met one of Ruth Benedict's megalomaniac-paranoids on an atoll.

## 4.2—ON THE HORNS OF A DILEMMA: A PROBLEM OF INTERCESSION

A group with whom I have worked is in the process of rapid migration to another country. Since 1950 this group has been moving in increasing numbers to the new host country. While the group runs the gamut of socioeconomic classes, by and large they are lower-middle class white-collar workers. In their move to the new country, these people are relocating in cities where they are seeking similar occupations. In order to aid this mass movement, the host country sent administrators to the country of origin to facilitate the relocation process.

In the course of my research, one agency administrator, Robinson, aided me in a number of ways. He allowed me to look through some of his files; he showed me the forms filled out by the immigrants; he invited me to sit in his office while he interviewed some prospective migrants; and he described in detail the local communal political structure.

Although at first I was impressed by the extent of his cooperation, I soon began to see Robinson in a negative light. As he allowed me to observe his behavior *vis-à-vis* those trying to emigrate, I frequently saw him adopting a hostile, sarcastic, and domineering attitude. He treated his staff—also members of the same community as the migrants—in a similar fashion. After observing his interviews and talking with members of the community and other agency personnel, I concluded that he was deeply involved in intracommunal politics.

Originally there had been only one political organization in the community. The leader of this group, a very proud man who had to be handled with kid gloves, had a run-in with Robinson shortly after his arrival. The conflict arose because the leader, expecting to be given special treatment because of his political status, was treated like everyone else. Incensed, he made a point of opposing Robinson whenever he could.

Because of the leader's refusal to cooperate, Robinson aided in the founding of a second political association, actively helping and supporting this factional group in the ensuing internecine conflict in order to abet his own ends. In addition, Robinson took every opportunity to demonstrate to the community at large that he was doing them a favor, that it was his country which was the benefactor, and that they should be grateful to be on the receiving end.

As the months passed and as my rapport with the people increased, I learned that a number of my informants were so afraid of Robinson that they were reluctant to apply for immigration papers. I was told that on occasion Robinson would harass applicants by calling them to his office and then sending the migrant away on the pretense of having found a problem in the application. As a result, the applicants incurred unnecessary travel and psychological costs. Those who did not submit to the harassment, I was told, would receive an unfavorable review of their application for immigration. I also learned from members of Robinson's mission that his behavior and actions greatly retarded the migration process.

Finally, some of the members of the emigrating community asked me to go to the agency office and intercede in their behalf. When I asked them why they didn't go themselves, they responded, "We are afraid of Robinson." These requests continued until I was feeling substantial pressure to act as a patron of sorts in behalf of these people. Based on my own observation and my informant's remarks, I was convinced that Robinson's behavior resulted in flagrant violations of human dignity—at least in terms of American cultural attitudes.

Before leaving for the field, I was warned that, as a participant-observer, I should remain objective and not allow myself to become emotionally involved in the research situation. Yet, here I was being drawn into an increasingly distasteful conflict. To compound my problem, I am a member of the same ethnic group as the people I was studying, and I share their deep feelings for the host society. I felt that the situation observed could not but blacken the image of the host in the eyes of those who were immigrating. As my investigation proceeded, I found that my evaluation of the situation was essentially correct: those who migrated did so with a very negative attitude toward the host society.

I wanted to inform Robinson's superiors of these unfortunate developments. As a human being, I felt that his treatment of the migrants as "niggers" should be stopped. As an anthropologist, I was on the horns of a dilemma. I had hoped at a later date to do a diachronic study of these people after they were settled in their new land. It was conceivable that Robinson could impede these plans by asking his colleagues to refuse my study application. In addition, I was faced with the very serious question of betrayal of trust. Robinson had given me time and help to facilitate my study. Was it ethical for me to work against the interests of a man who had played such an important role in my investigation? Also, if my intervention proved unsuccessful, would it be harmful to the prospective migrants? Would Robinson take his wrath out on them? I was faced with the basic problem of the undefined role of the researcher as interloper in the affairs of the research community.

Just prior to the end of my study, I was called to the office of a high emissary from the host country. He told me that he had been informed of Robinson's activities and that he knew that I had information which might help remove him from his post. According to this official, Robinson was "not a responsible person and not exactly healthy in a psychiatric sense." The official in question asked me to write a letter describing my observations of Robinson's behavior. He assured me that the letter would remain confidential.

After much self-examination, I decided to write the letter, despite the possible consequences. Shortly thereafter, I returned to the United States.

## 4.2 – On the Horns of a Dilemma: A Problem of Intercession

However, the situation was not concluded. Shortly after my return home, I received a letter from Robinson, who had somehow obtained a copy of my "confidential" letter. He stated that what I had written was "vile, filthy, malicious, and untruthful," and I was a "spreader of poison... all this, no doubt, in full payment for the cooperation which I showed you." He ended his letter by wishing me a "multiplication of pain and sorrow."

Needless to say, I was deeply disturbed over this turn of events, and the potential harm which could ensue. I wrote to the emissary to inform him of Robinson's letter and to find out what had transpired since my departure. I told him of my concern over possible consequences for the people and for my own future research plans. I received an immediate reply assuring me that my letter had been kept confidential but that apparently one of Robinson's friends in the host country's main office had seen it and informed him of its contents. More to the point, however, was the official's statement that Robinson would have to remain for another year since a replacement had not been found. He ended his letter by writing:

> Whether this [incident] would adversely affect the ... [community] is doubtful because too many people are scrutinizing what Robinson is doing, even though the community itself may not have the courage to protest. If I were you, I would forget the whole business and feel compensated by the fact that you did what you considered was your duty as an objective observer and an individual interested in the welfare of the ... [community].

## 4.3 – PLAYING THE ROLE OF INTERCULTURAL MEDIATOR

For the last decade or so the remote corner of the Canadian Northwest Territories where I did field work has been frequented by United States and Canadian sports fishermen who are flown in by small charter airlines. The first summer that I was there about forty men arrived in groups ranging in size from two or three to fifteen. This was a sizeable increase over previous summers. One of the airlines brought in two or three aluminum boats, but in order to accommodate the larger groups, the guides sometimes asked the Eskimo if they could borrow one or both of their canvas-covered canoes. The Eskimo, who rarely refuse requests made by white men, always acceded, but they didn't like giving up their canoes; it limited their freedom of movement and activity considerably.

As the only bilingual speaker in the area, I was employed by both sides as interpreter in the negotiations over the canoes. At one point, toward the end of the summer, after the Eskimo had been without their canoes for some time, one of the canoe owners—my adoptive "father"—told me that if the new group of white men who were expected to arrive asked to borrow his canoe I should refuse.

When the white men came, they asked to borrow the *other* canoe, which was reluctantly loaned. The next morning they brought it back with a large hole in the bottom—it had been ripped on the rocks. When I went down to the shore, they were in the process of attaching their outboard to the second canoe, while the owner watched in silence. The guide told me that since the first canoe could no longer be used, they had come to borrow the second one. The owner—my "father"—told me the same thing, adding that the guide had promised he would return the canoe when he was through with it. My "father" did not repeat his earlier directive that I should refuse on his behalf to lend the canoe.

At that point, I had a choice between saying nothing or telling the guide how the Eskimo—and my "father" in particular—felt about lending their canoes. Since I had not, at that moment, been asked to say anything, speaking up on my own would violate the canoe owner's autonomy. In the Eskimo view, one should not intervene in an interaction between other people unless specifically asked to do so. The Eskimo would also be likely to see my interference as both rude and dangerous *vis-à-vis* the white men. In their view one should not refuse requests, both because it is discourteous and because there may be unpleasant consequences, especially when the person making the request is more powerful than

---
Contributed by Dr. Jean L. Briggs, Memorial University of Newfoundland

you are. On the other hand, the canoe owner had told me, several days earlier, to refuse to loan his canoe if the white men asked for it. And if they ripped a hole in this one, too, it would be three months before we would be able to obtain repair materials. Meanwhile, we would be unable to fish or hunt efficiently; reach our food supplies, which were stored on a nearby island; collect twigs across the river for fuel; or visit with other communities. Finally, I knew that the white men were unaware that the Eskimo would comply with any requests they made, whether the Eskimo considered the request an imposition or not; they were unwittingly imposing on the Eskimo.

However, few of these arguments crossed my mind at the time. My Western values simply took over. In outrage, I defended the Eskimo's rights, telling the fishing guide about the length of time before the first canoe could be repaired, the difficulties that having no canoe would create for us, and the fact that the owner didn't wish to lend his canoe. The guide replied that if the owner didn't wish to lend the canoe they certainly wouldn't borrow it, whereupon I turned to the owner and told him that the white men would not borrow the boat if he didn't wish to lend it to them. The owner, in an unusually strong voice, replied that the white men should do as they pleased—a statement which I repeated to the guide. The Eskimo response to my interference was to ostracize me, from that time until three months later when we resumed contact with the outside world. Then, with the help of some Eskimo friends who were more acculturated, I was finally able to explain my behavior and was more or less accepted back into the Eskimo community.

## 4.4—AN UNWELCOME INTRUSION INTO THE HOST COMMUNITY

David Green spent a year doing field work in a small village community in a tropical country. The subject of his research was social organization and its relation to a distinctive form of subsistence economy. This economy had been undergoing rapid change for a number of years. Part of Green's research plan was to return to the community for a follow-up study four or five years later in order to test whether or not the connection which he postulated between social organization and certain features of the economy was valid. Also, in the course of doing field work, Green found that the villagers had a more elaborate religious system than he had expected. He was able to record only the general outlines of the system, and he felt that to study it fully would require at least another year in the field.

Personal and professional responsibilities prevented Green from making the return trip as soon as he had planned. However, when he was finally able to begin planning his return, a letter arrived from a Peace Corps volunteer assigned to the same general area in which the community was located. In the letter, the volunteer described meeting a young man who had been one of Green's field assistants and was now a secondary school student. He described how extraordinarily bright the young man was; but how his studies were cutting him off from his family and the village, and how the other students in the school mocked and insulted him because of his ethnic background.

This account did not surprise Green. He knew that the surrounding population regarded the villagers, who were ethnically distinct, as "uncivilized pagans" and that the two groups had as little to do with each other as possible. However, the volunteer concluded in his letter that he and his wife intended to move into the village where Green had worked and hinted that they planned to arouse in the villagers a sense of pride in themselves.

Green was concerned about the volunteer's plan. From his own experience, he knew that intergroup relations in the area were explosive. The villagers were not only in the minority but were politically vulnerable and economically dependent on their neighbors. Thus, any assertiveness on their part could be harmful to them. Furthermore, the political consequences could well be disastrous, not only to the villagers, but to any outsider, whether Peace Corps volunteer or anthropologist, who might wish to work with the community in the future. Finally, the presence of the volunteer and his wife in the village would almost certainly affect those changes in village life which Green hoped to study on his return.

## 4.4—An Unwelcome Intrusion into the Host Community

Consequently, Green replied by urging the volunteer to select another community in which to live because of the touchy political situation and his own research plans. Green received no reply to his letter. However, several months later he received a note from his former field assistant telling him that the volunteer and his wife had moved into the village according to their original plan.

## 4.5 – RELATIONS WITH THE PEACE CORPS IN BOROBORO

There were several Peace Corps volunteers in the region where I was conducting research. I frequently met them while conducting a survey and, on several occasions, they stayed with me while traveling through the village where I lived. These volunteers found it difficult to establish any rapport with the rural inhabitants of the area. Indeed, they felt they were the targets of an undercurrent of hostility. In contrast, they were aware that the people were friendly and cooperative with me.

The volunteers couldn't understand why the villagers were so friendly and giving to me when I had nothing to offer, while the Peace Corps workers promised them prospects of better living conditions. Part of the reason for their cold reception was their failure to adapt to rural life. They maintained all the characteristics that the people identified with the typical white attitude of superiority: manners, dress, condemnation of the local dialect, and strong disapproval of local farming habits. One frustrated and naive volunteer asked me why, after nearly two years, he had accomplished nothing with the people; they still did not understand that he was there to help them. I answered by reminding him he still did not understand or speak the language.

Some months later, in order to expand my survey, I moved from the village into the city. It was at this time that I met the area director of the Peace Corps. He was very pleased that I would be living in the city and requested that I assist him and the Corps, since I had a better knowledge of the rural areas than anyone he knew. He wanted to know which communities to send his volunteers to and which to locate females in. Primarily, however, he wanted to know why the rural volunteers thought they were not being successful. In response to the last question, I suggested, after much hesitation, that the Peace Corps community development program might be tied too closely to the local government's program. As a consequence, volunteers frequently were caught up in politics, both at the national and local levels. But more important, I remarked, was the strong element of ethnocentrism among the volunteers.

I offered the following example. One volunteer traveled throughout the rural areas in the region where I worked assisting the local schoolteachers. He taught physical exercises, folk tales, and children's stories. On those occasions when he stayed with me in the village, he often discussed his problems and asked my advice. I noted that most of the stories which he taught the children were American

---

Contributed by Dr. Norman D. Ashcroft, Adelphi University.

rather than national folk tales. I also questioned the utility of teaching rural children physical exercises—many of them had walked over five miles through the bush to attend school. The volunteer replied that the children were uncoordinated and that they needed training in how to play games. When I questioned this lack of coordination, he informed me that the children couldn't even throw a baseball correctly. I reminded him that cricket was the national game which these children played as well as American children played baseball.

Another example of ethnocentrism which I passed on to the director concerned a rural summer camp for city girls. I visited the camp one day and noticed the severely regimented schedule of activities. Moreover, about forty girls were closely supervised by five volunteers. Parietal rules were strictly enforced at night, and the girls were not allowed to associate with the young men of the village. Since most of the girls were fourteen and fifteen years of age, I assumed that many of them considered this rule unfair.

I asked the volunteers to relax the restriction; after all, I explained, this is not an American Girl Scout camp. To relax the rules, I was informed, would bring disaster. One volunteer told me that the boys were "terribly wicked" in this community and if she were to let the girls go about on their own, there would be "hell to pay" from parents. I asked if village boys were any more "wicked" than city boys, but she responded by insisting that the girls were her responsibility not mine. So the volunteers "protected" their charges to the amusement of the villagers and the chagrin of the girls.

I was unsure of the area director's reaction to my criticisms but was reluctant to become too closely involved in Peace Corps problems. So I said nothing more. Nevertheless, he asked me for the names of anthropologists who were experts in the area and suggested I recommend a bibliography of reading that might be helpful in training. I provided this information willingly.

Some weeks later the director asked me if I thought it wise to place a couple in the village where I had lived. Again, I reluctantly became involved. After meeting the couple, I suggested that it might be better to place them in an urban setting; in my opinion, they would find it hard to adapt to rural living conditions. My suggestion was ignored and they were sent to the village.

Three weeks later, the couple resigned from the Peace Corps and left the country. I saw them on their last day in the village and listened to their complaints: these were the most unfriendly people they had ever met; they were full of prejudice toward white people, did not like them from the start, and never appreciated the advice they had to offer. The wife told me she tried to convince the mothers to bathe their children more often and to change their hygenic habits. The mothers ignored her suggestions. The villagers later told me their side of the story; the two volunteers were the most unfriendly people they had ever met. They spent most of their time in their house and never once had the courtesy to come to the villagers' homes and introduce themselves. The villagers wondered if all Americans were so impolite and difficult to get to know.

The director later explained to me that the husband was physically ill and thus had to terminate his assignment early. When I indicated that there might have been other reasons, I was told to stop interfering in Peace Corps affairs. He noted that I had done nothing but criticize the Corps since he had met me and that I constantly interfered with development programs. In his opinion I not only misunderstood the rural situation but misunderstood the country's problems as a whole. And I certainly misunderstood the mission of the Peace Corps, he said. I asked what the mission was. The reply: the Peace Corps was to help improve American image abroad and to help implement American foreign policy.

## 4.6 – A CONFRONTATION WITH A PRIEST

The anthropologist often comes into conflict with the local missionary, whose beliefs the anthropologist may have specificlly rejected. Yet he must also appreciate the missionary's sincere desire to help the people among whom he is working as well as the time and effort he spends.

The events that follow occurred in a small administered territory in the Pacific.

Father Samuel Brown had been in the territory about a year when he was appointed to the mission station at Boro. Our conflict occurred after he had been there for about three months. At that time he was in the early stages of learning the local language and culture. Although he was aware of what he needed to learn, he perceived sufficient similarity between his former post and Boro to think that he already had some understanding of his new flock.

Malu, a resident of a local village, was in the mission hospital at Boro for what was diagnosed as a psychosomatic ailment. Feeling somewhat improved, he was ready to leave the hospital when he met Patiti, a sorcerer by reputation, although he denied the charge. According to Malu, Patiti bewitched him so that, upon returning home, Malu began to feel ill again. Fearing Patiti's spell, Malu left his own home to stay with relatives in another village. Two native doctors tried to cure him, but Malu's condition worsened. Through a medium, it was learned that Malu was being possessed by several powerful ancestral spirits at Patiti's behest. The only man who knew the appropriate rituals for dealing with these spirits was Tako, who lived in a nearby village. Malu's relatives arranged with Tako to perform the cure.

At this point, Father Brown arrived. I should mention that Malu was, at least nominally, a Christian. Father Brown tried to persuade Malu to return to the mission hospital. He hoped to cure him through a combination of sedatives and occupational therapy. But Malu refused to go. Should he return to the mission, he declared, he would surely die. Father Brown persisted but Malu remained adamant.

Shortly afterwards, I encountered Father Brown in the center of the village. Although I had not been present during Father Brown's discussion with Malu, I was aware of the purpose of his visit. In a loud voice in English, Father Brown accused me of hindering his work. He argued that if I cared about Malu's welfare, I should try to persuade him to return to the mission hospital. I retorted

---

Contributed by Dr. Matthew Cooper, McMaster University

that if Malu really believed in Christianity he would return of his own will. Obviously, I argued, Malu believed more strongly in the power of the ancestral spirits, and he should be allowed to choose the treatment in which he had faith.

Father Brown was incensed by my heatedly delivered remarks. Implicitly I was saying that the problem was psychological in origin and that the Christianity and the traditional religious scheme, at least in these circumstances, were merely alternative psychotherapies. We continued arguing loudly for several minutes before a crowd of interested, although largely uncomprehending, villagers. Finally, he declared, "You don't know the difference between good and evil." At that point, I realized that for the priest the ancestral spirits were real; they were manifestations of evil. Realizing the futility of further argument, I said, "Father, this isn't getting either of us anywhere." I invited him to my house for a cup of tea. Without saying more, we finally agreed to let the disagreement stand unresolved. When we met later, neither of us mentioned the incident. Malu remained in the village, went through the curing ceremonies and eventually got well.

## 4.7–HOW FAR TO GO IN DECEPTION: A CLASH OF VIEWPOINTS

Before I left for the field, some of my advisors at the university expressed their concern about a woman doing field work alone in such a remote and dangerous area. They suggested that I tell the members of the society I planned to study that I was married. Some even advised me to arm myself with a fake biography of my husband and children, including photographs, a wedding ring, and so forth. My advisors were also concerned that as an unmarried woman I might not be allowed access to certain ceremonies or other events, such as childbirth. Thus, the false role of a married woman would not only be a protective device but also an aid to my research. It would put me into a normal category in terms of adult roles in the society. So I went into the field armed with the paraphernalia for this fake role, including a wedding ring provided by a friend and a picture of his sister's children.

After I had been in the field about three weeks, the people brought up the question of my marital status. This arose because at the government's insistence I had spent a weekend at the nearest government post which was occupied by a government patrol officer. He was the closest government official responsible for my safety, and he advised me to hire the houseboy who had been working at the post, which I did. But the houseboy told the people who lived in the valley where I worked that I was married to the patrol officer. After I had been there for several weeks, some people asked me if this story was true. My knowledge of the language was still only rudimentary; however, I managed to communicate the fact that I was indeed married, but not to the government official. I showed them the borrowed picture and explained that this was my family. They responded with great enthusiasm.

Unfortunately, the local missionaries heard that I had been telling the people that I was married. They got upset about this, and eventually one of them took me aside one day after I had been in the field for three of four months. He said I should not lie to the people. He and his fellow missionaries were trying to teach Christian ethics, and they never lied to the people.

I argued that I really didn't think I was lying in that sense. If the missionaries were so concerned about my protection and my physical safety, they should see that my story was a useful kind of subterfuge, one intended to assure my safety; it was not morally detrimental to anyone. But the missionary maintained that it involved false pretenses, and if I didn't tell the people the truth, he would have to do it himself.

Well, I never did tell the people the truth and, as it turned out, my marital status really wasn't an important factor. I was so much of an outsider that they could not place me in the usual male or female categories anyway.

Nevertheless, I found myself in an interesting position *vis-à-vis* the missionaries and their relations with the people in my village. The missionaries were preaching in such a way that their message was being misinterpreted. Part of the difficulty arose from their elementary linguistic skills, but they also permitted some of the misinterpretations to continue. For example, the people were convinced that their skins would turn white if they memorized enough gospel verses. Furthermore, they believed that my memorizing these verses they would never be sick again, they would have eternal life and the dead would come back to life.

Visitors would come to me and say: "Teach me the life words!"

And I would reply, "I do not know the life words. I am not a Christian."

"You are lying. All white people are Christians."

"No, not all white people are Christians. I am not a Christian."

"Missionaries say all white people are Christians."

"Well, they are not talking about me; they are talking about other white people. I am not a Christian."

Balak was a close friend and a good informant; he was also an important political figure in the valley. One day he asked me to help him learn the gospel verses so that he could bring his beloved daughter back to life.

"Will you help me learn them?"

"I can't help you learn them, Balak. That is the missionary's job. If you want to learn the life words, go talk to the missionary."

"Well, do you think what they said will really happen?"

"I don't know... No! I don't think so!"

"They told me my little girl would come back to life if I just memorized enough of the life words. Why won't you help me memorize the life words?"

"I don't know the life words!"

"Do you think my daughter will come back?"

"No. I think you've misunderstood the missionaries. You should talk with them again."

There were several other incidents like this. This was probably the one thing that I agonized about most in the field. Finally, I decided to talk about it to the missionaries.

I received a variety of answers from them, none of which really acknowledged the problem. Finally, I talked to one of the most intelligent and experienced of the missionaries when he came back from leave. He spoke the local language fluently and knew the most about the ways of the people. But it turned out he, too, was protective of the missionary movement, which was successful largely because of these misinterpreted messages. I told him that the local people did not understand and that there could be practical consequences of this misunderstanding when they didn't turn white or their children didn't come back to life. I pointed out that they could attack the missionaries and kill them; they could attack me as well. But he insisted that "If God wants them to be enlightened, He will enlighten them."

## 4.8 – THE LOCAL MISSION AND ITS PRIEST

The mission station was located about twenty miles out of town; we had to pass through mission grounds to get to the Indian village we were studying. When we first met the priest at the station, he was friendly. He said, "My house is your house, and please use it any time you want."

The priest ran the mission station as if it were his chiefdom. He operated a store for the Indians and charged exorbitant prices, supporting the mission on its profits. The mission was also in the process of putting in a large plantation, and the priest hired the local Indians to work for very low wages.

A Volkswagen bus came out to the mission evey week, and the priest sold tickets to the Indians at reduced rates for the ride into town. But he would refuse tickets to those he was trying to coerce for some reason, telling the bus driver not to let these individuals board the bus.

The priest was also in the market for Indian artifacts which, after purchasing at an unbelievably low price, he then sold out of the country. A short time before we arrived, a collecting team from a European museum came through the area. The priest had refused to allow them to go through the mission grounds in order to reach the Indian village. He complained that the museum people were paying the price the Indians asked for artifacts, which was too high. But everyone was paying more for artifacts than the priest did.

All this we learned later, after our first confrontation with the priest. Since he had offered us the hospitality of his house, we at first stored our equipment there and then went back into town for other supplies. But when we returned, he demanded to know what we were doing there, and he asked to see our credentials. He looked at each piece of equipment, asking what we intended to use it for. When he saw our outboard motor, he said, "I don't know why you brought that. You're not going to give it to the Indians, are you? I don't want that motor in this territory. They don't need it. They'll just go running around with it."

After this confrontation, whenever we went into town or returned, we would go through the mission lands as quickly as possible without stopping. Then he removed the bridge that we had to use to cross over a tributary stream.

The missionary also ran a brothel for government officials and important merchants and politicians, providing girls or boys depending on taste. Every Sunday, he would invite people to the station to get drunk and have fun. We learned about this from one of our European friends, who told us how he fell into the river while he was screwing an Indian girl; and how the priest had been with a little boy, because he liked them better. The priest was a strange man, as he liked girls too.

A larger conflict with the priest arose over the young man he had employed to be our guide and interpreter. He was a good man, and the only Indian in the area who could speak the lingua franca. The priest wanted to use our guide to bring in a group of Indian workers for his plantation. Even now it's unclear to me to what extent the priest really intended to employ this man and to what extent he simply wanted to sabotage our research efforts.

His motives in any event were very complicated, because he not ony wanted the young man to work for him, he wanted to establish him as a kind of chief. He had this mad idea from a book he had read by Edgar Rice Burroughs that every group of Indians had a chief and the chief gives orders and bosses people around, which is a misconception of the political organization of these Indians, particularly since our guide was only 18 or 19 years old. But even if you were the most powerful man in the area, you still wouldn't hold this type of authority, since the local chief's powers are religious, the prestige of which only permits him to give suggestions.

Our guide was terrified of the priest. He knew that chiefs do not have the authority to coerce. And he had seen what had happened in a government settlement when an elderly man had been given this prerogative. The man lost all his previous prestige and status and even his religious powers. The whole settlement experienced a cultural collapse as a result, with drunkenness, incest, and amoral behavior ensuing.

To put pressure on our guide, the priest refused to let his father use the bus. His father was the real chief, but he was forced to walk into town. The priest also threatened the villagers by warning them that he would deny access through the mission lands if they did not cooperate with him.

Our guide became more and more upset over this conflict. The Indians cannot stand anyone putting pressure on them. For example, our guide had a bicycle to use in town. Some of the Indians nearby the mission station gave him a hard time about it, demanding rides, and so forth. His response was to take the bicycle and throw it in the river. Indians under such pressure were also known to disappear into the jungle. And after a while our guide began to say, "I'll go off into the jungle some place and die away."

Finally, he asked us to go over the missionary's head and talk with his superior. But we were reluctant to do this; we had heard about the power of the church and how it protected its clergy no matter what anyone said. We were afraid that if we discussed this situation with another missionary we would suffer the consequences.

There was really no solution to our case. As outsiders, we were powerless in the situation. We felt sorry for our guide, but we knew that giving him up would be no solution. The priest would still insist that he perform a task which he didn't want to take on—a task quite divorced from any role that he could possibly see in his own culture. Any protest on our part would simply result in our removal from the area, and everything would continue in exactly the same way as before.

Our only recourse was to tell the Indians how badly they were being cheated. We also tried to encourage them to set up their own business, with the help of some concerned people in the town. But I don't know if these efforts were successful.

Eventually, after we had left, our guide and his father took the motor and went away, way up into no man's land, looking for a lost family of their tribe that was supposed to be living there and whom they thought might be relatives.

## 4.9 – THE TRADER AND HIS MONOPOLY

The trader's store was located up the river about a five-day journey from town. Anyone working in that area was completely dependent on him to provide supplies and services. He was a very wealthy man, worth several million dollars. Not only did he control trade and transportation in the territory—he owned the only outboard motors in the region—he also controlled the postal services. Furthermore, he had a monopoly on chicle production in the territory.

When we first arrived in the company of another man, who was fairly well respected in the region, the trader was very friendly to us. After purchasing supplies at his story, we continued up the river to a point where we were picked up by the Indians we planned to study and taken to their village, located on another tributary of the river.

We stayed with these Indians for two weeks, trying to decide whether to do field work with them. During our visit, we learned that these people usually spent six months of the year working for the trader, gathering chicle in the mountains. This meant that they disrupted their aboriginal way of life for half the year, during which time individual families moved about and the village dispersed.

While we were asking them questions about their yearly work cycle, they apparently decided that instead of collecting chicle that year they would stay in the village and the "rich" Americans would support them.

In order to get back to town at the end of the second week, we had to go back down the river. We planned to go to the trader's store and find a boat there. So when it came time to leave, an Indian paddled down to the trader's store to buy gasoline for our return trip. While there, he told the trader that he thought he wouldn't work for him this year gathering chicle, as he was going to work for the American anthropologist, who would support him and all his people.

Well, the trader didn't send up any gasoline for four days. Finally, after sending down another person to find out what had happened, the gasoline was provided, and we went back to the store, where we had to stay for two days waiting for a boat.

The trader's attitude had in the meantime completely changed since our first meeting with him. Previously, he had made a point of telling us that the prices he charged the Indians were far above what they were in the nearest town. "Well, one price for you, another for the Indians!" he had told us. Now, suddenly, he was demanding exorbitant prices for the supplies we needed.

## Section 4: Relations with Representatives of Outside Agencies

He put us in a rat-infested hut and provided a cook who stole all our food. He refused to speak to us and turned his back whenever we approached. It was frightening in addition to being unpleasant, since he was the most powerful man in the territory.

During our stay with the Indians and while we waited for a boat at the store, we learned more about the trader's operations. He paid the Indians to collect chicle with goods from his store. But his scale was rigged. Even so, the trader owed money to many of the Indians who worked for him, although they were led to believe they were in debt to him.

We later decided to work in another area, even though we were still dependent on this trader for our supplies. When we next saw him, he asked where we had decided to work. We told him we were planning to work in another area with a different group of Indians. From that time on the trader was friendly and cooperative. He sold us supplies at low prices and joked with us whenever we stopped at his store.

# 4.10–MISSIONARIES AND ANTHROPOLOGISTS

When missionaries have been faced with acute difficulties in understanding why indigenous peoples behave in a particular manner they have sometimes posed the question, "Isn't there some anthropologist who could help us with this problem?" And similarly, anthropologists have commented, "Why don't missionaries obtain the help of an anthropologist if they really want to understand the patterns of behavior foreign to them?" But despite the fact that an "alliance" between missionaries and anthropologists would seem to be so appropriate and easy,[1] the truth of the matter is that numerous obstacles stand in the way of any extensive collaboration or rapprochement.

## MISSIONARY-ANTHROPOLOGIST CONTACTS

There are many missionaries, for example, whose personal contacts with anthropologists have tended to disillusion them with regard to the possibility of significant assistance from these specialists in culture and human behavior. For one thing, most missionaries have at one time or another had contacts with anthropologists who have been studying peoples in their part of the world. Even when anthropologists have not shown themselves hostile to missionary activity (which not infrequently they are), they quite often show evident disapproval of changing a society. In fact, perhaps without quite realizing it, many anthropologists are devotees of the cult of the exotic.

Professionally, it is of course much more tidy to describe a culture which seems relatively isolated from the outside world rather than in the maelstrom of cultural change. Perhaps as a kind of expression of revolt against Western society, some anthropologists unconsciously nurse some of Rousseau's romanticism about the "noble savage." In fact, more than one missionary has become quite amazed at the seeming cultural blindness on the part of an anthropologist who may be hostile toward the mission's efforts in changing society, while he seems relatively unconcerned about the rapid and sometimes tragic changes which are being instituted by economic interests which introduce huge plantations, sprawling mining compounds, or satellite slums, with resulting breakdown in tribal authority, widespread drunkenness, and mounting venereal disease. Particularly galling to many missionaries is the polite congeniality of some anthropologists when they

---

By Eugene A. Nida. Reprinted from *Practical Anthropology* Vol. 13, No. 6, November-December 1966, pp. 173-177, 187, by permission of the author and publisher.

accept the missionary's hospitality, but their overt and often bitter hostility toward missionary activities when they are with the indigenous people.

Perhaps, however, a more important basis of misunderstanding between so many anthropologists and missionaries is the fact that a high percentage of anthropologists feel constrained to study a culture in the abstract rather than to become involved in trying to help people. In fact, many anthropologists not only prefer to see the indigenous culture remain the way it is, but they also feel a certain professional pride in refusing to make recommendations as to how situations might be improved. Moreover, some anthropologists have been so impressed with a functionalist view of society that they seemed utterly blind to areas of dysfunction.

Many missionaries, furthermore, have had the experience of being "pumped dry" by anthropological investigators who seem keenly interested in obtaining all the information they can about the peoples whom the missionary knows well. Usually such anthropologists either promise or imply that they will be happy to reciprocate in sending the results of their studies to the missionaries. Unfortunately, in very few circumstances do anthropologists ever comply with their promises. Perhaps they feel somewhat embarrassed because the results of their analyses seem critical of the missionaries. Or they may assume that their results will be in too technical a form of language for the missionary, of whom they are basically contemptuous. They are interested in circulating their work among academic peers, from whom they can get prestige. Sometimes years elapse between the collection of data, and publication. The missionary, in the mean time, has long since been forgotten. It is therefore no uncommon experience on the part of missionaries to feel that anthropologists have been interested primarily in oneway communication, without any reciprocity.

At the same time, of course, anthropologists have not always been exemplary in their personal behavior, so that not only in terms of the standards of the missionaries, but in those of the indigenous culture itself, their conduct has been cause for severe criticism by the indigenous leadership.

## ANTHROPOLOGISTS AND MISSION ASSIGNMENTS

Despite such problems of basic misunderstanding and difficulty which have arisen, some missions have realized the significance of anthropology for their work, and have actually hired anthropologically-trained persons to assist them in technical phases of their work and investigations. But in a number of instances even this has not proved very satisfactory. For one thing, some of these anthropologists have actually not been fully qualified, particularly in field experience. They have seen their work as an opportunity to get experience and advance their own careers. Therefore, as a result of either lack of proper academic orientation or of acquaintance with field situations, their advice has sometimes been almost worse than nothing.

Then again, difficulty has resulted from the fact that anthropologists who have undertaken to help missionaries directly have concentrated so much attention upon establishing good rapport with the indigenous population that they have sometimes consciously or unconsciously tended to alienate the missionary community. Having been assigned to study the local culture, they have felt that this is their proper object of concentration, and accordingly have more or less dismissed the problems and needs of the missionaries as being irrelevant to their task. Occasionally their identification with at least some elements in the indigenous community have resulted in anthropologists becoming indirectly the leaders of dissident factions. This has, of course, been a tragedy, for the anthropologist's role in missionary work is not to "take sides" in controversies, but to bring sides together. He needs to be the catalyst in bringing about real understanding, and to do this he cannot afford to become partisan with one constituency or the other.

Sometimes anthropologists in the employ of missions feel that they have completed their work when they have submitted their reports to the church and the mission. Unfortunately, these reports tend to be written in at least semitechnical language, and as a result are rarely fully understood. Moreover, they frequently contain many theoretical arguments and observations, all of which seem unrealistic and unimportant to the layman.

The greatest difficulty, however, with some anthropologists who are attached to Christian missions is that too frequently they are not willing to become a part of the very problems which they are studying. In other words, they do not want to become involved, to make decisions, to take the consequences of decisions, being prepared to pick up the pieces if the whole project collapses. That is to say, they are not really missionaries at heart, and under such circumstances are rarely prepared to communicate effectively with missionaries whose involvement is no mere "balcony approach" to the scene of life but an earnest and intense living at the very vortex of human problems.

## DEVELOPMENT OF CULTURAL INSIGHT

Quite obviously, it is impossible to train all missionaries as anthropologists. The very volume of information which must be assimilated, the complex techniques and methods which must be mastered, and the range of field experience which must be acquired, all prohibit any attempt to train the average missionary to be an anthropologist. On the other hand, it has not proved satisfactory merely to have professional anthropologists provide technical analyses of various customs and beliefs of an indigenous people. For the most part, missionaries simply do not read such documents, or if they do read them, they usually do not understand how to apply the insights which they may contain. The only practical solution to this problem would seem to require a degree of mutual involvement; but if missionaries cannot themselves learn the content of anthropology and if anthropologists are unwilling or unprepared to engage in applied anthropology for long periods of time in a particular tribal area, what is the solution?

At least one aspect of this solution may be found in the techniques which Dr. Loewen has developed in helping missionaries to learn how to ask the right questions in the right way.[2] This he did so significantly in connection with investigation of Indian problems among the Mennonite settlers in the Chaco of Paraguay. If missionaries themselves can learn how to ask the right questions in the right way, and if at the same time they have rid themselves of the typical prejudices which tend to distort and skew the evidence which they obtain, there is then a real possibility that the missionaries themselves can arrive at the right solutions, particularly if their fundamental motivations for serving others are genuine.

The problems of anthropological insight are, however, not restricted merely to missionaries. In working with Bible translators who are themselves translating the Bible into their own mother tongue, we have seen certain very startling facts emerge. In the first place, these translators normally know their own language well, for they have learned it as children before going away to boarding school, and they have continued to speak it with fellow tribesmen at school, in nearby cities, or during the few months a year when they return to their own homes. They have no problem with the language as such, but they do with the cultural context in which the language is normally used, for their formal education has been almost entirely outside of the tribe.

They know the words, but they do not understand the variety of cultural settings in which these words are employed. As a result of the Western, institutional education many "trained leaders" in the church have been educated away from their people and have never been reabsorbed, for they have been out of the tribe at that crucial time when their peers were obtaining adult status through the informal procedure of initiation and apprenticeship. Accordingly, many African translators, for instance, do not know precisely what certain key words mean. This is not because the words are themselves obscure or ambivalent in meaning, but simply because the contextual setting of these words has never been experienced by the speaker himself. These translators themselves need help in analyzing the cultural patterns of their own indigenous society.

Unfortunately, the type of Bible school and seminary training which has been so extensively employed in various parts of the missionary world has been oriented almost exclusively toward the structure of thought as it is formulated in various European languages: English, French, Spanish, and German. In a course in homiletics a student may have been permitted to preach in his own mother tongue, but more often than not the content, as revealed in an outline submitted in the European tongue, is judged almost exclusively on the basis of culturally alien standards. There has rarely been an attempt to deal significantly, critically, and creatively with the fundamental problems of inter-cultural communication. It has only been taken for granted that pastors would find the appropriate terms in their own language to communicate the alien concepts which have come to them in a foreign language. It is scarcely any wonder, therefore, that we are faced with a significant hiatus in both learning and understanding.

As is becoming increasingly evident, therefore, there is a real need for meaningful cooperation between missionaries and anthropologists; but if this is to be relevant, missionaries and educated national Christian leaders must themselves become involved in the very process of finding answers to questions. It is not enough merely to have them read the anthropologist's report. And anthropologists, on the other hand, must be willing to identify more fully with both missionaries and nationals. In other words, they must identify with the church, if the real problems of the church are to be resolved. The anthropologist himself cannot hope to communicate to the people all of his theoretical knowledge or his store of detailed technical information, but he can have a very significant role to play in helping people learn how to ask the right questions in the right way in order to arrive at valid solutions. Perhaps the real crux of the problem is asking questions *in the right way*, for this requires a degree of empathy and self-exposure which leaves little room for professional pride or academic detachment. Probing into the problems of human maladjustment cannot be done from the psychological distance of the outsider. One cannot find the truth until he becomes a part of it.

**NOTES**

1. See Jacob A. Loewen, "Missionaries and Anthropologist Cooperate in Research," *Practical Anthropology* Vol. 12, No. 4 (July-August 1965), pp. 158-190.
2. op.cit.

## 4.11 – COMPETITION FOR ACCESS TO THE COMMUNITY

For the past six years I have been engaged in a study of the emotional concepts and behaviors of a small Eskimo community, its theories of psychodynamics and interpersonal motivation, how these are utilized in actual interpersonal behavior, and how they are taught to children. My research requires a thorough knowledge of the dialect spoken by this group, as well as the development of close relationships with selected individuals in the group. I had made two field trips to the area under study and was planning a third trip for the year 1970. For that purpose I had arranged to be relieved of teaching duties for the year.

However, in March 1969 I received a letter from an eighteen-year-old freshman at another university who informed me that he planned to spend a year living with the Eskimo group I was studying—from July 1969 to July 1970. Unaware that I was currently engaged in research in that community, he was writing to me because somebody had told him that I knew more about that group than anyone else. He thought that I could tell him who to be adopted by and what equipment would be useful for him to take for himself and for the Eskimo. He had always wanted to live with the Eskimo, he said, and he had obtained permission both from the Canadian government and from his university, which was giving him a year's credit in biology and anthropology for living as the Eskimo do and for making parasite and pesticide counts in animal livers. His parents also approved of his plan. This would not be his first visit to the community; he had been there already, once, on a fishing trip of a few days with his father, and a second time with a tourist outfit for a week, helping to build a tent camp. On these occasions he had made the acquaintance of a boy about his own age—one of the two or three young people in the group who speaks a little English—and had corresponded with him periodically for several years.

I felt considerable sympathy with the young man's enterprise. His plan seemed to be carefully thought-out and seriously motivated. On the other hand, it raised serious obstacles to my own plans; I felt that the community of twenty-six people was too small to bear the weight of two foreigners simultaneously. The Eskimo had told me so themselves; they had said to me once: "We don't mind your being here because there's only one of you, but several white men together buzz like mosquitoes and are a nuisance."

Nevertheless, I didn't feel that my research was more important than the enrichment of this student's life experience. I don't believe that knowledge is an absolute

---

Contributed by Dr. Jean L. Briggs, Memorial University of Newfoundland

value. Moreover, if there was only room for one foreigner, I thought the Eskino had a right to choose who that should be; after all, I don't "own" them. But I also knew that if I didn't go there as planned, I might not have another opportunity. Not only were my funds and available time limited, there was also the fact that these Eskimo might be about to move into a larger settlement containing Eskimo and whites from many areas—a settlement where the psychodynamics and interpersonal interactions would be quite different.

I responded to the student in detail, giving the advice he had requested on equipment and adoption. I told him who to apply to for sponsorship and described how he should behave so as to be a minimal burden on the Eskimo, warning him that it would be difficult to avoid being a burden to some extent on a community that size, especially because of his probable culture shock reactions—which I described.

I also told him the nature of the dilemma he was creating for me and said that, if he proved to be a burden to the Eskimo, it would make it impossible for me to return to the community while he was there. I didn't ask him to go elsewhere, but I told him I thought his decision should be made with the full knowledge of the implications it would have for other people.

Unfortunately, my letters only succeeded in making him highly resentful of my interest in these Eskimo. He replied that he couldn't possibly go anywhere else, both for economic reasons and because he was very interested in this particular group. He said that it would also be impossible for him to go at any other time but that because he is a male and competent in fishing, hunting, and canoeing he felt sure that he could both obtain his own food and contribute to the supply of the group; and he saw no reason why our simultaneous presence in the camp should inconvenience the Eskimo.

It turned out that he did experience several of the difficulties that I had envisaged, and he found it advisable to leave the community after a few months. On the whole, my research has not been damaged by these events, but it has been changed. I was unable of course to return to the area in 1970. By the time I did return, the Eskimo, as predicted, had moved into the larger settlement. My conditions of observation and participation were considerably more limited in the new settlement than they had been in the old. Nevertheless, much of their behavior has not yet changed; and insofar as it has changed, the differences themselves provide interesting data. The Eskimo talk about both of their foreign visitors and judge each of us on our own merits.

# SECTION FIVE
# RELATIONS WITH OTHER SOCIAL SCIENTISTS AND RESPONSIBILITIES TO THE PROFESSION

## INTRODUCTION

The ethics of the relations between social scientists are not well delineated or understood. Part of the problem lies in the fact that the nature of property rights in science has not been adequately considered. This issue has been submerged because it conflicts with the basic ethical tenet of science that knowledge must be free and available to all. I have discussed these issues more fully in Appendix 2, where I review the problems produced by overcompetition.

Certainly overcompetition was not a problem in the early days, in the Dreamtime of anthropological research, when anthropologists were thin on the ground and their rewards were limited. These individuals were primarily motivated by the personal satisfaction of living in a foreign society and recording its dying culture for all mankind. In this early period of anthropological research, the social modality of interrelationships was more one of communitas than of structure, to use Victor Turner's terminology. Then came "big anthropology," with professional rewards going to the swift and the not so ethical. Anthropologists who produced basic texts appeared at professional meetings with their wives in fur coats, ignoring the concern over the world-wide destruction of fauna. As communitas among professionals faded, the clamor for ethical guidelines became more audible.

But the problem of professional relations is not confined to the borders of our own society. Claims have been made that the American professor in a developing country has certain obligations to his colleagues there (cf. Whyte 1969); and many feel that interpersonal and interuniversity reciprocities should be established. But one must be aware that the Western European ethic of scientific inquiry is still not shared by professionals in all other societies. I have heard of instances in which professionals in another country have published under their own names articles written by American colleagues working in that country. In other countries, close association between a visiting scientist and the local social science community can result in the visiting scientist being asked to leave, since the scientific community is in conflict with the government.

Also, there is the problem of having to pad one's pay roles with local social scientists so that the research can be accomplished. Is this not in itself unethical?

Does this not add a further intrusive factor into an already sensitive field situation? Unfortunately, I have been unable to collect representative case materials dealing with these problems, in one instance because the individual feared he would not be allowed back into the country to continue his research.

In Appell (1973a), I discuss in further detail some of these problems and how social scientists might approach them.

## RELATED CASE MATERIALS IN OTHER SECTIONS

*Section 3: Relations with Host Government:* A Request for Informant Names by a Government Official; Field Work in a Restricted Region.

*Section 4: Relations with Representatives of Outside Agencies and the Public with Respect to the Host Community:* An Unwelcome Intrusion into the Host Community.

*Section 6: Dilemmas in the Use and Misuse of Social Science Knowledge:* The Discovery of Drugs: A Difficult Ethical Question; Differential Access to the Results of Anthropological Inquiry: A Dilemma in Professional Responsibility.

*Section 7: Publication: Responsibilities and Liabilities:* Problems in Urban Ethnic Research.

*Section 8: Relations and Responsibilities to Funding Agencies:* A Request from the National Foundation to Review a Research Proposal.

*Section 9: Issues in Teaching:* The Introduction of Deviant Ideas by the Instructor; A Student Recounts his National Foundation Interview; A Matter of a Teaching Contract.

## 5.1 – A PROPOSED RESTUDY OF NEW BUTU

Walter Grant had recently returned from his second field trip to New Butu and was in the process of preparing a monograph on the social organization of the society he studied there. He hoped to have the book finished within two or three years so that he could return to New Butu to continue his study of the society and investigate the social changes that had occurred. However, he received a letter from a friend that caused him to reevaluate his research plans. His friend had enclosed a photocopy of a letter he had received from Dick Considine, an anthropologist who was planning to conduct research in New Butu. One paragraph in Considine's letter particularly concerned Grant. It read as follows:

> I have applied to several foundations for funds to carry out research in New Butu on the history of ethnographic investigations there. I will be engaged in a study of how theoretical constructs of social systems, assumptions with regard to social processes and human nature, as well as personal idiosyncracies, influence anthropological inquiry in terms of the selection of a problem, choice of locale for field work, and the collection and interpretation of field data. I expect to hear within the next few weeks the results of my research proposals, and if they are favorable, I plan to leave immediately for New Butu to visit the locales where previous ethnographers have worked. I hope to be able to investigate on the scene the manner in which the ethnographic investigations were undertaken by visiting all communities studied by the previous ethnographers, talking with informants that were used, and collecting what pertinent information I can. At the completion of my research, I should have enough data to contrast with the published materials of those who have worked in New Butu and determine to what degree the conceptual tools used and personal characteristics of the investigator have affected their collection of data and interpretation of empirical reality.

This was the first that Grant had heard of Considine's plans, and since there seemed to be an element of time involved, Grant wondered how he should react to this news and what course of action he should take.

## 5.2 – THE BREAKING OF A DISGUISE

Marie Adams, a medical anthropologist, worked in one of the large, new nations of Africa, studying the indigenous system of medicine of a tribe living in a remote section of the country. During her research she observed a number of incidents that had a direct bearing on one aspect of her project, the impact that Western medicine was having on the traditional system of medicine.

Most of the medical personnel, from district medical officer down to the level of dresser, were drawn from the politically dominant ethnic community. Adams frequently observed that medical personnel were demanding small payments for their services in the form of cash or agricultural produce. Those being treated would often complain about this to Adams. Then, during a major smallpox epidemic, she discovered that a local chief was hiding from the government medical teams those people in his village who had become infected with the disease as they were afraid they might be taken away from the village.

On her return from the field, Adams was asked to write a general article discussing the problems of introducing Western medical practices. To illustrate her argument, she described some of the incidents she had observed with regard to the behavior of medical personnel, including the problem of the smallpox epidemic. However, she disguised the locale and the people involved to avoid causing any embarrassment to the government, to any of the individuals involved, or to her informants. She believed that without using such a disguise the government might not welcome other foreign research personnel in the future and would perhaps prohibit her return to continue her research. Also, there was the possibility that members of the dominant ethnic group might punish her informants, particularly the local chief.

Several years after her article had appeared, Adams was shocked to discover that a younger colleague had deliberately broken her disguise. In an article in which he reviewed all the research that had been conducted in the country, her colleague referred explicitly to the disguised article, providing the true identities of the tribe, its location, and specific individuals.

Marie wondered what action she should take, if any.

## 5.3—A CASE OF POACHING?

For the past three summers I have been working in an Indian community in northern Mexico. Just before I left the field last summer I spoke to my principal informant about my plans for the following year. I told him I planned to return the following summer to investigate spirit possession. I asked him to help me in the meantime by finding out all he could about the subject in his spare time and locating all the shamans in the general area.

After returning to the university, I learned from a colleague that another anthropologist had been funded for a year of research, starting this autumn, to investigate shamanism in the village where I had been working. Rather disturbed by this news, I called up a close friend of mine and told him my problem over lunch.

"Well," he replied to my question of what I should do, "I'm really rather unsympathetic to this kind of situation. Your reaction to the possibility that someone else may use your informant is part of a larger problem. This is the anthropologist's attitude that a whole community or an area is his personal property. I think there is something insidious in speaking of 'my Indians' or 'my informant.' You are saying that these are *my* Indians; that this is *my* exclusive research problem; and don't tread on *my* property. I think this attitude overlooks the human rights both of the members of the community who may not want to be regarded as somebody's Indians and of the informant, who might be quite willing to work with somebody else. And why shouldn't he?"

"I suppose you do have a point," I replied, "especially in extreme cases. I used to be very self-conscious about referring to 'my people.' But once when I was doing field work in another area, I heard myself referred to as 'our white man' by the members of the village in which I was residing. Consequently, I don't feel too strongly about it any longer. In any event, this situation is different. The anthropologist has not contacted me about his field work plans. And I have spent a number of months and a considerable amount of money training my informant. I told him when I left the field this September to begin thinking about the problem of spirit possession, and I asked him to contact the shamans in the area so that when I return next summer we can begin to investigate the subject without delay. This other anthropologist could intervene before my return and obtain all the information on spirit possession which my informant is collecting for me—leaving me with nothing. Whether you agree with me or not, is there anything I can do?"

## 5.4–COMPETITION FOR HOST COMMUNITIES

The notion of "ownership" of a village, tribe, or people has long been derided within the profession—as well it might be. However, by assuming that any locale is fair game for any investigator, some embarrassing situations have arisen. The most common problem is that more field workers are present at one time than the society is able to absorb comfortably. There is also the hazard that oversaturation will lead to a disinclination to cooperate with any anthropologist.

Before going into the field several decades ago, I checked with colleagues who had already been in the region. I was told to feel free to go to this area, but was also told why the area might not be suitable for the research I had in mind. Wisely, I elected to "stake out new turf."

Some years after I had completed my initial research and had published some of my findings, a colleague inquired about the possibility of sending one of his students to the same community to do a follow-up study. The answer was an enthusiastic yes, coupled with a request that the student contact me so that I could provide him with introductions, names, etc. However, seven months later, a letter from the family with whom I'd lived in the town arrived saying that a nice young man from still another university had come to make a study of the town and was living with them! I had never heard from this student or his professor. Fortunately, the first graduate student did not go to that community. If he had, the situation might have become difficult.

On a recent return visit to the same town, I accidently ran into old friends who, it turned out, had been engaged in informal studies there for several seasons. Why hadn't they communicated with me during this long period of time? Should some mechanism be set up to avoid the anthropological invasion which besets many populations today? I see the problem not as a question of ownership but as one of dual courtesy: both to the people who generously share their home with outsiders and to other anthropologists who may have useful information to share.

## 5.5 – TENSIONS IN A NORTHERN COMMUNITY

While studying Eskimo social organization, I was struck by the hostility among the whites who lived in the main settlement. The manager of the trading store was hostile toward the local administrator and the police; one of the missionaries was cold with the police; the local nurses had strong feelings against the teacher; and so forth. Indeed, this white community formed a small sociocultural group that exhibited strong pathological symptoms that resulted in adverse consequences for the Eskimo. This type of situation is not uncommon in the North, and, theoretically, it would have been an interesting topic of study. Furthermore, I was in a good situation to do so, since I could use my research with the Eskimo to disguise my interest in the dynamics of the white community. In any case, the whites were very willing to talk to me. They hoped that I might exercise a positive influence on their future when I returned south; thus, each of them tried to win my support.

What stopped me from doing this study was a concern for other anthropologists. If I had published the results of this research, all other anthropologists going into northern settlements might have been considered spies, and their field work could have been much more difficult. On the other hand, it might be argued that in deciding not to do this study I ignored the very real interests of the Eskimo, for such a study could have resulted in the amelioration of the governmental administration of the North. However, I decided that such an outcome was rather problematical; it appeared to me that the authorities usually do not take much interest in the results of anthropological research or allow them to influence their administrative actions.

## 5.6—A PROBLEM OF RESPONSIBILITIES

At luncheon in the faculty club, Dr. George Meadows turned to Dr. Donald Wilson and said, "Did you know that the Government Research Institute is going to publish Bleighton's thesis?"

Wilson, having heard the whole story of Dick Bleighton's research, was quite surprised. Meadows had the unfortunate experience of beginning a long-term research project in the same village where Bleighton had spent two months doing research for his thesis several years ago. Meadows had a difficult time there initially and was scornful of Bleighton's work because the latter had apparently so antagonized the community that informants refused to cooperate with him.

Meadows continued, "You know, this is terrible. Bleighton's materials are completely skewed by his failure to develop rapport in the community and much of what he reports is just plain wrong. If his thesis is published, it will take years to correct the record, if ever, and he'll do lasting damage to the community because of his unfavorable opinion of it."

Wilson agreed with Meadows but wondered what he, or anyone else, could do about it.

## 5.7 – FIELD WORK AMONG THE KINANI INDIANS

In the autumn of 1968, as Jan Benson was entering his third year of graduate training in cultural anthropology he began to make plans for field work during the following summer. His main area of interest was Africa, but there seemed little chance that he would be able to obtain funds to support research there for the summer. His second area of interest was North America, and he contemplated spending the summer among an Indian tribe. He thought that this would give him important field experience so that he would be in a better position to apply for funds for his African research the following year. If no funds became available for this, Benson concluded that he might spend several summers among the same Indian tribe to obtain enough data for his thesis. Then, with a doctoral degree to bolster his credentials, he might be able to secure the funds to support his strong interest in Africa.

Consequently, Benson began searching the literature and talking to anthropologists and archaeologists who had worked in Canada in order to locate a tribe of Indians that had not yet been studied and that was as little acculturated as possible. In the course of this search, he learned that a small group of Indians called the Kinani lived on one of the rivers draining into Hudson Bay. Apparently, these people maintained their aboriginal economy to a large degree.

Benson decided to visit the Kinani the next summer; he began searching for sources of funds to support his field work. He was unable to secure any funds except a small amount to cover some of the cost of his equipment. Since he was determined to go in any event, he decided to use some of his limited personal savings to cover the costs of transportation to and from the field.

While searching for literature on the Kinani and talking to various anthropologists experienced in Canadian anthropology, Benson learned that an anthropologist named Leon Black was devoting his career to the study of the Indians of eastern Canada. Several professors suggested that Benson contact Dr. Black in order to find out if he had any information on the Kinani or any plans to study them himself.

At a spring meeting of the American Ethnological Association, Benson introduced himself to Dr. Black and spoke to him of his plans. Benson specifically asked Dr. Black if he had any intention of studying the Kinani in the near future, as he did not want to interfere with Black's research plans since his primary interest and professional commitment was to Africa. However, Dr. Black stated that he had no plans for studying the Kinani, and in any case, he would not be free to undertake such a study for several summers. Black encouraged Benson, remarking that it was a good idea to study this unacculturated group of Indians before too much change took place.

At the end of his spring term, Benson flew to Fort Severence, where he purchased a canoe for the rest of the trip. His plans were to go by canoe down the Severence River, a journey of several weeks, and then travel for some miles along the shores of Hudson Bay until he came to the Kinani River, up which the Kinani encampment was located.

On the trip down the Severence River Benson passed a couple of settlements of Indians more acculturated than the Kinani were alleged to be. About ten days out of Fort Severence, Benson came to Fort Defiance. Since this was the last post on the Severence River, he expected to resupply there and notify the local government representatives of his plans. When Benson introduced himself to the local constable and asked permission to continue on to the Kinani encampment, the constable mentioned that he had heard that Dr. Black was there. He told Benson to check with the game warden, Ian McPherson, who had told the constable about Black's activities and who also had a firsthand knowledge of the Kinani Indians.

Ian McPherson was a half-breed who had married a woman from the Pokano tribe at Fullerton Inlet. Benson learned from him that Black had in fact been flown into the Kinani encampment about a week earlier by the government and that he planned to spend the summer there. McPherson also told him that there were only fifteen Kinani families living in the encampment at this time of year and only one Indian among them could speak English and act as an interpreter.

Benson returned to his tent to decide what his next move should be. This was going to be a difficult decision since he had limited funds for travel to another area for field work.

## 5.8 – IN THE FIELD WITH AN INTELLIGENCE AGENT

Ben Smith had been in the country for six months when he learned through a friend in the local government that another American anthropologist, Roger Hartley, was shortly to arrive to do some field work in an area along the border of the country. Smith planned to call on Hartley but was unable to do so for several months because of his own research concerns. When the opportunity finally arose, he wrote Hartley and asked if he might visit him in the field to discuss their mutual interests. He never received a reply.

A month later, while visiting the capital of the country, he ran across Hartley in the hotel and engaged him in conversation, which led to a drink. It became clear after several beers that Hartley was not an "academic" anthropologist; Smith began to wonder if he was not in fact a disguised intelligence agent for some agency of the United States government. If he was an agent and this fact was discovered, Smith was afraid that the local government might require all American anthropologists to leave the country, whether they were agents or not. Consequently, he wondered what he could do to verify his suspicions and, if they were true, what steps he should take to protect his own research project and those of other legitimate scientists who might wish to visit the country in the future.

## 5.9 – THE DISCOVERY OF AN EARLY-MAN SITE AND ITS SUBSEQUENT EXCAVATION

During the summer of his first year in graduate school, Neil Borg was visiting various archaeological sites in Central America. While in Guatemala, he made a survey of the upper reaches of a river basin and discovered a prehistoric site showing evidence of early man. Without either the time or the funds to do an extensive excavation, Neil determined the extent of the site and made surface collections. On his return to graduate school, he prepared a brief summary of his find and published it in *América Indígena*.

As Borg continued his graduate studies, his interests began to shift from archaeology to ethnology; he was unsure whether he would return to excavate the site. At the end of his third year in graduate school, Borg was given the opportunity to join an expedition into the Congo as the ethnographer. As a member of this expedition, he would be able to spend about two years with the Batawa people, during which time he could gather the necessary material for a thesis. Attracted to the idea, Borg decided to join the expedition. He left for the Congo after completing his Ph.D. orals.

Toward the end of his second year in the field, Borg received a letter from a friend who was on a dig in British Honduras. He wrote that on the basis of the information presented in Neil's article in *América Indígena* an expedition had arrived at the prehistoric site in Guatemala and was excavating it. Borg was disturbed with this news. He wondered if he had any claims over the site as its discoverer, and, if so, how he could exercise his rights in this situation.

## 5.10–DEALING WITH ANIMOSITY ARISING FROM A PREVIOUS STUDY

As anthropologists have begun to conduct research among literate people, new ethical questions have arisen (see Kluckhohn 1940, p. 331; Gallaher 1961, p.8; Barnes 1963, p. 118; Henry 1966, p. 552). One of the main issues is the fact that the natives of these literate societies read the published accounts of information supplied by them, as informants, and reworked by the investigator. This fact alone presents a preliminary choice to the field worker as to how to present the purpose of research (see Henry 1966, p. 552). Apparently, some anthropologists have found it necessary to cover their professional identity or true objectives in order to secure the data for their intended research problem (see Adams 1963). My purpose is not to evaluate the ethical standards of anthropology as a discipline and profession but rather to illustrate the inherent problems of field research in a literate community and, particularly, the problem of a subsequent study (see Gallaher 1961, p. 8).

Whether doing a subsequent but different study in the same community or a restudy, the behavior of a previous researcher is critical. If an investigator resorts to unethical behavior, (i.e., misrepresentation for the purpose of gathering data) future research and reinterpretive work can prove to be abortive. People do not easily forget and forgive an outsider who misrepresents his behavior in the name of science. Even if a previous researcher has been completely forthright and ethical in his dealings with a community, a subsequent investigator may find the community has developed a negative or even hostile reaction to the publication of the research and the conclusions drawn.

When Gallaher visited Plainville, Missouri, after the publication of West's *Plainville, U.S.A.* (1945), he found that he was handicapped by the residents' mistrust of social scientists. He explains (1961, p. 8) that the community had welcomed West yet felt that the publication was a direct insult to their town. Gallaher also notes that the inhabitants of this small Missouri town understood neither the purpose nor the significance of the research (1961, p. 4).

*A Community in Stress* (1964) was the culmination of a study conducted by Whitney Gordon in the Reform Jewish temple of Middletown. According to Gordon, the study was descriptive. He used the research techniques of participant observation previously employed by the Lynds in their original studies of

---

Contributed by Dorothy E. Finnegan, Colby-Sawyer College. I want to thank Dr. Whitney H. Gordon for his kind cooperation in the presentation of this case.

Middletown. Gordon took the study one step further, however, by attempting to demonstrate the existence of stress within the individuals of the Jewish community. His underlying objective was to show that the stresses the Jews of Middletown experienced in both their community relations and their personal and interpersonal relations in the temple were caused by their ethnicity.

My research constituted another study of the congregation of the Reform temple. At the inception of this research, I told the congregation that I was a graduate student in anthropology at a local university attempting to complete an assignment for a course entitled "The Anthropology of Religion" and that I wished to learn about the involvement of active field work. My intentions were clearly communicated to the initial informants, including the rabbinical students who "care" for the congregation.

I began this project with little knowledge of the community's response to Gordon's published work. Although a colleague did inform me of possible repercussions, I encountered no negative reactions to my initial investigations and observations. Thus, my study progressed smoothly throughout the first month without mention of Gordon's name. However, during my fifth week of research, I was attacked during an evening session at the temple. The abuse was initiated and directed by Joseph Moshier, a semi-influential member of the congregation who apparently was personally hurt by Gordon's research.

On this particular evening, the congregation was celebrating the naming of a child. After the service, all the members retired as usual to the basement for refreshments. I circulated among the people for a short time until two men invited me to join them at one of the long tables in the room. I sat down with them and explained the purpose of my study and my presence at the temple. As we talked about the various rites of passage observed in the temple, I overheard Moshier complaining about my presence.

Once Moshier recognized that I was listening to him, he increased the volume of his tirade to include me in his audience. Moshier was protesting to his listeners that I should not be trusted, reminding them of "what Gordon did to us." I tried to explain I was a graduate student in anthropology and was neither a sociologist nor a student of sociology and that my main interest, as far as this project was concerned, was in the religious beliefs and rituals practiced by the congregation. I also indicated that, with the permission of the members, I desired to continue the study as the subject of my Master's thesis.

My explanation did not stop Moshier's harangue. He replied that Gordon had told the temple members the same thing at the onset of his study ten years ago. "Why, now, should we trust you?" he asked. Moshier continued to insist that Gordon had misrepresented himself, entered into their homes, and joined in their social and religious activities only to publish a book uncomplimentary to the congregation and to some members individually. Upon asking several members who were listening to the conversation, Moshier found that few people had actually read Gordon's book. Only one of the men, Mr. Golden, with whom I had been previously engaged in conversation, had been a member of the temple during Gordon's work. Golden quietly explained to Moshier that my questions in no way resembled the material in which Gordon had been interested; I had particularly asked about religious beliefs.

## 5.10—Dealing with Animosity Arising from a Previous Study 167

Moshier was still very upset and was not calmed by the reassurances of Golden. I felt that the time had come to defend my position. Again, I quietly explained my intentions to Moshier. Furthermore, I offered to sign a witnessed affidavit describing my goals. This statement seemed to quiet Moshier for a short time. He made a few more negative comments concerning my study and behavior, but the harangue had clearly been dissipated.

During the debate, I fully believed the study to be aborted, although I was not aware of the power which Moshier exercised within the social structure of the congregation. It was only later that I discovered that Moshier was a quasi-influential member of both the community of Middletown and the temple. Although the leaders of the congregation assured me that I would be allowed to continue my work, they also indicated that several doors would remain closed to me as a result of the discussion with Moshier. Observing the temple's governing board, for example, which was previously permitted, was now out of the question. I was also warned to be cautious in approaching topics outside the general realm of religion. However, most of my fears over the success of my research were calmed at the following week's service: previous informants were confident that the incident was not significant since Mosher did not attend too many services.

After this incident, I learned that many reactions to Gordon's book were negative, although most people had not read it. The membership of the congregation had changed somewhat in the ten years following Gordon's study. The newcomers had heard of the outcome of the previous field work from the older members, but few were concerned enough to read the book. One member of the congregation explained that the study was not significant and therefore did not trouble him. Others said that they had merely skimmed the book. Some indicated they had meant to read it and would definitely do so now that their interest was stirred. Thus, most of the members, due to their lack of familiarity with Gordon's published work, were not significantly affected by it.

In his book, Gordon employed specific quotations from temple members to show the ambivalent feelings of these individuals in business and social frameworks. The members of the congregation were sufficiently disguised in Gordon's writings by the mere fact that no names or even pseudonyms were used. Nevertheless, those members of the congregation who read the book carefully could identify some of the more prominent members. I believe that it was this easy detection which caused the negative response to the book and its author.

The members also reacted unfavorably to the use of certain quotations which they felt were presented out of context. Members indicated that due to Gordon's seeming duplicity they originally had chosen their words in response to an entirely different context than that which appeared in the book.

From this, one can see how the role of ethical behavior comes into play in field work and how it affects subsequent restudies. Gordon himself explains (1964:xxiv):

> The research worker may meet the ethical standards of the anthropologist insofar as he does not change the situation, damage individuals or leave the field in a condition such as would bar later entrants. But the investigator is rarely open in either his goals or his

means. The study here was a purported inquiry into the life of Jewish families in a midwest American city. There was no mention of the orientation towards stress.

To the extent that one does not damage or harm human relations in field research, he may meet the society's formal and ethical requirements. But an element of duplicity may be operating in many sociological studies and a touch of moral chicanery was present in the present work.

After the publication, Gordon (personal communication, June 1970) asked for a meeting with the congregation to clarify any points in the manuscript, although this option was never acknowledged by the president of the board.

The ethical behavior of the previous researcher is neither meant to be placed on trial nor scrutinized here. The dangers of spoiling the field for future work are inherent in field research in the social sciences. Yet anthropology cannot move forward in an unreceptive field. In my own study several approaches could have been employed to discuss the events I have described with the congregation in order to defuse it.

I could also have gathered much more information from the incident with Moshier. However, my initial purpose was to study the religious behavior of the congregation. Therefore, soliciting any more information concerning this incident would be a breach of my ethical principles. If I had entered the temple with the intent of replicating or re-evaluating Gordon's work, it is doubtful that I would have been allowed to continue after Moshier's attack. Yet, had I been permitted to conduct a re-evaluation, I could have in good faith delved more deeply into the problem. In either case, there are inherent dangers for both the literate "natives" and for the social scientist in the growing study of urban anthropology.

## BIBLIOGRAPHY

Adams, William Y. 1963. Shanto: a study of the role of the trader in a modern Navajo community. *Bureau of American Ethnology Bulletin* 18.
Barnes, J.A. 1963. Some ethical problems in modern field work. *British Journal of Sociology* 14:118-34. Reprinted in *Anthropologists in the field,* eds. D.G. Jongmans and P.C.W. Gutkind. Assen: Van Gorcum.
Gallaher, Art, Jr. 1961. *Plainville, fifteen years later.* New York: Columbia University Press.
Gordon, Whitney. 1964. *A community in stress.* New York: Living Books.
Henry, Frances. 1966. The role of the fieldworker in an explosive political situation. *Current Anthropology* 7:552-54.
Kluckhohn, Florence. 1940. The participant-observer in small communities *American Journal of Sociology* 46:331-43.
West, James. 1945. *Plainville, U.S.A.* New York: Columbia University Press.

## 5.11 — ANTHROPOLOGISTS THREE

The field anthropologist who is first on the scene in a region inevitably establishes the ethical framework at several levels. As long as he remains the only social scientist in the area, his ethical problems are relatively localized, confined mostly to his relationships with indigenous people and the possible implications of such relationships for future studies by other social scientists. When additional anthropologists enter the situation, the domain of ethical considerations expands sharply. Added to the matrix of complex personal, economic, or political situations that already exist is a new overlay of potential tension and conflict among social scientists seeking to establish or protect their vested interests in the society. Thus, the idea of "property rights" comes to the fore.

This kind of situation occurred a few years ago in the emerging nation of Suliya. As in many such nations, Suliya has been making extensive use of external assistance in attempting to develop its economy, modernize its institutions, establish its identity in the world community of nations, and instill a sense of unity among a diverse ethnic population contained within arbitrarily imposed national boundaries. The tribal-dominated regional power groups, formerly held in delicate balance by a ruler, the most powerful of the tribal leaders, is rapidly being replaced by a new parliamentary and ministerial system of centralized government patterned after the Western European model. However, the centralized government remains elitist and largely representative of the dominant tribal groups. Because of poor communication facilities, many ethnic enclaves remain relatively uninfluenced by national developments, and a few are openly hostile toward the modernization movement.

Robert Adams drifted into Suliya almost by accident and lived with one of these untouched ethnic groups located in one of the remote areas. These people had not been observed systematically since the days of the early explorers a century or more earlier. Adams was an anthropologist only in attitude and interest, having set off to see the world after completing a Bachelor of Arts degree. Various jobs took him from place to place in Europe and adjacent continents. He developed a growing fascination with other cultures that led to a year spent living among one of these groups.

Faced with a depleted bank account at the end of the year, Adams accepted an offer of a job in Suliya. There his continuing interest in remote groups led him to the region in question. Adams found several distinct ethnic groups, considerable cultural diversity, and some unique patterns of social organization, ecological relationships, and methods of conflict resolution. He spent much of his free time in this area, at some distance from the site of his paid employment. He developed many contacts and was able to move easily within the region.

After several years of this work-field study combination, Adams returned to the United States to pursue graduate studies in anthropology, during which time he made major contributions to the literature. When he finished his graduate degree, he returned to accept a nongovernmental administrative post in Suliya which provided him with significant time and freedom to continue his field studies. Up to that time, only linguists had evinced much interest in the area, and they had confined their work to gathering samples for analysis at their home universities. Adams remained the only person to have spent any extensive time in the field. In so doing, he had slowly and carefully established his credentials and reputation with the central government authorities. These officials knew a little about the region and were highly suspicious—even fearful—of the residents, and uncertain of the motives of a foreigner who wished to spend time among them. Nevertheless, Adams was one of few individuals—and the only foreigner—who was able to obtain blanket permission from the Ministry of the Interior to reside in the area without having to undergo intensive investigations and follow seemingly endless bureaucratic channels.

Harrison Bean had entered the region unexpectedly and unannounced. He had completed academic requirements for an anthropological degree. In the course of his studies, he had become intrigued by reports concerning the region where Adams was working. However, Bean found no funding sources interested in supporting studies in that region. All of them had their own priorities of interests and were willing to support him if he would undertake studies in "their" areas but would not support his own interest. Therefore, he saved enough money to finance the trip to Suliya himself on a tourist visa. Once in the country, he set about trying to obtain permission to remain for a field study. He knew of Adams's publications but had not known Adams was back in the country. When he learned of Adams's presence, he sought out Adams for advice and assistance.

Adams was favorably impressed by Bean, who turned out to be bright, well-read, and adaptable. Adams provided considerable assistance in securing official permission for Bean to conduct a study within the restricted area and also in helping Bean select a village site and get settled. No real problem of conflict of interest emerged between the two researchers. Although Bean was generally interested in social organization and overall cultural patterns, his primary interest in indigenous medical systems was viewed by both men as supplemental to Adams's study. Bean found a good local informant and spent over a year in the field, having managed to secure several small sources of financial support after his arrival in Suliya.

Bernard Cross entered the scene about nine months after Bean's arrival, but with a difference. Cross also had completed his anthropological degree requirements in the United States and was undertaking his first foreign field work to acquire data for a dissertation. The major difference between him and Bean was that Cross was funded for a full year with a grant from a major American agency. He had secured a residence visa for Suliya prior to departure from the United States but had not specified the geographical region in which he planned to work. The Suliya embassy in Washington apparently assumed that Cross intended to reside in the capital city while studying adjacent villages—for whch no special permission was required from the home government.

Cross also had prior knowledge of Adams's published work but he did not know of either Adams's or Bean's presence in Suliya. He made no extensive inquiries about the current political situation nor did he make any preliminary contacts in Suliya beyond obtaining official permission to reside there. He was explicitly interested in the area where Bean was located and somewhat disappointed at finding Bean already established there. Cross was even more dismayed to find that he was not free to travel within Suliya but was required to obtain special permission from the Ministry of the Interior. The ministry, in turn, was reluctant to allow still another foreign anthropologist to establish himself in this remote region. Furthermore, ministry officials suspected that Cross had ulterior purposes for visiting the country and seeking to enter the region in question.

Several external considerations were coincidentally influential at this time. One of these was a controversy concerning indirect support of research by the United States Central Intelligence Agency through various obscure channels. Also, the central government, in conjunction with a multinational funding agency, was planning an economic development project for the region in which Cross and the other anthropologists were interested. This plan would cause major social and cultural changes; further, it had not been discussed with any of the local people of the region and the government had no intention of doing so prior to going ahead with the project. Adams and Bean both knew of the plan and were fearful of the probable conflict should the government attempt to implement the plan without prior involvement of the local people.

These considerations influenced the ministry's response to Cross's application to enter the region, as well as Adams's and Bean's responses to Cross's request for assistance. They offered several suggestions of alternative sites which would provide Cross with an opportunity to conduct his field observations in areas where no anthropological field work had ever been carried out but still near enough to the city to fall within limits of the original residence permit. Adams and Bean both offered considerable advice, and Adams even persuaded ministry officials to permit Cross to enter an area somewhat further from the city than the ministry had intended, in the general region of Adams's own studies but short of his locale.

Much of the advice Cross received from Adams and others was negative, or he regarded it as such; he began to feel threatened. Believing he was being blocked at every turn, he began to suspect that a conspiracy existed to prevent him from pursuing his legitimate aspirations. The fact that his interests broadly overlapped with those of Adams bolstered his belief that Adams in particular was blocking him for personal reasons.

Adams also recognized this possibility. His work responsibilities left him only a few weeks throughout the year to pursue his field studies. He knew that both Cross and Bean would complete their full-time field work and return to publish their findings considerably sooner than he could manage. At first, he even considered using his own considerable influence at the Ministry of the Interior to prevent Cross from locating anywhere near "his" region. However, Adams did not do this; his considerable assistance to Cross was probably a matter of overcompensation prompted by guilt.

Cross's behavior during his first months in Suliya was less than reassuring to Adams and other observers. It is unclear how much of this behavior could be attributed to Cross's suspicions of a conspiracy and how much was his usual personality. In any case, he seemed to be plagued by difficulties; nothing he undertook worked out right, whether is was ordering a meal in a restaurant, purchasing supplies, or making a trip. His conversations were increasingly loaded with accounts of his problems; his audiences tended to be those individuals who were willing to listen to such accounts in return for food, drink, or transportation. Cross developed a pattern of nighttime socializing in public places in the city among the more deviant of the elite indigenous population, who enjoyed identification with foreigners. He eventually selected one of these people as his principal interpreter and began to move out into the village area where he had received permission to do field work.

Cross's trips to the village area seemed as troublesome as his residence in the city. Invariably, he returned to the city earlier than expected because of new problems. Roads were impassable; another form or permit was needed; supplies were stolen; or illness interfered. Also, Cross attempted to extend his area somewhat further than the permit intended, and in so doing, he encountered confused reactions from local officials and leaders. Furthermore, his research was offensive to some of the local leaders in terms of the ideas it introduced and because Cross's interpreter was essentially a foreigner in the villages. He had to find a bilingual resident at each place where they stopped so that conversation had to go through two translations—from the local language to the first language of the interpreter and then to English. Cross's interpreter shared the general fear, suspicion, and antipathy toward these "primitive" peoples and was unable to hide his attitudes. Thus, the whole communication process was less than optimal, and local village leaders eventually complained to government officials about Cross's activities.

As the situation worsened, Adams became concerned about his own reputation with the central government, since he had, in a sense, vouched for Cross. Adams was further concerned about the impression which Cross made as an anthropologist conducting research. A negative impression would impede not only his own work but that of future investigators. The Ministry of the Interior, although reluctant to offend or to appear repressive, increasingly saw Cross as a disruptive element. Feeling impelled to act, the ministry came up with a solution that prevented the situation from getting any worse—but did nothing to resolve the basic ethical problems. At a time when both Adams and Bean were elsewhere and Cross was in the capital, the ministry declared the region beyond the immediate urban area closed to all foreigners for reasons of security. It was gently suggested to Cross that he return to his own country and postpone indefinitely the proposed study.

Some time later, when Bean and Adams were ready to return to the region for further studies, permission was readily granted, although the official "closure" remained in effect. Following the experience with Cross, the central government now makes it much more difficult for social scientists to conduct research than when Adams first arrived.

## 5.12 – POLITICS, PERMITS, AND PROFESSIONAL INTERESTS: THE ROSE CASE

**INTRODUCTION**

In June last year questions were asked in Federal Parliament about the refusal of a request from Professor Frederick Rose, of Humboldt University, East Berlin, for permission to enter an Aboriginal reserve on Groote Eylandt, in the Northern Territory. Rose had done anthropological research on Groote Eylandt in 1941 and his proposal to follow up this work with new inquiries had received financial support from the Australian Institute of Aboriginal Studies (hereafter AIAS).

In almost all of the instances during the last ten or fifteen years when an Australian adminstration has refused a scientist entry to a reserve or territory, no reason has been made public. Hence it has been difficult to determine what issues of policy might be implicated and hard to judge whether the refusal was justified. In this case, the Minister for the Interior stated that permission had been refused because Rose is a Communist, a fact that Rose has confirmed. This suggests that opposition to Communism is the only issue at stake, and may justify the government's decision to many members of the public. Nevertheless, before the matter was raised in parliament, the social anthropology section of AIAS passed a resolution criticizing restrictions on entry into Aboriginal reserves.[1] Later, the Federal Council for the Advancement of Aborigines and Torres Strait Islanders condemned the operation of the "permit system" of controlled entry into Aboriginal reserves,[2] and the Australian branch of the Association of Social Anthropologists protested against the use of the permit system to impede scientific work.[3]

Despite these resolutions and letters of protest in the press, there has been little debate about the important issues involved. These go far beyond opposition to Communism and relate not only to the rights of Aborigines as citizens but also to the proper conduct of social inquiry and the distinction between the actions of social scientists in their professional roles and as ordinary citizens. Only a few facts about the Rose case are publicly available, and fewer still about other recent refusals. Therefore we shall first discuss general principles and then apply them cautiously to the limited evidence.

---

By J.A. Barnes, Australian National University. Reprinted from *The Australian Quarterly* Vol. 41, No. 1, March 1969, pp. 17-31, by permission of the author and publisher.

## THE POLITICAL ENVIRONMENT OF SOCIAL RESEARCH

Governments everywhere sometimes obstruct research by withholding information or financial assistance but research in social anthropology is particularly liable to obstruction through entry permits. An anthropologist typically studies *other* people, and hence has to travel before he can get to work. Sometimes he requires permission to carry out a specified research plan in addition to the usual traveller's visas and entry permits. In a foreign country he has to accept bureaucratic hurdles as a given part of the social landscape, to be tackled with the help of the same qualities of tact, sympathy and patience that later will be crucial in his scientific work. He may argue that his inquiries will be of substantial benefit to the community and country or, more plausibly, that they will be quite harmless, but if the authorities are unyielding he can only pack his bags and try elsewhere. With luck, he will gain the approval of the local authorities and even their active co-operation, but this is always a courtesy extended to him and never a matter of right. In some countries the outsider has virtually no hope at all of beginning research. For example, Fried, writing of China in 1963, says:

> All societies attempt to direct and control research, but some do so only by indirect, informal, and subtle means, such as the offering of differential rewards. In societies like contemporary China, however, the difference is a qualitative one: social science is defined by the government, tasks are carefully set, the personnel is carefully chosen and performs under restraint.[4]

If he is able to go ahead, he may meet further hazards. He probably finds himself working in a poor country and is likely to come up against the difficulties and dangers of what Galtung calls "scientific colonialism." He may encounter the notion of anthropology as a by-product of imperialism and of knowledge as a form of national property; nowadays he has to deal with the aftermath of Project Camelot, that *cause celebre* of United States political interest in social science research in Chile.[5]

Much of the discussion that has gone on recently within the ranks of anthropology, sociology and political science about professional codes of ethics has related to these colonial and neo-colonial situations. It is important to realize why the Rose case is essentially different. We have here a domestic matter, even though Professor Rose works in East Berlin. The Aboriginals he wished to re-visit are neither foreigners nor dependent peoples in a distant colony, but Australian citizens and voters, just as Professor Rose is apparently an Australian citizen.[6] His case has prompted resolutions and protests by social scientists and other members of the Australian community. These academics are rightly concerned with many issues of public policy which lie outside the range of their professional interests and specialization but for which, as voters, they share responsibility, however diluted this may be. Even those who feel that it is inappropriate for Australians to proclaim against the exclusion of an anthropologist from South Africa, or the banishment of a psychologist from Tanzania, cannot avoid being concerned with administrative decisions within Australia. There is a much stronger case for taking action within one's own political community, and indeed a responsibility to do so, as well as a greater likelihood of achieving some practical result. For Australians, actions by Australian governments are matters of civic concern in what we may call the strong sense, in contrast to actions by other governments about which Australian citizens may feel moved to comment, but for which they have no direct responsibility.

## CIVIC AND PROFESSIONAL ISSUES

These considerations apply to all enfranchised members of the community and not in any special way to anthropologists. As professionals with more knowledge of the local scene, and with a greater awareness of the likely outcomes of alternative policies, they may be expected sometimes to initiate and guide public action but they do so in their capacity as informed citizens rather than as anthropologists. Not surprisingly, they differ among themselves about what should be done, for public policies usually impinge not on their common interest as specialists but on their diverse interests as citizens. Anthropologists do not all support one political party, nor, for example, do they all support the interests of Aboriginals against graziers. On the other hand they do have a common professional concern with the pursuit of truth, with the transmission of a body of knowledge, with the maintenance of academic and intellectual standards, and so on. The Rose case, as I see it, contains some issues which are clearly civic, in the strong sense as defined above, some other issues which are clearly professional, and yet others whose classification is a matter for argument.

## ENTRY TO RESERVES

Why should entry to Aboriginal reserves be restricted at all? This seems to me to be largely a question addressed to citizens and I can answer it only as a citizen. Restrictions on access to Aboriginal reserves were introduced for segregation as much as for protection and had the effect of protecting administrations from public criticism as well as protecting Aboriginal women from prostitution. There was never any justification for protecting administrations in this way, and this form of protection has become less appropriate as Aboriginals themselves have become more articulate about their living conditions. Do they any longer need protection additional to that provided by the laws of trespass and the right of access to the courts available to any member of the public? Aboriginals are still poorer and have had less schooling than the rest of the community, but they are now sufficiently aware of their rights as citizens to be able to put their case before the public. Although help from welfare departments and non-Aboriginal sympathizers may be valuable, Aborigines should be encouraged to defend their own interests rather than rely on the support of others. On the other hand an Aboriginal's home is scarcely his castle. The shacks and humpies of the countryside and the camps of the outback are not suburban villas into which Aboriginals can withdraw, safe from the intrusions of missionaries, tourists, philanderers and scientists. Aboriginals may need some kind of special means of securing privacy, not because they are natives to be protected but because they do not have the same kinds of homes as the rest of the population. Yet it would not solve the problem to treat the whole of a large reserve as if it were an Aboriginal front doorstep, and hence to deny outsiders permission to enter except as guests of the residents, just as it is not reasonable, in my view, to treat a large grazing property as if it were a suburban market-garden. Visits to rural settlements where there are no organized facilities for the accommodation of visitors always present some difficulties, whether in New Guinea, or Indonesia, or even in the remoter parts of Europe. But Australia is the easiest country in the world to camp in, and it is comparatively easy for fieldworkers to make their own arrangements for accommodation and supplies. Administrators and missionaries are certainly right to resist interminable demands on their limited facilities for providing hospitality and transport, but this should not be made an excuse for excluding fieldworkers with their own facilities who can look after themselves in the outback. Some arrangement is needed whereby Aboriginals who do not live in normal houses and who carry on much of their social and ceremonial life in the open should be able to achieve the same measure of privacy as is enjoyed by those of us who live within four walls and who can hire the R.S.L. hall for our corroborees.

The present system does not achieve this end. Entry is only by permission of the welfare department concerned, and for entry to settlements run by Christian missions, approval from the mission is also needed. Aborigines living on grazing properties are the most inaccessible of all. Some attention is beginning to be paid to the views of Aboriginal communities but the only instances I know of are those in which a group of Aboriginals is said to have expressed dislike of a proposed visitor. I have not heard of any instance where permission to enter has been granted to a non-Aboriginal merely because the local Aboriginals wanted him to come. On some reserves, Aboriginals cannot invite even their own relatives without administrative permission.

The present system excludes more people than necessary, but also fails to provide Aboriginals with the privacy to which they are entitled. The tourists who visit certain Aboriginal settlements with government and mission encouragement provide a ready market for the sale of local artefacts. Probably few Aboriginals would want to abolish the trade and maybe in the long run this process of commercialization is the only way of preserving Aboriginal culture at all, as the evidence from Hawaii and Tahiti suggests. Nevertheless, the exploitation of Aboriginals themselves as living tourist attractions is a pernicious form of cultural prostitution and we should remember Mr. Wentworth's warning: "... Aborigines are too important to be considered as a tourist attraction."[7]

The failure to provide privacy stems from the widespread Australian assumption that Aboriginals are sub-people with only limited rights which have lower priority than the interests of approved White people. For instance, if a scientist is given permission to visit an Aboriginal settlement, the administration expects Aboriginals to answer his questions, provide him with samples of blood, let themselves be weighed and measured, and so on. What is worse, some scientists seem to take the same view; one suggested recently that the fingerprints of all Aborigines should be on file so that they might be permanently identified throughout their lives. The same attitude, whereby Aboriginals are regarded primarily as scientific curiosities suitable for study rather than as fellow citizens, is seen in the proposal to establish a computerized personal data bank for, or rather about, aboriginals who, presumably, are thought to be less aware than other sections of the community of the threat to civil liberties entailed by this operation. Given strong administrative support, it is feasible to conduct an adequate inquiry into Aboriginal health, or physical characteristics, or even intelligence and perception, with an unwilling and unenthusiastic set of subjects, for these investigations depend much less on establishing those good relations of mutual confidence and understanding essential to fieldwork in social anthropology. Sometimes it may be in the public interest to carry out investigations compulsorily, as for example in a TB detection campaign, but there is seldom justification for applying compulsion selectively to Aboriginals merely because they are different from Whites. The present system of controlled entry to reserves does not provide Aboriginals with protection from this form of compulsion but rather provides the mechanism for applying it.

Whatever may have been appropriate in the past, a new system is now needed whereby Aboriginals are able to protect themselves from unwanted interference in their daily lives, and yet at the same time visitors, whether tourists, missionaries or research workers, are able to make contact with Aboriginals in a context in which Aboriginals are free to decide for themselves whether or not they wish to sell boomerangs, play the didgeridoo, sing hymns, discuss trade union organization and cross-cousin marriage, or whatever else they or their visitors are interested in. A Christian mission also has its own rights to privacy which should be respected, but it should not use its monopoly of communication facilities to deny Aboriginals in its vicinity any effective choice of visitors.

This should not be difficult to arrange. In general, entry to an Aboriginal reserve as a short-term visitor should be open to all, and Aboriginal communities should be encouraged to provide facilities for such visitors. Longer-term visitors would stay only with permission from the Aboriginal community concerned. Research workers would be dependent on the voluntary co-operation of members of the community, as they are anywhere else. Missions would be free to extend or withold hospitality to visitors but not to deny them the use of facilities such as air strips and postal services.

The argument so far is what I have called a civic argument; it sets out my views as a citizen about matters of public policy. If we accept this argument, a Communist or Jesuit or scientologist (not in all states) or Black Muslim or trade union organizer would be as free as anyone else to go to Groote Eylandt or any other Aboriginal reserve to make contact with Aboriginals and to persuade them of the sweet wisdom of his particular creed. This follows from the basic premise of the assimilation policy, that Aboriginals are fellow citizens.

## SOCIAL ANTHROPOLOGISTS

But what about anthropologists? Are they less free than Jesuits and Communists? Presumably not, at least as citizens. But in the field they are not just citizens. They are usually supported financially to do a specified job. At this point our discussion shifts from civic to professional issues. We are concerned not with the rights of Aboriginals or Communists or anthropologists as citizens but with how research can be competently carried out in conformity with a professional code of ethics. Like any other profession, social anthropology makes special demands on its practitioners. Because any aspect of human activity *may* prove to be relevant in social anthropology, these demands are both more embracing and more vaguely defined than, say, in medicine or the natural sciences. In the field the social anthropologist may sometimes have to be on the job twenty-four hours a day. Whether he has any "private" life depends on the community he is studying, for in many societies the distinction between public and private is drawn differently or not drawn at all. The opinions he expresses, or declines to express, about local affairs, and the effects of his presence on social events, all form part of his field data. Investigators in other disciplines are not constrained to this extent.

Unfortunately a concern with professional ethics, and indeed with most othe other problems of fieldwork, has developed only in recent years.[8] There is still no authoritative consensus about the extent to which a social anthropologist, while in the field, should express himself freely on topics that are controversial or sacred to the local community, or attempt to alter the course of events. In my view, if he is pressed an anthropologist has always to state his own opinion on any topic honestly, however distasteful this may be to his questioners; but in general he should listen sympathetically and avoid parading his own opinions. He should be ready to help members of the community achieve a greater understanding of the likely consequences of alternative courses of action rather than to introduce changes on his own account, and he should take responsibility for the advice he gives. But however diffident and circumspect he may be about his own opinions and actions, his range of inquiries must be far-reaching. His main task is to understand social systems. Hence, along with ostensibly safe topics like kinship, he cannot ignore, and sometimes must concentrate on, sensitive matters like bribery and corruption, political and religious movements, intergroup tension and illegal activities, areas of social life which an administering authority may well prefer to remain in obscurity.

Social anthropology demands a substantial measure of detachment from the values of any one cultural system, including that of the society to which the anthropologist himself belongs. Hence the discipline tends to attract students who are already critical of their own society. Much anthropological fieldwork is carried on in social environments which lack any tradition of organized political contests or public debate, where the necessary background statistical information, normally freely available for a metropolitan community, can be obtained from official sources only as a favour, and where a visitor may have to depend in some degree on officials for accommodation, supplies and transport since these are not available commercially. Although the administrator may realize that his long-term interests lie in the greater understanding of social processes that should accrue from painstaking empirical inquiries, in the short-term the fieldworker may appear merely as a trouble-maker who expects to use scarce facilities only to produce inaccessibly published articles of little use to the practical man.

**THE SPONSOR**

Given this critical attitude, it is not surprising that in recent years many social anthropologists have become more aware of the importance of their relations with groups and individuals who are in one way or another connected with the community that provides the focus for their research, as well as with members of the community itself. The need for some form of code of professional ethics is accepted. Since there is no generally agreed code, the sponsor should specify how its workers should behave in the field, so that the legitimate interests of the various groups and individuals affected by their work are protected and so that the practical and theoretical value of empirical research may become more widely appreciated. If a prospective fieldworker cannot accept the conditions laid down for work in a particular place on a particular topic, he must change his plans.

Some conditions, such as not divulging information disclosed in confidence and paying due respect to local notions of propriety, can be phrased so as to apply in all field situations. Others will vary. For example, if an anthropologist is to study a community that is partly Christian and partly pagan, he must take a tolerant attitude towards both Christianity and paganism, and must be prepared to be regarded as a disappointing ally by both sections of the community. To study rites and ceremonies, the anthropologist has to attend performances, and to study beliefs, he has to stimulate discussion and argument. Hence in some phases of his work he may come to be identified clearly with one side rather than the other; but in his analysis he needs to comprehend both points of view. Likewise he should not seek to propagate his own political views, but should be a sympathetic listener to the views of others. Thus it is that while many people become anthropologists because of their nonconformity, in the field they have to become partial conformists, even if to an exotic code of behavior.

Many universities are bound by their charters not to discriminate against persons on grounds of religion, sex, race, nationality and political affiliation. Some people argue that this principle of non-discrimination must apply not only to appointments on the campus but to support for field research as well. Although this can be done easily in many disciplines, an extension of the principle to cover proposals for field research in social science on specific topics in specific localities is quite unworkable. The method of close observation and controlled participation characteristic of social anthropology yields its best results only when the fieldworker can enter as fully as possible into the life and thought of the community he lives among, even though he should never lose his identity as an outsider. Therefore a sponsoring institution is quite appropriately concerned with many aspects of a fieldworker's personality and beliefs as well as with his strictly academic competence. But as soon as these other qualities are taken into account, there is an obvious danger that a sponsor may be led to reject an application merely because it dislikes the applicant's temperament or his religion or political beliefs, rather than because these characteristics will result in unsuccessful field research. The best guard against this danger is for the sponsor to be ready to inform the applicant, if he so requests, why it is unwilling to support him.

The sponsor is concerned with the fieldworker's personality and beliefs in three ways. A fieldworker who is strongly committed to an all-embracing and rigid political or religious ideology is often quite unable to envisage any new interpretation that may be suggested by the facts before him. He may strongly believe, for instance, that all non-Christian religious ceremonies are satanic, or that all non-Europeans are like children, and may be unable to accept any field evidence that might possibly conflict with these beliefs. The books and articles an anthropologist has published should enable a sponsor to judge how conscientious he is in recording facts that do not fit his theories and how ready he is to modify his theories to fit awkward facts.

The sponsor also wants to know whether the fieldworker's political and religious affiliations will make him unacceptable to the community he wishes to study. Thus, for instance, some fundamentalist Protestant communities would reject a Catholic fieldworker, however accommodating he might be. The age and sex of the fieldworker, whether he is married or unmarried, black or white, may limit the choice of possible research fields. The sponsor has to match the applicant's characteristics with whatever prior information it may have about the prejudices, values and convictions of the community concerned. It has to be careful not to treat these prejudices with excessive caution, and even more careful not to adopt them itself.

Thirdly, the sponsor has to assess whether the political and other views of the fieldworker may interfere with his work as an anthropologist while he is actually collecting his data. In any field situation, there are likely to be many things an anthropologist, as cirizen, would like to see changed. If he feels in private duty bound to devote much of his energies to making political or religious converts or effecting ameliorative social change, that is not part of his research task, he is deflecting his efforts from the job he is paid to do, as well as raising the other difficulties just mentioned. In my view a sponsor committed to the support of scientific research should require a fieldworker not to try to make converts of any kind while in the field. An anthropologist unable to accept this condition should seek support from missionary or political organizations, so that his scientific research is clearly seen as a spare-time activity. On the other hand, a fieldworker is still a citizen with political and religious convictions even while he is in the field. If he wants to change the state of affairs he encounters he should do this unequivocally as a citizen after he has left the field and is free of the special constraints of the field-work situation.

If a prospective fieldworker who has gained sponsorship is refused entry to the Aboriginal reserve where he hopes to work, the interests of both sponsor and fieldworker are affected. The sponsor seeks to promote research. If there is a policy of obstructing research, whether implemented by a government agency, a mission, or a local Aboriginal group, the sponsor should exert what influence it has to bring about a change of policy. If the refusal is aimed at one particular fieldworker rather than at research in general, the sponsor may still be concerned. Anthropologists are not all interchangeable, and since most social anthropologists work alone rather than in teams, each usually has experience and expertise not shared with others. Sometimes a research job can be done economically by only one particular person, and his sponsor then has a professional interest in seeing that he gets an entry permit. If the job can be tackled by any one of several anthropologists, and if the objection to a particular fieldworker has nothing to do with his professional competence but is based, for instance, on his political affiliation, then it seems to me that the sponsor's interest in promoting research is not immediately affected, though it may have other interests which are.

## ROSE

How does this analysis apply to Rose as potential fieldworker, the AIAS as sponsor, and the Northern Territory and the Federal Government as the entry-refusing agencies? Rose's book, *Kinship, age structure and marriage,* was recognized as a major contribution to Aboriginal studies.[9] On the evidence of professional opinion overseas the AIAS acted correctly in sponsoring Professor Rose to carry out further research on the same topic in the same Aboriginal community.

Two aspects of this sponsorship need special comment. In parliament, Mr. Wentworth said: "It was realised that there might be some political difficulties in this matter, and I think the Institute very properly took the view that these political matters were not its concern, particularly since it did not have available to it information on which it could evaluate those matters."[10] In the current political climate, there are many politicians and citizens who might object to the AIAS knowingly sponsoring research by a Communist, however, well qualified he might be, and Mr. Wentworth may have made his statement to protect the AIAS from this possible criticism. By contrast, my view as a citizen is that at the present time we live in a democracy where, within the framework of the law, there should be no discrimination against political dissenters and where scientific research can flourish under conditions radically different from those, for example, described above for China.

Alternatively, the Minister's remarks may suggest that even if the AIAS had all the information it wanted about Professor Rose, his political activities would be of no concern to it. Again, I disagree. I think that the AIAS would have failed in its task of promoting good research if it had closed its eyes to Rose's political affiliations, for these cannot be separated from his fieldwork. In Rose's words, "As a Marxist, I believe science cannot be divorced from politics ... the political connotations and consequences of the work are unavoidable."[11] The way in which Professor Rose acted in the field on past occasions, and the way in which he is likely to act in the future, are very properly the concern of the AIAS, even though the bald fact that he is a Communist is irrelevant. If it could be shown that on earlier occasions Rose had set out to make political converts and to form Communist party cells among Aboriginals, then it might reasonably be argued that his inquiries into kinship were only a by-product of his political activity. The AIAS should then decline to support a new field project whose outcome was likely to be largely political and only incidentally scientific. In the same way, it should not support a Christian missionary, however well trained as a social scientist he might be, if his main activity in the field was likely to be evangelism rather than research. Rose's two scholarly monographs and his travel book suggest to me that he was a conscientious field worker on Groote Eylandt in 1938-39, 1941 and 1948, and at Angas Downs in 1962. His use of political pressure to gain an entry permit to Groote Eylandt in 1965 doubtless annoyed the Administration and he was then accompanied into the field by a member of the Welfare Branch. In his popular book he mentions his political activities in eastern Australia and Darwin but although this book is presumably aimed at Communist coffee tables, he makes no claim to have stimulated political activity among Aboriginals in the field.[12]

The Minister went on to say that Professor Rose "has a particularly bad record of treachery and of prostituting his position as an anthropologist for the gains of the Communist party.... The Matters in relation to which Professor Rose has prostituted his position as an authority on the Aboriginals have been in the Communist interest." I do not know what matters Mr. Wentworth refers to. However, it seems both odd and unconvincing that the Federal Government should appear as the defender of anthropology. If, for instance, Rose had prostituted his position as a Communist in the interest of anthropology, then presumably this would be the proper concern of the central committee of the party. Similarly, if Rose did what the Minister attributes to him, then it is the anthropological profession rather than the Federal Government who should be concerned. Since anthropologists have not been told in what way Professor Rose has abused his professional position, I can only guess that his fault, in Mr. Wentworth's eyes, is that he has given information about Aboriginals to his Communist comrades. I cannot see that this action would contravene his professional status, for there are many Communist anthropologists, particularly in Communist states. I infer that the Government's real objection to Professor Rose is that he is a Communist, as stated by Mr. Nixon,[13] or that he is seen as having "a particularly bad record of treachery," as indicated by Mr. Wentworth, or both, rather than that he is an anthropologist who has disgraced his profession. The mention of "a particularly bad record of treachery" is presumably a reference to those actions by Rose which were inquired into by the Royal Commission on espionage in 1954-55, which followed the Petrov incident.[14] A ban imposed because of a record of treachery is quite different from a ban imposed merely because of membership of a legal opposition political party. Even so, we have to remember that no charge of treachery has been laid against Professor Rose, and the proof of such a charge has to be established. More importantly in this context, even if a charge of treachery had been proven, it would not necessarily provide an adequate ground for preventing Professor Rose from carrying out an anthropological inquiry that has no military significance whatsoever.

To sum up, as an anthropologist I think that on the limited evidence available, the AIAS was right to sponsor Professor Rose. However, if it can be established that in a significant sense Professor Rose has "prostituted his position as an anthropologist," then the AIAS should hear about it, for this fact, rather than whether he is a Communist or a true-blue Tory, may reflect on his professional performance in the field. It still appears to me that the Government's ban on Rose was based only on political grounds, and not on political and professional grounds combined. As a citizen I think that Rose, like any other member of the public, should be free to visit Groote Eylandt and that the Aboriginals he wishes to re-visit should be the people to decide whether he can stay and for how long.

What action can be taken? The present system does not require the Director of Welfare to state his reasons for refusing entry, nor does the law provide any formal machinery for appeal against his decision. Thus the only courses open are to raise the matter in parliament, as has been done, and for individuals and organizations to make representations to those in power and to seek public support through the press and other media.

The AIAS, as a statutory body linked financially to the Federal Government and concerned with Aboriginal *studies,* is poorly placed to bring pressure to bear on matters of Aboriginal administration, and even less so on the issue of the rights of Australians as citizens, whether Aboriginals or Communists or neither. It does have a duty to promote research into the culture and way of life of Aboriginals. If Professor Rose's proposed research can be carried out economically only by him and by no-one else, then the AIAS should indicate how much importance it attaches to the research, so that this may be weighed against the importance attached by the Federal Government to excluding him.

The Association of Social Anthropologists is the professional organization of social anthropologists in the British Commonwealth. Professor Rose is not a member but he is professionally qualified and appears to be in good standing with his colleagues. The Australian branch of the Association has spoken in support of him as a colleague, though its resolution does not mention him by name and refers to entry into Papua and New Guinea as well as into Aboriginal reserves.[15] The resolution is limited to a protest against obstacles to scientific research, in which members have a common interest, and says nothing about Aboriginal rights, civil liberties, or the administration of reserves. These are matters about which members of the Association, as well as members of AIAS, are certain to have divergent views and about which they can and should speak as citizens.

**CONCLUSION**

As usual in these cases, facts are scarce. The Government takes its decision partly on the basis of facts that are not disclosed and hence cannot be discussed publicly. Therefore I have presented my arguments, far too tortuously alas, in terms of general principles and have then applied these to the few facts I have. If more facts became available the same principles might yield a different answer.

I hope that these arguments will find supporters. Nevertheless I have to note that I am at odds with those of my colleagues who advocate the entire abolition of the permit system of controlled entry to Aboriginal reserves, and also with those who object to any obstacle to free inquiry. Instead I advocate a system whereby Aboriginals decide on their visitors and on the extent to which they will co-operate in scientific inquiries. I am at odds with Mr. Wentworth and many of my colleagues who hold that a fieldworker's political and religious beliefs are not the concern of those from whom he seeks sponsorship. On the contrary, I think that the extent to which these beliefs influence his behaviour in the field and his analysis of his data is of great concern to a sponsor. As a citizen, I am also at odds with the Federal Government which, contrary to the aims of assimilation, seeks selectively to protect Aboriginals from Communist influence with a ban whose only practical effect is to prevent some interesting anthropological research work. Finally, I am completely at odds with Professor Rose when a few years ago he wrote that the Australian Aboriginals had "legally and constitutionally the lowest status of all suppressed people in the world," and that it is impossible "within a capitalistic society to carry out policies to bring about equal rights for a coloured minority."[16] However, I do not see this as an adequate reason for stopping him from doing fieldwork. I hope the day will come when fieldwork on Groote Eylandt would show him that he was wrong.

Academics usually make poor politicians, and it is folly to expect an academic organization to become an effective political pressure group. The art of the possible calls for qualities of compromise and tactical sensitivity that combine uneasily with the quest for enduring principles and underlying causes. It is easy for academics to criticize decisions taken by busy men who have to balance many incompatible interests. But though criticism may be easy it may still be correct. In any case, even if academics cannot hope to have an immediate influence on political decisions, they nevertheless have a duty to determine what interests are at stake.

## NOTES

1. "Australian," 1 June, 1968.
2. "Aboriginal quarterly I" (3), July-September, 1968, p. 7.
3. "Canberra Times," 18 December, 1968.
4. Morton H. Fried, "Foreword," in William R. Geddes, "Peasant life in communist China," Ithaca, N.Y., Society for applied anthropology, 1963, p.2.
5. Johan Galtung, "Scientific colonialism," "Transition" (Kampala), 6 (5), 1968, April-May, pp. 11-15; Irving Louis Horowitz, ed., "The rise and fall of Project Camelot: studies in the relationship between social science and practical politics," Cambridge, Mass.; M.I.T. press, 1967.
6. The Minister for the Interior, Mr. Nixon, is reported as stating that Professor Rose has Australian citizenship ("Sydney Morning Herald," 1 June, 1968), though Rose, who was born in England, states merely that he is a British subject, and that "I regard myself as an Australian" ("Australian," 13 April, 1965). Cf. F.G.G. Rose, "Ureinwohner, Kanguruhs, Dusenclipper," 1966, Leipzig; Brockhaus Verlag, pp. 7-8.
7. House of Representatives, "Debates," 26th Parliament, first session, first period, pp. 1670-1671 (3 May, 1967).
8. Cf. Donald J. Tugby, "Towards a code of ethics for applied anthropology," "Anthropological forum," 1 November, 1964, pp. 220-231, and references therein; J.A. Barnes, "Some ethical problems in modern field work," in Douwe Geert Jongmans and P.C.W. Gutkind, eds., "Anthropologists in the field," Assen; Van Gorcum, 1967, pp. 193-213; Gideon Sjoberg, ed., "Ethics, politics, and social research," Cambridge, Mass.; Schenkman publishing co.; M. Brewster Smith, "International conference on social-psychological research in developing countries," "Journal of personality and social psychology," 8, 1968, pp. 95-98.
9. Meyer Fortes, "British journal of sociology," 13, 1962, pp. 81-82; P.E. de Josselin de Jong, "A new approach to kinship studies," "Bijdragen tot de taal-, land- en volkenkunde," 118, 1962, pp. 42-67; Jane Goodale, "American anthropologist," 64, 1962, pp. 664-667.
10. House of representatives, "Debates," 26th parliament, 2nd session, first period, p. 1887 (4 June, 1968).
11. "Banned professor interviewed," "National U," 4 (8), 1968, p. 13.
12. "Classification of kin, age structure and marriage amongst the Groote Eylandt Aborigines," 1960, and "The wind of change in central Australia," 1965, Berlin; Akademie-Verlag; "Ureinwohner, Kanguruhs, Dusenclipper," pp. 175-277.
13. House of representatives, "Debates," 26th parliament, 2nd session, first period, p. 1886; cf. Senate, "Debates," p. 1352 (4 June, 1968).
ceedings." Pp. 321-324, 1385-1405, et passim. Report, pp. 132-136. F.G.G. Rose, "Ureinwohner," pp. 49-52.
15. "Canberra Times," 18 December, 1968.
16. F.G.G.Rose, "Grundlage und Entstehung der 'Northern Territory Welfare (Native) Ordinance' von 1953," "Ethnographisch-Archaologische Zeitschrift," 3, 1962, pp. 59, 71.

## 5.13—MIND ASSAULT

Stanley Milgram's "The Experience of Living in Cities" provides a little internal evidence on the quality of life in the city. Milgram reports that Miss McKenna of the City University of New York contrived an experiment in which telephone callers misrepresented themselves as long-distance callers "who had through error been connected with the respondent by the operator." The callers in this experiment then proceeded to diddle the subjects by representing themselves as persons in need (of information). That dialogue established, the subjects were put to a greater test when the caller asked, on some pretext, that the respondent "please hold on." The caller would put the phone down for almost a minute, and then would ask yet further questions, in the cases where the respondent had continued to make himself available. "Scores were assigned the subjects on the basis of how helpful they had been."

On the calendar in front of me, I have just come upon this quotation from Henry Thoreau's *On the Duty of Civil Disobedience*. "It is not so important that many should be as good as you, as that there should be absolute goodness somewhere; for that will leaven the whole lump." Inverting Thoreau's sense, I draw the uneasy conclusion that the small leavening of absolute duplicity that Miss McKenna unloads onto the lump of troubled city life may do more to increase those troubles than to alleviate them. The informed citizen of our city will henceforth consider the dangers of mind assault as well as body assault when he wonders whether he should open his door, or heed the phone call of a stranger.

Miss McKenna may have introduced a ghost into the machine which she will reencounter if she repeats her experiment at a future time.

Jules Rabin

*Northwood Campus, Goddard College*
*Plainfield, Vermont 05667*

---

Letter submitted to *Science*, an edited version of which appeared in *Science* 23 May 1970, Vol. 168, p. 919. Copyright 1970 by the American Association for the Advancement of Science.

# SECTION 6
# DILEMMAS IN THE USE AND MISUSE OF SOCIAL SCIENCE KNOWLEDGE

## INTRODUCTION

The misuse of social science knowledge presents many complex issues with few clear solutions. It is not confined to such major incidents as the selection of bombing targets in Southeast Asia on the basis of anthropological information, as has been alleged. The misuse of knowledge also occurs in many apparently insignificant incidents, which in total can contribute to an erosion of human freedom and dignity and an acceleration of the processes of objectification and dehumanization of man. There are social forces in our society that are producing increased dehumanization, and the social sciences have to be cautious not to become the handmaidens of these. As Kelman (1968, particularly Chapter 2) argues, the social sciences should be used for the *humanization* of society. The cases in this section are primarily oriented toward this problem. Also see Appell (1973a), Beals (1969), and Perloff (1964) for a discussion of these issues. Cain (1967) presents a useful case illustrating the misuse of sociological inquiry to influence public opinion.

Some anthropologists, fearing that the results of their research might be misused by repressive governments, have chosen not to publish their data. Thus, the fear of misuse can impede the growth of knowledge and its communication. This raises the question of how social scientists can communicate their findings so that they do not become accessible to the layman to use for his own purposes. In other words, can social scientists retain responsibility for the use of the knowledge they create?

Related questions are: How can the individual scientist take action when the knowledge he has created is misused? What responsibility does the social scientist have in instances where action is taken on the basis of information that he knows to be false or inadequate, particularly when he has more adequate knowledge?

## RELATED CASE MATERIALS IN OTHER SECTIONS

*Section 2: Relations and Responsibilities to Respondents and Informants:* Conflict in the Roles of Friend and Informant During Feedback of Research Results.

*Section 4: Relations with Representatives of Outside Agencies and the Public with Respect to the Host Community:* On the Horns of a Dilemma: A Problem of Intercession.

188  Section 6: Dilemmas in the Use and Misuse of Social Science Knowledge

*Section 7: Publication: Responsibilities and Liabilities:* A Problem of Publishing on Identifiable Communities and Personalities.

## 6.1 – MISUSE OF THE ANTHROPOLOGIST'S INFORMATION

This incident occurred in a country where the Indian population is still exploited by a racially mixed class holding political and economic power and speaking the language of the old colonists. This exploitation has now been subtly worked into the legal system in much the same way that segregation in the southern United States was legalized in the first part of this century.

The trouble resulted from my idly passing on some information to the chief magistrate of the region in which I worked. An ambitious and powerful man, he used this information against my informant, who was also his assistant and the local magistrate in the Indian community where I was residing.

The chief magistrate is the head of government in the capital town of the region; this and other regional posts are held by members of the dominant class. It is the only government body recognized by the state and national governments, which means that the state and national officials deal only with regional officials in seeking the representation of the entire region or in giving the people some form of aid. The Indian communities also have their own form of independent government. However, as these native forms receive no official recognition by the state or national powers, the members of the Indian communities must articulate themselves to the structure of the regional government through the local magistrates in order to get the benefits from economic relations with the dominant class or to get benefits from the state and national governments. The local magistrates are appointed by the chief magistrates as his representatives in the small Indian communities.

The power of the chief magistrates is felt most forcefully in the capital town. Within the national and state political structure, the local magistrates are the lowest and least powerful members. At the community level, the people have a hand in choosing these individuals, and very often they are those who have high standings in the native community government. Thus, the local magistrates are in an ambiguous position. They owe their authority in part to the respect they command within their local community and in part to their representation of the chief magistrate. These local magistrates must try to fit into both worlds.

One of the methods that the local magistrates use to handle the problems created by their dual role, as I learned later, is to restrict or modify information that passes from the community to the chief magistrate and vice versa. The chief magistrate depends on the local magistrate for information on activities in the

Indian community and for support to carry out his wishes. The greater his dependency on information supplied by the local magistrate, the less he can directly influence the actions of individuals in the Indian community.

The economic life of the capital town is also controlled by the dominant class, which exploits the Indian community. For example, at the weekly regional market held in the town, the Indians receive low prices for their products and pay high prices for their purchases.

The chief magistrate also acts as a "commercial agent" by charging the Indians fines so that they may be relieved of further prosecution for crimes of which he has knowledge. If a person refuses to pay, the chief magistrate has the power to imprison him. Or he may allow the case to pass on to the local judge, who has greater punitive powers. The Indians see this judicial process primarily as an economic one in which they pay a certain amount as the price of having committed an antisocial act.

In the Indian community where I worked I learned from my informant, the local magistrate, that he also performed certain duties in the church which had always been associated with the position of local magistrate in this Indian community. One day I mentioned this fact to the chief magistrate. I thought he would be interested in this aspect of the civil-religious hierarchy of the community.

Later, I learned from the local magistrate that the chief magistrate had reprimanded him for participating in religious affairs. The chief magistrate wanted to make sure that the local government in the Indian community maintained a strict separation of church and state, according to the national constitution. He might also have been motivated by the desire to introduce a Protestant sect into the community. Indeed, he had managed to undermine the autonomy of the local government in another Indian community by acting as peace maker in a bloody conflict between Catholic and Protestant factions.

On learning of this, I told the local magistrate that I did not agree with the chief magistrate and that the less said about the matter to him the better. From that time on I was friendly with the chief magistrate, but I did not volunteer any more information. I was not pressured anyhow, because the chief magistrate would never admit that he needed information from an American who obviously did not know what he was doing living with Indians.

I have also decided to do my best to insure that my published works do not get back into the town. They could be utilized by the literate dominant class as ammunition against the autonomy of the Indian communities. This would pave the way for further economic exploitation of these people. In consideration of my Indian friends, I feel that the best place for my ethnographic writings about them is with my various colleagues in the several institutes of Indian studies associated with the national government. There, the interests of the Indian class will be respected, and the writings will most quickly find their way into the hands of people who wish to help these people.

## 6.2 – THE DISCOVERY OF DRUGS: A DIFFICULT ETHICAL QUESTION

I was working on a project investigating the system of treatment for drug addiction. This project was financed by a city agency and conducted under its jurisdiction. One day, while I was visiting a locked treatment ward with a prison guard on duty outside the door, one of my chief informants showed me a batch of heroin, saying, "What's the point of these wards? The whole thing is idiotic! Anybody who wants to can use drugs in the wards."

I said to him, "Oscar, put it away! I don't want to see it."

I didn't want to see the heroin, as I look back upon it now, because it would have put me in a very difficult moral bind. Not only was he committing a criminal act, but the very presence of the heroin on the ward meant that the whole treatment program was, in a sense, a sham. Anybody could use drugs, and they did. Drug addicts only go into treatment to reduce their habits so that they can support them. Instead of a $40- or $50-a-day habit, they push it down to a $5-a-day habit, and therefore they have to steal less. The economics of how much they can steal in a community determines the time point at which they enter the hospital.

If I had acknowledged the presence of the drug, I would have felt obliged to notify my superiors on the project. They were all ethical people who believed that the research data should stay with the research staff only. So I knew the information would have remained with the members. But in this case we would all have been party to a criminal situation. We would also have been party to a disruptive hospital situation that worked against the whole treatment philosophy. Somone on the wards, probably one of the guards, was obviously being bribed to smuggle in drugs. Nevertheless, this type of treatment facility does reduce the amount of drugs consumed in the community, even if it does not effect cures. And if we had published this aspect of the treatment program, those who did not believe in this sort of approach to drug addiction could have used the information against the program. Consequently, no matter what I did, there were ethical implications that were not to my liking.

## 6.3–WHETHER OR NOT TO DEPOSIT FIELD NOTES IN AN ARCHIVE

In 1969 I received a grant from the National Institute for Mental Health to conduct research for my doctoral dissertation among a group of Indians living on a reservation in one of the Mountain states. This grant was supplemented by funds from my university on the stipulation that some "product" should result from the research. After a year in the field, I returned and began writing my dissertation, finally taking a teaching position in another state while completing it.

Shortly after taking this teaching position, I began to receive letters from the administrator who was in charge of the supplemental funds that I had received from my university. He wrote that my funds had come from a university endowment and the university was now establishing archives for all research materials resulting from studies aided by this endowment. I was asked to deposit copies of all my pictures, notes, and so forth.

My research among the Indian group had been unusual in two respects. I became aware shortly after my arrival that the local police were intimidating the Indians whenever they left the reserve. There were frequent unlawful searches of automobiles and persons; occasionally Indians were threatened and beaten. The police seemed to take considerable pleasure in harassing the local Indian community at every turn, and as I became more intimate with my Indian informants, I too began to engage the interest of the local police. Several times I was subjected to searches or threats. Once, after I had attended a drinking party with some Indian friends, the police threatened to report me to the National Institute for Mental Health and to take the matter up with my university.

The Indians, on the other hand, operating in this very repressive situation, were engaging in a number of illegal acts. And as my research proceeded, I became very interested in this aspect of the Indian community structure. As a result, I had considerable materials in my field notes that detailed murders, thefts, and disputes within the Indian community and between the Indian and the white communities. The Indians' fear of reprisal was so strong that one of my major informants would not be seen talking into my tape recorder. Before he agreed to provide me with information, I had to swear that his materials would never be identified with him. We made arrangements to meet in a small room in town with no windows and two

### 6.3—Whether or Not to Deposit Field Notes in an Archive

doors. We entered and left by different doors and about ten minutes apart each time. However, I was able to obtain very rich data on this informant's life history, which included his participation in several illegal acts.

Since I had not agreed to deposit my field notes prior to receiving the university grant, I did not respond to the first letter from the administrator. In a second letter, he stated that the university would pay for all duplication of notes and other materials. Specifically, copies of field diaries, duplicates of taped interviews, duplicates of negatives, and all categories of field notes were required. I was assured that because of the confidential nature of my materials they would not be available to anyone without my permission. However, an index of all materials with dates, places, and the context of all interviews, including names of informants, would be an open file.

Inasmuch as this index might be used to compromise my informants, particularly after I had published my materials, I wrote back refusing to provide such data.

The administrator replied that unless I agreed to deposit my materials I would not receive my degree. Finally, I complied to the extent of submitting innocuous materials which I believed would not compromise my informants such as genealogies, kinship data, and linguistic notes. But I refused to send any additional materials.

## 6.4–ON THE PREPARATION OF ETHNIC HANDBOOKS FOR THE ARMED FORCES

Shortly after returning from the field, I was approached by a representative of a private corporation that frequently performed contract work for the government. The corporation had conceived the idea of preparing a handbook for the use of the United States Armed Forces on the tribal peoples of a region in Southeast Asia where I had worked. The region was far removed from the scene of conflict in Vietnam. But the corporation's staff reasoned that hostilities might arise there at some point in the future. The Department of Defense would, therefore, be interested in having information available on the tribal peoples, particularly since the army had found that the tribal peoples of Vietnam who inhabited the interior had been friendly to the United States forces. The corporation was in the process of preparing a proposal to submit to the government for funding the project.

I had been approached because of my research in the region, and the staff representative wanted me to work on the project. The handbook was to be prepared on the basis of published ethnographic materials, and my job was to evaluate the reliability of these materials and generally provide guidance in use of the literature.

There was no question that I needed employment while I finished my dissertation, and the salary offered was very generous. Furthermore, reviewing the ethnographic literature would be of considerable value to me in writing my dissertation. But I knew from my own research that many of the tribal people in question had not been willing to commit themselves to either side of the hostilities during World War II. Consequently, I wondered about the real value of the project.

However, my main dilemma was whether or not I wanted to be associated with such a project, for I had strong feelings against the Vietnam War. I believed that the United States government had grossly misused the tribal peoples there and in the surrounding regions.

On the other hand, the information in the ethnographic literature was available to anyone and the project would probably be carried out whether I joined it or not. Also, there was always the possibility that false information might be included in the handbook which could eventually result in actions detrimental to the tribal peoples involved. Thus, by refusing to join the project I could be neglecting my responsibilities to the tribal peoples.

## 6.5 – THE INADVERTANT FEEDBACK OF RESEARCH CONCLUSIONS

I was part of a research team studying the nature of race relations and interaction between Europeans and blacks in an African city. In particular, my research focused on how the Europeans accommodated the conflict between their utopian values of human equality and their stereotypes of the black community, which they used to justify their behavior toward the blacks. I discovered that the Europeans were completely unaware of this value conflict and that the blacks accepted the stereotype as a mechanism for facilitating social relations with the dominant group. I finally reached the conclusion that the failure to recognize this dissonance in values had the adaptive function of minimizing overt conflict between the two communities.

On returning home I gave a paper at an anthropological meeting detailing my conclusions and sent copies to the various members of the research team. I asked them not to send copies to individuals in the community under study. My concern was not that community members would read the paper but that I would not be there to explain those points made in the paper which they might at first interpret as personally damaging.

However, sometime later I learned that the member of the research team in charge of relations with the local European government had sent copies of my paper to the borough council and to other members of the white elite community. Many of these people became incensed by my observations so that, when I returned several years later, they were not willing to cooperate with me in my research.

## 6.6–DIFFERENTIAL ACCESS TO THE RESULTS OF ANTHROPOLOGICAL INQUIRY: A DILEMMA IN PROFESSIONAL RESPONSIBILITY

My research was concerned with the social structure of the Silikan, a swidden-agricultural society in Southeast Asia. For a number of years a Protestant sect had been proselytizing among a neighboring ethnic group, and the Silikan were aware of their work. Occasionally, a missionary would visit the Silikan as well, and the people in my village frequently asked my opinion of such missionizing, for the visiting missionaries promised great rewards to those who would convert to Christianity.

The Silikan believed that the natural world was populated by spirits who were potentially hostile to human beings. These spirits dwelt in groves of trees that surrounded springs as well as other natural features, such as landslides. If an individual cut down any trees in these groves while preparing a swidden, he would be attacked by the disturbed spirits, who would cause the offending man or a member of his family to become ill.

The missionaries argued that if the Silikan became Christian they could cut these trees with impunity and so could become rich from the harvest they would reap on these virgin lands. Thus the Silikan perceived that the missionaries were promising not only abundant harvests but protection from sickness as well.

The Silikan, however, showed better ecological sense than the missionaries. They argued that if they did cut down their groves of trees around springs, the country would eventually become drier.

The Silikan also raised pigs, which they used as offerings to the hostile spirits when they became angry and made someone ill. The missionaries insisted that if the people converted to Christianity they could sell the pigs for a profit, rather than keeping them for sacrifices, which they then ate. The missionaries were thus ignoring the impact that a diet of reduced protein would have on the Silikan, whose protein intake was already at a minimal level.

During my field work, the Protestant missionaries built an agricultural station and elementary school about ten miles away from my village. They wanted to enroll Silikan children in the school to teach them modern agricultural techniques as well as Christianity. While the agricultural station was still under construction,

## 6.6 Differential Access to the Results of Anthropological Inquiry

I was visited by the station manager, a European missionary. He was interested in teaching the Silikan how to plant fruit trees. I pointed out to him that they had always planted a large variety of fruit trees, groves of which could be seen throughout the countryside. In fact the name "Silikan" arose from a descriptive term indicating that these people lived surrounded by fruit groves. I then asked the missionary whether he could help me identify some of the more unusual crops raised by the Silikan, such as millet, sorghum, and so forth. But he unfortunately was apparently less informed on this subject than I. He excused his ignorance with the statement that if this were Europe he could easily identify such crops.

Several years later, after I had left the field, I received a letter from the head of the agricultural station asking for reprints of any articles that I might have written on the Silikan. I did not know how to respond. Finally, I did send him a complete set of reprints, feeling that I was ethically obliged to do so. I believed that the results of scientific research should be available to all and hoped that the missionaries would use my article in the best interests of the Silikan.

However, after several conversations with other anthropologists I wondered if I might have done the wrong thing. Certainly the results of my research were not freely available to all—the Silikan could not read them but the missionaries could. Thus, my analysis of the Silikan social organization, which included articles on residence, family organization, bride price, land tenure, and village organization, gave the missionaries a decided advantage in their attempts to impose cultural change. On the other hand, the Silikan leaders were possibly put at a disadvantage— if in fact my articles were of any use—in opposing the wishes of the missionaries or in trying to move their people in a direction that was not favored by missionaries. There was the added problem that the Silikan were politically unorganized beyond the village level. Yet the changes that they were being forced to deal with affected them all, and they were thus particularly vulnerable to the missionaries' efforts.

# SECTION 7
# PUBLICATION: RESPONSIBILITIES AND LIABILITIES

**INTRODUCTION**

> *One of the needs of science . . . is to keep the monkeys away from the typewriters.*
>
> Norbert Wiener (1964, p. 18)

The ethical responsibilities of the social scientist in publishing the results of his inquiry are seldom examined. Fichter and Kolb (1953) in fact argue that there is a state of normlessness in this area. This is a critical problem as the publication of research results always has the potential of harming the subjects. Becker (1964a) goes so far as to argue that the relationship between the social scientist and those he studies inevitably contains elements of conflict. This is because social inquiry necessarily delineates the disparity between the real and the ideal, reports things that the host community would prefer not to have brought to public attention, and pierces the social defense mechanisms that enable the society to function.

The social scientist characteristically describes deviations from the rules or an ideal about which, in many instances, nothing is being done. Making these public puts the society in the embarrassing situation of having to take action when it perhaps would rather not. Social inquiry also destroys the public image of the society that has been constructed to ease social friction and motivate people to keep its organizations functioning. It makes the lines of factionalization appear more rigid than they are by the very fact of drawing them.

Social inquiry also deflates people's view of themselves and their lives by treating what is precious to them merely as instances of a class. It discovers things that if made public would violate the subject's privacy and possibly damage reputations. Thus, Becker (1964a, 1967) argues that the problem is not to avoid harming people but to decide which people to harm.

Hicks (1977) discusses the problem of disguising subjects and communities to protect them and the implications that this can have on the growth of knowledge. Colvard (1967) provides an interesting case of the issues involved in disguising identities and reporting verbatim accounts.

In anthropological inquiry there is the growing problem of the literacy of informants. Also with the increase in world travel, the publications of the anthropologist can bring down on his host community the burden of the simple-minded tourist seeking new experiences and the insensitive curious.

**RELATED CASE MATERIALS IN OTHER SECTIONS**

*Section 1: Relations and Responsibilities to Host Community:* A Problem in Political Identification and Co-option.

*Section 2: Relations and Responsibilities to Respondents and Informants:* A Case of Privileged Communication; Conflict in the Roles of Friend and Informant During the Feedback of Research Results.

*Section 5: Relations with Other Social Scientists and Responsibilities to the Profession:* The Breaking of a Disguise; A Problem of Responsibilities; Dealing with Animosity Arising from a Previous Study.

*Section 6: Dilemmas in the Use and Misuse of Social Science Knowledge:* Misuse of the Anthropologist's Information; The Inadvertant Feedback of Research Conclusions.

*Section 9: Issues in Teaching:* A Case of Uncredited Editorial Work.

## 7.1—PUBLISHING AND BAD SCIENCE

There's another illusion that the more papers are being published, the more science is being done. However, a large number of *bad* papers means less science is being done. I'll bring up the old figure of speech of the monkeys and the typewriters....

Well, monkeys or typewriters working in this way, given enough millennia or millions of years to work, would certainly get every possible combination of a certain number of letters. Among these would certainly be the combinations which are the works of Shakespeare. But how much would the monkeys and the typewriters have contributed? Not one thing! For this reason: In getting the works of Shakespeare, they would also have gotten all of the conceivable trash and balderdash in the world. In order to get Shakespeare, it is not enough to have Shakespeare together with this other, but to have Shakespeare separate from the other. It would be at least as difficult a task as writing the works of Shakespeare to separate those works from all other possible works. Shakespeare's works would no more exist in that mass than a sculpture does in a block of marble. You may say that all the sculptor does is to remove the unnecessary marble. So, in separating the non-Shakespeare from the Shakespeare, you would be doing exactly what the sculptor does in separating the superfluous marble from the statue. We call that making a statue, and I think we can call this writing the works of Shakespeare.

Extreme cases like that don't occur. But suppose you have a large mass of low-grade scientific work: If it is your duty to look through it all in order to find the high-grade scientific work, the mass of it makes finding the high-grade scientific work much more difficult. You have no alternative but to neglect a large part of the work and work on such criteria as knowing who's done it and going through the titles and finding one which has a trace of imagination in it. The existence of the other work doesn't help you find the really fundamental scientific work one bit. It makes this a harder task. So I say that one of the needs of science at the present is to keep the monkeys away from the typewriters.

---

An excerpt from Norbert Wiener, 1964, "Intellectual Honesty and the Contemporary Scientist," *Technology Review* April, p. 18. The original article was drawn from a tape recording, provided by Rabbi Herman Pollack, of the author's informal remarks to students at a B'nai B'rith Hillel Foundation meeting held in 1963 at M.I.T.

## 7.2–A PROBLEM OF PUBLISHING ON IDENTIFIABLE COMMUNITIES AND PERSONALITIES

The Eskimo group with whom I have worked for the last six years has, during this time, become increasingly exposed to Western civilization, including our language and literature. Also, the children are now going to school and learning to communicate in English. With increased literacy in the community, I've wondered how these people will react to the book I wrote about them and what I should do about it.

The book is a personal account of my life in a small Eskimo camp during the two years I lived there as a member of one of the Eskimo households. My aim was to describe the ways in which the Eskimo people handle people who "misbehave." Thus, a good deal of "bad" behavior—from the Eskimo point of view—is described in the book. Worse, since the book is written in a narrative, anecdotal style, the dramatis personae can be identified. And, finally, the publisher asked that pictures be used to illustrate the book, preferably pictures of the characters described.

The problem is, of course, to reconcile two mutually conflicting obligations. On the one hand, I feel a responsibility to contribute to scientific knowledge and to report honestly to the scholarly community the results of my research. On the other hand, I feel that I am equally responsible to the Eskimo, who have welcomed and nurtured me during my visits and that, in return for their hospitality, I ought to avoid making statements that they might find embarrassing or that would create tension in their interpersonal relationships. I also have less altruistic concerns. I am afraid that if the negative statements I make about individuals do reach them, their displeasure will jeopardize my future work with them, as well as that of other scientists who may wish to work in the area. Unkind gossip is an offense that is not lightly regarded by the Eskimo.

To help me resolve my dilemma, I consulted with an Eskimo missionary couple who live in a neighboring community and oversee the religious welfare of the group I studied. They had sponsored my entrance into the group. The wife of the missionary is bilingual and is closely acquainted with Western society, having lived in it for a number of years before returning to live with the Eskimo. I also knew that she was concerned with the Westerner's stereotype of the Eskimo as "Stone Age men" or "happy children."

---

Contributed by Dr. Jean L. Briggs, Memorial University of Newfoundland

I told this couple that I had written a book about the community, describing the style in which it was written and those aspects of its contents that worried me. I asked them whether they thought I should publish the book. I added that I was afraid the members of the community I studied would be offended if the book came to their attention, but that I believed it was necessary to describe "bad" as well as "good" aspects of the way Eskimo treat each other if Westerners are really to understand the Eskimo and their life.

The missionaries told me that I should certainly publish the book because what is wrong with most accounts of Eskimo life is that they are not sufficiently detailed. The missionary's wife felt that while the book might make the community "a little bit unhappy" for a short time, they would soon begin to appreciate having their traditional ways recorded as they move farther and farther away from them toward Western ways.

I allowed myself to be convinced that I should publish the book, but decided to make several compromises, none of which seems to me on reflection completely satisfactory. First, I decided not to conceal the geographic location of my work or the name of the group. I reasoned that the work would lose ethnographic value if the statements could not be put in historical and geographical perspective. I also knew that an attempt to conceal the locale would probably fail in any case because anyone interested in the area already knows or can easily find out where I did my field work.

Second, I decided to disguise individual identities by using pseudonyms, even though in some cases—notably those of the missionary couple and my Eskimo father and mother—identification can easily be made by role. I reasoned that, with the exception of these four individuals, most people in the book could only be identified by other community members, by the missionary couple, or by a few non-English-speaking Eskimo in a neighboring community. Outsiders would have difficulty in determining the identities of individuals mentioned in the book because the composition of Eskimo households changes frequently due to migration, birth, and death. Furthermore, the government census is not very accurate, and only the community members are sufficiently familiar with local genealogies to identify individuals by tracing relationships on my kinship diagrams.

Also, I omitted any information that could be used against individuals in the community or against the group as a whole by interested outsiders, with the possible exception of the missionary and his wife. Although the latter could use information I provide in judging the grace of their parishioners, they are already aware of most of the "bad" acts I describe through local gossip.

I have not disclosed any information that an informant has labeled "confidential." Neither have I repeated gossip that I heard from sources outside the community; that is, information that the community members do not know I have. One might argue that it is not fair to write an account of behavior in the community without the members' permission, since the people I describe had no conception of how public their lives would become through my account. Had they known they might have responded differently or chosen not to respond at all. On the other hand, they did assume that I would give a verbal account of my trip to my friends and colleagues at home. This may be a weak argument, but the same problem applies to any case study or biographical material.

I asked the missionary couple to tell the community about the book and to try to explain my reasons for writing it as I did. I also asked them to describe the measures I have taken to conceal the identities of community members, but to be frank in admitting that these measures might not be effective in all cases. I hoped that the missionary couple would be able to present the situation in such a way that the people could see the value of an honest description of their behavior.

I also requested that the missionary ask the people whether they objected to my putting their pictures in the book. I asked him to explain that I would not label the pictures with the names of the individuals and that I planned to use pictures which I took several years after the period described in the book, thus confusing readers who might try to match faces and ages with the characters in the book. Essentially, then, I left the decision about including photographs up to the people in the community.

The missionary wrote back to me that the Eskimo "didn't mind" my publishing a book about them and that they would be "proud" to have their pictures in it. The book was subsequently published in 1970.

When I returned to the community a few months after publication, I asked the missionary's wife to tell me more about the people's reaction to my book. She said that the Eskimo had agreed to the publication but that they had not really understood why I wanted to record the "bad" happenings as well as the good ones, because the Eskimo way is to forget the bad as soon as it is over. She tried to reassure me that the Eskimo were now beginning to understand. When I expressed doubt, she said: "We have a saying that a man doesn't have a man's backbone if he is bothered by what a woman says."

All the members of the community welcomed me warmly, and my adoptive parents told me that they remembered both the annoying and the pleasant things that had happened when I first came, but that the good outweighed the bad. I gave copies of the book to the missionary and his wife and to my adoptive family. I explained to the latter that the title of the book, *Never in Anger,* meant that they had never gotten angry with me even when my behavior was annoying to them, a fact for which I was very grateful. They were pleased with my gift and the explanation of the title. However, I am still waiting to find out whether they are offended by the contents of the book.

## 7.3—PROBLEMS IN URBAN ETHNIC RESEARCH

As anthropologists increasingly turn to research among urban and literate communities, they inevitably face ethical decisions when publishing their data. I shall attempt to outline some problems I encountered in such a study.

I had lived in a country in southern Europe, teaching and doing field work there. When a new position brought me to a western United States city with about 4,000 members of that nationality living there, I saw a chance to do research on this ethnic group.

I began to focus on the unassimilated old men, who lived in the downtown area of the city which had once been the residential center for most immigrants from the home country. These men had for various reasons remained culturally unassimilated while successive waves of their countrymen had become economically successful and semi-assimilated, eventually moving to suburban areas. The old men were still living in the area of their original settlement, frequenting the one remaining coffee house. Most of them would die soon, and the coffee house was about to be razed to make way for an urban renewal project.

I made daily visits to the coffee house and surrounding area, which also contained a homeland grocery store and several other dying establishments run by members of this ethnic group. I became close friends with most of my informants—about forty in all. I learned of their disillusionments, frustrations, and disappointments. They complained of their life in the United States, their fellow countrymen, and their local church and priest. I felt that these criticisms should be reported and discussed in my study.

At the same time my wife and I became involved in the affairs of the community center and church of the suburban members of this group. The original immigrants from the home country gravitated first to the downtown area. As they grew more prosperous, they moved out of the downtown area. In the 1920's the city, where a new church was built. By the early 1950's a new community center and church had been built about six miles from the center of the city. This is where the majority of the 4,000 members of the group lived. The ethnic group as a whole is prosperous, firmly Americanized, and middle class. Most are now second- and third-generation Americans.

---

Contributed by Dr. G. James Patterson, Eastern Oregon State College

In discussions with these assimilated members, 80 per cent initially denied that a minority of their group was unassimilated and would not admit that they knew of the existence of a homeland coffee house downtown. The one local priest, who was American born, also shied away from discussions of the old men. The point of view of the majority was that their people had come from a poor land to one of great opportunity; they had worked hard and been good Christians; and they had prospered. It certainly was true that the unassimilated old men were exceptions. But most of the assimilated pretended that the others did not exist. Although few may actually not have known of their existence, most, when pressed, admitted their knowledge of the old men but criticized their old-country way of life and lack of Americanization.

Conversely, my research among the unassimilated old men revealed severe criticism of the United States and of most successful members of their ethnic group in the city. They complained that the priest had never visited their coffee house and that they felt he was embarrassed about their existence and way of life. They resented his avoidence of them.

These old men, who were mostly uneducated and uninformed about social science, refused to take me seriously as a researcher. They simply accepted me as a young man who had lived in their country, knew their language, and liked the congenial atmosphere of their coffee house. This was all true, and my rapport with them was good. The problem was that they did not believe I would publish their stories. Furthermore, although most of the old men could not read English, the majority of their ethnic group could do so. They would probably be angry and embarrassed if they were to read the old men's strong criticism of them. I felt that the priest especially would be angry and probably hurt. The problem was compounded by the fact that all these people shared an idealized value of care and respect for the aged, something they were not giving the old men.

One additional problem arose. There was considerable illegal activity in and around the coffee house, including bookmaking and other forms of gambling, sale of stolen goods, and drinking of alcoholic beverages in an establishment which had no liquor license. The police were aware of most of this activity; they periodically accepted payoffs for their silence. This information could be embarrassing and perhaps harmful to my informants if published.

My solution was not completely satisfactory. First, I wrote the entire study, complete with verbatim case histories, for my Ph.D. dissertation, which was the original impetus for the study. I gave all living persons pseudonyms and asked permission of the men to tell their stories. They all agreed, although they had little understanding of what I was doing. I avoided making my study or its results explicit to the priest and to the more assimilated of the group because I did not want to deal with their negative reactions. The dissertation is on file in the library of a university thirty miles from the city studied, and it is also on university microfilm.

Second, in preparing a paper on my research for publication in an anthropology journal, I did not emphasize the depth of the alienation of the bitterness of my informants, although I did refer to it. As with my dissertation, I made no attempt to disguise the city or the ethnic group. In the paper I made no reference to the old men's illegal activities.

My solution, then, was to plunge in and make my findings known—although in diluted fashion in the paper—despite possible negative reactions to it by assimilated members of the ethnic group. My primary loyalty is to the old men, my informants, and I feel that no harm would come to them as a result of anyone reading the study, since they have little contact with the majority of the ethnic group and would not be adversely affected by their criticism. The reference to illegal activities, briefly mentioned in the dissertation, cannot hurt them since the area is about to be razed, the coffee house destroyed, and the men dispersed.

The pride and self-image of the majority, and the priest, would be wounded if they should read the findings. But the ethnographic facts and attitudes had to be written for the sake of honesty. Perhaps in the future anthropologists will have less freedom to work with the majority of the group in this city, but they are losing their ethnic characteristics to the extent that anthropologists probably will be less and less interested in them as a group. The unassimilated old men are representative of the last of an era in the history of this ethnic group in the United States, and I felt that their attitudes and behavior should be recorded, even if the information disturbs or insults others of the same ethnic background.

## 7.4–AN ATTEMPT TO CONTROL THE CONTENTS OF PUBLICATION

My research in an administered territory in the Pacific was focused on changes in political organization. One of my general concerns was the transition from small-scale, informally organized polities comprising, at most, a few villages to organizations encompassing the island, district, and territory.

As part of my research, I planned to study the working of the District Council. The district included 40,000 people from some ten language groups. Neither the district nor the council had any precedent in aboriginal political organization. Members of the council were elected by universal suffrage. The chairman and other officers were elected by the council members. Nevertheless, the council's activities were largely controlled by the district commissioner and members of his staff.

Being ignorant of the proper procedures, I asked an informant, who was a local council member, whether I could attend the upcoming meeting. He seemed nervous about my request and suggested that I ask the district commissioner for permission. When I approached him, he replied that I could attend only if I promised to allow him to censor anything I might write about the council.

I felt the problem to be one of protecting my professional integrity. But I also realized that freedom to pursue further research depended, at least to some extent, on the good will of the district commissioner. So I suggested a compromise to him. He could read anything I wrote before publication and append a reply, if he felt one necessary. He thought this procedure to be fair and granted me permission to attend the meeting.

Shortly thereafter I learned that council meetings were open to the general public; it was unnecessary to obtain permission to attend them. But rather than confront the district commissioner with his deception and attempt to take advantage of me, which I would have liked to do, I avoided him whenever possible except for a few ceremonial occasions.

---

Contributed by Dr. Matthew Cooper, McMaster University

## 7.5 – THE PROBLEM OF PUBLISHING ON ILLEGAL ACTIVITIES

During my field work I did not actually discover illegal activities. Everyone knew that they had taken place and who the guilty parties were. But the two men—Harold Jones and Tom Smith—were never arrested. Smith disappeared and there was insufficient evidence against Jones, who remains a highly influential member of the community. However, everyone lonws where he got all his money.

Jones was the vice-chairman of the District Council, and Smith was the treasurer. Checks made out in the name of the council were always cosigned by both men, who thereby effectively controlled all monies being paid out by the council. However, in 1963 an auditor was brought in to investigate the apparent impoverishment of council funds. Smith quickly disappeared after destroying all the key records. Nevertheless, the auditor in his report was able to show that Smith had defrauded the council of over $15,000 during the years he was treasurer.

That same year, Jones opened up a construction business in the district capital, which required a considerable investment in machinery. He also became involved in national politics and began to build up a political following in the capital, which culminated in his running as a candidate in the general elections.

Everyone in the small town which Jones comes from says they know where Jones got his initial capital; however, they do not challenge him because he is a powerful man, generally described as a crook and a twister.

My problem as an anthropologist is how to present my field data. Jones is an important political figure, and there is sociological significance in the way in which he was able to make the transition from local to national politics, simultaneously building up a commercial enterprise and a political following. This requires considerable investment, and Jones is becoming a model for others who want to enter the political arena. Consequently, part of my task as an anthropologist describing how individuals move from one level of politics to another is to trace the source of the capital which makes such a transition possible. If I interpret events as I observe them, I must also mention the probability that Jones is a criminal. The area where I worked is easily recognizable to anyone with only a slight knowledge of the country, so it follows that major figures are also recognizable. However, since there is no solid evidence against Jones, it is also possible that in putting my interpretations of events into writing I may be sued for libel. To further complicate the issue, I wish to return to the region and continue my field work. I am unsure how to resolve all these conflicting aspects of a sensitive ethical dilemma.

## 7.6—THE POSSIBLE EFFECTS OF PUBLICATION ON THE SOCIETY STUDIED

Frank Featherstone had majored in foreign languages in college. He had wanted to go to graduate school, but he lacked the funds. Instead, on graduation he took a job in the Tribal Administration Service of a Middle Eastern country, hoping that this would give him the opportunity to improve his knowledge of Arabic while earning money to continue his education.

While in that country Featherstone did linguistic research and published a major paper on dialectal boundaries. Despite this work, Featherstone discovered that his interest was slowly shifting from the language that people spoke to the people who spoke the language. After seven years at this job, Featherstone decided to do graduate work in anthropology. He entered a graduate school in the United States and pursued a "generalist" approach, taking a balanced load of courses in various subfields. He felt that he was basically a field worker rather than a theorist. With this orientation to the profession, Featherstone did not look for an academic appointment on graduation. Instead, he accepted a job as a research analyst with an oil company in another country in the Middle East.

Featherstone knew a number of things about the country where he was going to work. It was a theocratic country, ruled basically along the lines of benevolent paternalism, although there were rare occasions when this paternalism could turn into violent fury. He was also aware that the Middle East was characterized by a surprising uniformity at the surface coupled with a mind-boggling diversity—ethnic, political, religious, economic, and so forth.

At one point during his field work Featherstone decided to concentrate on the religious aspects of the culture. His employers had sent him as a field supervisor to direct a malaria control program in one of the largest oases of the country. The area included 25,000 acres of cultivated land, over 2.5 million palm trees and some 150,000 people occupying one large town and 35 smaller settlements—all of which meant an extended assignment. This oasis was also unique in that its population was about equally divided between the orthodox Sunnite branch of Islam and the largest unorthodox branch, the Shiites. Featherstone was familiar with the basic differences between these two denominations and the historical development of

---

Contributed by Dr. Federico S. Vidal, Southern Methodist University

## 7.6 – The Possible Effects of Publication on the Society Studied

each. He also knew that the few sociological or anthropological studies of the Middle East area had been mainly concerned with homogeneous population centers or aggregates in terms of their religious sectarianism. Thus, any information he could gather on the social integration of these two sects, which were represented in one place in such large numbers, could be of considerable anthropological significance.

The government officials, as well as the upper classes and the majority of the country's population, were not only extremely orthodox but also followers of the most puritanical form of orthodoxy. These people, Featherstone realized, would not be good informants about the Shiites. They would tend to dismiss any problems concerned with their presence and take refuge in the oft-repeated statement that "there are no differences between Muslims." Featherstone had discovered that this declaration represented an ideal pattern *for* behavior rather than an actual pattern *of* behavior. His information would have to come from his own observations and from the Shiites themselves.

In this regard, Featherstone was in an excellent position and knew it. His linguistic background and previous experience in the Middle East made it possible for him to dispense with the services of an interpreter. In the joint arrangement between the government and the oil company to split the cost of the malaria project, interpreting services would have been furnished by the government. The interpreter would have been a Sunnite, not only likely to misrepresent questions and answers when dealing with Shiites but also likely to be a government informer. Featherstone had a deeply rooted distrust of interpreters and hated to be at their mercy. He kept recalling the Italian dictum *traduttore, tradittore*—"a translator is a traitor"—and that in Spanish the now obsolete word *truchiman,* derived from the Arabic *turujman* or "interpreter," meant "rascal." Featherstone liked to take an interpreter along only as a safety precaution when he met with high government officials under circumstances in which he might have to make a commitment in the name of his employers, or when talking to highly educated people, who were in the habit of using the most flowery classical Arabic. In such cases, the use of an interpreter gave him twice as long a time to think about a proper reply. The other point in Frank's favor was that since his duties included inspection of all public or private structures in the oasis which were to be sprayed with an antimosquito chemical, he would have free access to all settlements in the area, whether Sunnite, Shiite, or mixed.

Concentrating on the religious aspect of the culture, Frank discovered a number of things about the two sects. First, they were definitely not culturally integrated, except in economic terms. The unorthodox Shiites were considered heretics by the Sunnites. While not openly or violently persecuted, the former were more than just ignored; they were grossly discriminated against. There was not one Shiite in government service, the police, the military, the courts, or among the upper-class merchant group. The Shiites were servants, cooks, waiters, garbage collectors, sewage diggers, disposers of night soil, or, at best, semi-indentured day laborers in the palm gardens. Featherstone's field notes recorded many instances of discrimination:

October 12th. Went to Tawilah this morning to check on the spraying process. I am very interested in this village. Abdullah tells me that it has more than four hundred houses, so it must be one of the largest villages in the oasis. Also, I was told a few days ago that this is one of the few villages with both a Sunnite and a Shiite population. Most of the others are either/or. Parked the car outside the walls and walked through the west gate (does it have a name?) searching for the foreman of the spraying crew, or someone who could tell me where the village headman lives. Was soon surrounded by a passel of kids who kept pestering me with questions, and kept milling around me. Another group of children was following us, some twenty-five or thirty yards behind. At one point I stopped and started making small talk with the children (all boys, of course): What's your name?, do you go to school?, do you help your father in the fields?, what is the name of the village headman?, etc. Then, pointing at the other group of kids, who had also stopped but had kept their distance, I asked: "Are these other boys afraid of me?" The answer was: "Don't worry about them; they are just Shiites."

Another diary entry a few weeks later showed the same sort of discrimination among adults and at the highest social level:

November 8th. Nothing much to do today; since it is the 9th of Muharram, one of the most holy days for the Shiites, I have given them three days off. With half of the population engaged in devotional pursuits, the town looks quite deserted, and I decided to pay a social visit to the governor. On my way I bumped into 'Abd al-Nabi, whom I haven't seen since he retired from the company a couple of years ago. After the usual and lengthy exchange of Arabic greetings, I told him where I was headed. 'Abd al-Nabi said that he has not seen the governor for some time and asked if he could come along. No objections.

At the palace we were immediately ushered into the official reception room. As usual, it was crowded with visitors, petitioners, and bodyguards armed to the teeth.

After the normal greetings, and the inevitable coffee-and-tea routine, the governor and I engaged in a little talk, with me mostly reporting on the progress of the spraying program. Then he turned to my friend.

"Well, 'Abd al-Nabi, I hear that you just bought a new car a couple of days ago."

"That's right, Your Excellency, and may your days be made long by Allah."

"Now, considering these days we are in," added the governor, "I hope you chose a black car with black upholstery!"

This was a tasteless reference to the fact that Shiites are observing the holy day which commemorates the martyrdom of the founders of their sect, and, therefore, my friend's new car should be in mourning black.

The governor laughed out loud at his clever remark, the attendants and visitors giggled; 'Abd al-Nabi (who most likely had been the target of similar remarks before) blushed visibly; and I was not only embarrassed but more than a little irritated. We took our leave shortly.

## 7.6 – The Possible Effects of Publication on the Society Studied

With free access to the Shiite villages—after all, the malaria mosquito does not discriminate on the basis of religion—Featherstone soon became friendly with a number of the village headmen. He learned of their persistence in maintaining their religious beliefs; some of their special religious rituals and their holy days in commemoration of the births and deaths of the early leaders of their sect. On such days they would gather, not in a mosque, but in a special building called a *husayniyah* (in memory of Husayn, one of their early martyrs) to put on a passion play, or recite old stories, or read from religious books concerning the origin of their sect. They also described the persecution which they endured because of their religious beliefs. On occasion this would lead to wailing, weeping, and, perhaps, even self-flagellation.

Featherstone also learned that the government had originally established schools only in Sunnite villages, thus forcing Shiite children to attend school in nearby Sunnite villages. In fact, when the government finally opened schools in Shiite villages a few years later, the appointed teachers were all Sunnites. For this reason, the Shiite elders usually managed to smuggle into the country a *mullah,* or religious teacher, to give the religious instruction to the Shiite children. Featherstone met and interviewed one such *mullah.*

After his field assignment had ended, Featherstone prepared to write up his field notes. The majority of the material he had gathered on the Sunnite-Shiite opposition in this part of the Islamic world had not previously been recorded. Therefore, his anthropological training was pushing him toward early disclosure. However, if he reported in writing on the blatant local discrimination, his informants would be identified and located; they, as well as other Shiites, could become the targets of intensified discrimination, if not outright persecution. Featherstone abhorred the possibility that those who had befriended him would be persecuted as a result of his published material. Moreover, future investigators, or perhaps even casual travelers, might either be forbidden access to the area or might find themselves under close surveillance by the local authorities, who could dictate which topics of research or which informants were acceptable and which were not.

Should Featherstone publish his notes on the Shiites? Is there another alternative?

## 7.7 – COMPETITION WITH ONE'S INFORMANTS

As editor of an anthropology journal, I was contacted by Luis Santiago, a scholar from a Third World country. Santiago wrote to ask whether he might submit a manuscript he had written on the concepts of disease held by the ethnic group of which he was a member. The topic was inappropriate for my journal, so I took the initiative of contacting a colleague who edited another journal. I thought he might be interested in the manuscript.

The editor replied to my inquiry by asking whether Santiago was the same Luis Santiago who had originally worked with one of his graduate students, Fred Collins, while he was gathering material for his dissertation among Santiago's people. The editor concluded that if it were the same person, it would be reasonable to send the manuscript to Collins for his critical reading.

This put me in a very difficult situation. I had received a number of letters and verbal reports to the effect that Collins seldom answered his professional mail, including inquiries with respect to his own research. Certainly he never answered my correspondence. And I concluded that probably Santiago had in fact originally written to Collins to ask him about the manuscript and had received no answer.

Consequently, in fairness to Santiago, I replied to the editor that Santiago was the same person who had been a research assistant to Collins. However, I believed that sending the manuscript to Collins posed some ethical problems. First, I noted that because Santiago had contacted me in the first place about his manuscript, this might indicate that there was some coolness in the relationship between the two men. I also pointed out that the manuscript presented a discussion very closely related to a paper which Collins had already published. It might be informative to compare the interpretation of a native-speaking scholar on the subject with that of a nonnative. However, this might not be acceptable to Collins, who was the original researcher, and it could put Santiago in an embarrassing position. In any case, asking Collins to review the manuscript would entail a conflict of interests for him. Consequently, I thought it might not be fair to either individual to ask Collins to review the manuscript.

I never received a reply to my letter and heard nothing further from Santiago.

## 7.8—SOCIAL ORGANIZATION OF MANU'A (1930 AND 1969), BY MARGARET MEAD: SOME ERRATA

At the end of 1969 what has been described as a "revised edition" of Margaret Mead's *Social Organization of Manu'a* (originally published in 1930) was issued by the Bishop Museum Press.[1] This new edition has a handsome front cover, a new introduction and a chapter of conclusions, by Dr. Mead, "outlining her current thought concerning the theoretical formulations and factual findings of the original work," together with "two bibliographic appendices."[2]

The original text of *Social Organization of Manu'a* has not, however, been revised in any way, having been reprinted with all of the errors (including the many literal errors in the Samoan language), which disfigured the edition of 1930. Moreover, coming as it does from the Bernice P. Bishop Museum (an institution with an established reputation in the field of Polynesian scholarship), it is well possible that unsuspecting readers of the reprint of this "classic in the field of cultural anthropology" will themselves be led into error. I have, therefore, in the interests of the accuracy upon which ethnography depends if it is to be of any scientific value, compiled a list of errata to go with the 1969 Bishop Museum Press reprint of Mead's *Social Organization of Manu'a*.

In the case of an ethnographic study such as Mead's *Social Organization of Manu'a* which is likely to be used as a source of information by scholars engaged in comparative study of the Polynesian region, it is obviously of importance that all citations in the vernacular should be accurately recorded in a consistent orthography. For an ethnographer working in a little known or hitherto uncontacted region such accurate recording of a local language may pose formidable difficulties, but Miss Mead, when she began her researches in Samoa in 1925, was fortunate in having for her guidance the 4th revised edition (1911) of Pratt's scholarly *Dictionary of the Samoan Language,* as well as Krämer's *Die Samoa-Inseln* (1902), which contains numerous texts in Samoan (in a consistent orthography, based on Pratt), as well as a glossary and an index of proper names.

Two of the most important conventions of Samoan orthography established by Pratt (who spent some 40 years in Samoa) are the use of an inverted comma to

---

By Derek Freeman, Australian National University. Reprinted from *The Journal of the Polynesian Society* Vol. 81, No. 1, March 1972, pp. 70-78, by permission of the author and publisher.

represent the glottal stop, and of a macron to mark phonetically long vowels.[3] Thus, in his grammar, Pratt (1911:2) notes that the glottal stop (or "break," as he calls it) is "a very important distinction between words otherwise similar in spelling, and must be carefully observed"; and among the examples he gives are: *ulu* "head" and *'ulu* "breadfruit," and *ta'e* "to break" and *tae* "excrement." The orthography of a Samoan word containing a glottal stop (or stops) is thus not complete without its correctly placed inverted comma (or commas).

It will be evident then that in ethnographic reports on Samoa, the correct marking of the glottal stops present in Samoan words is of vital importance, for this not only ensures grammatical and semantic accuracy, but also facilitates etymological analysis, the glottal stop in Samoan corresponding to the consonant "k" in other Polynesian languages. Similiarly, the inclusion of a macron, when this is integral to their orthography, is essential if some Samoan words are to be identified correctly in writing or in print.

Mead, unfortunately, although she had Pratt's *Dictionary* to guide her, did not, in the 1930 edition of *Social Organization of Manu'a,* use either the inverted comma (marking a glottal stop) or the macron (marking a phonetically long vowel) in a consistent way. Occasionally, as in the phrase: *'o le nu'u* (p. 15), the glottal stop is correctly shown, but very frequently it is omitted. Sometimes we are offered two versions of the same word on the same page, e.g. p. 174: Aga'e (correct) and Agae (incorrect); p. 196 Aso'au (correct) and Asoau (incorrect). On other occasions a glottal stop is shown where it does not belong, e.g. p. 103, where *toe* (meaning: again) is incorrectly printed as *to'e* (meaning: a sea eel; c.f. Maori, *toke,* an earth worm), and p. 201, where *tia* (meaning: a funeral cairn) is incorrectly printed as *ti'a* (meaning: A slender rod used in a game of darts; cf. Tikopia, *tika,* a dart).

One of the most hallowed of the institutions of Ta'ū was the Fale 'Ula (lit. crimson house; cf. Maori, *Whare Kura),* in which the genealogies and oral traditions of the Samoans were preserved. Mead spells this correctly in places (e.g. p. 149), but she also makes use of the erratic forms: *fale-ula* (p. 168), *fale ula* (p. 190) and *faleula* (p. 199), which are misleading, for whereas *'ula* signifies crimson, *ula* means to be facetious. As the title of the sacrosanct supreme chief of Manu'a we are offered the forms: Tu'i Manua (p. 148), Tui Manua (p. 188) and Tui Manu'a (p. 188), only the last of which is correct. Further the form "Tu'i Manua" is untoward, for whereas Tui is the honorific term for a chief of paramount rank, *tu'i* means: to pound into pulp or to curse.

Again, the macron, while used correctly in some instances (e.g. p. 213 *māfaufau),* is frequently omitted, some of these omissions being not unimportant semantically; on p. 115, for example, Mead records that one of the terms used in Western Samoa to refer to the death of a high chief is *gasoloao,* and suggests that this form is derived from *gasolo,* to slip down (i.e. as thatch slipping out of place on the roof of a house; cf. Pratt, 1911:161). The correct orthography of this honorific term from Western Samoa as recorded by Pratt is, in fact, *gāsoloao,* and, as the macron indicates, its etymology is very different from that proposed by Mead. The form *gāsolo* means: to pass along, as in procession; while *ao,* which is used to refer to an exceptionally high title, has the root meaning of a cloud. Thus *gāsoloao* euphemistically describes the passing away of a title-holder of high rank by poetically likening this event to the way in which towering cumulus clouds pass across the skies of Samoa. That any Samoan would use the word *gasolo*, meaning: to slip down, to refer to the passing away of a high chief is, in any event, entirely contrary to the values of Samoan culture. In other cases, the macron is shown where it does not belong: e.g. Falē (p. 11), *āli'i* and *solē* (p. 133).

The orthography of some Samoan words calls for the use of both an inverted comma and a macron. One such word is the name of the island on which Miss Mead carried out her principal researches in Samoa. In the new edition of *Social Organization of Manu'a* we are offered three different versions: Ta'u (p. xviii), Taū (p. 157) and Tau (p. 162). All are imprecise, the correct orthography being: Ta'ū.

In another instance, a macron is omitted, and a glottal stop gratuitously inserted, to produce a particularly inappropriate solecism. Fitiuta is one of the most distant and proudly dignified polities in the whole of Samoa. The term which Samoans use to refer to such a place is *faigatā*, a word commonly translated: "difficult," but which, in this instance, carries the connotation of a place where (because of the high rank of its chiefs), the approach of any *malaga*, or party of visitors, has to be painstakingly punctilious, this being for the reason that a polity, with chiefs of such exceptionally high rank, is quick to take offense at the slightest impropriety. Mead, however, has described Fitiuta (p. 196) not as *faigatā*, but as *fa'igata*, a neologism, which has the literal meaning of: "defunct banana."

Mistakes like this may be laughable to some but they are decidedly out of place in what purports to be a scholarly ethnography of Manu'a—the highest ranking region, traditionally, of all Samoa. A comparable error occurs on p. 173 where, in the course of a discussion of the origin of the name Manu'a, a reference is made to: Manua Tale. This should read: Manu'a Tele, which has the literal meaning: "great wound," a reference to the rending of the earth during the creation of Samoa. *Tale,* when used as an adjective (as in this instance) means: "coughing"; and so the version published by Dr Mead: Manua Tale, has the ludicrous meaning of "coughing wound."

On the same page (p. 173), the title of one of the highest ranking chiefs in Western Samoa, Malietoa, is twice misspelt: "Maleetoa," and on p. 185 the personal name of Tui Manu'a Eliasara, the last Samoan to hold this august title, is misspelt: "Etisela."

On p. 206, the portion of a shark *(malie)* which is, by tradition, ritually due to Sai and Faoa, two of the high-ranking titular chiefs *(ali'i)* of the island of Ofu, in eastern Samoa, is said to be the *sogo*. The correct word for the portion in question (the dorsal fin) is, in fact, *gogo;* while *sogo,* in terms of Samoan values, has the highly objectionable meaning, especially in a situation where is concerns titular chiefs (cf. Milner, 1966:213), v. (of urine, etc.), smell, stink.

Again, on p. 94, the Samoan word for the coconut-leaf platter on which *fā'ausi* (a taro delicacy) is served to titular chiefs is given as: *maile. Maile,* means: dog, and is a common word, the use of which is interdicted in the presence of chiefs. The correct term for such a coconut-leaf platter is: *ma'ilo.*

On p. 103, a girl when making kava in an assembly of chiefs is said, after the bast strainer has been returned to her free of particles of kava root, to *soli lea i luga o le tanoa,* which literally means: "to trample on the kava bowl," *soli* meaning: "to tread on or trample." This passage should read: *sōloi fa'ata'amilo lea o 'augutu 'o le tanoa,* a reference to the ritualised wiping of the flat rim of a kava bowl with a bast strainer, *sōloi* meaning: "to wipe."

Yet another catachrestic usage deserving of especial mention is Mead's listing (p. 214) of *taupo* as the term for "the titled girl of a chief's family." Pratt (1911:303) correctly gives the form *tāupou,* as the term for a ceremonial virgin, but this orthography Mead specifically rejects, stating that she prefers the "simpler phonetic spelling" of *taupo.* This, as anyone with an understanding of the Samoan language will recognise, is a very odd statement, for it betrays not only an inadequate ear for a basic Samoan diphthong, but also a failure to appreciate quite elementary points in Samoan cultural behaviour and etymology. A *tāupou,* as the holder of a title of rank, has the right, similar to that of a titular chief *(ali'i),* to sit, on certain occasions, in chiefly company, at one of the posts *(pou)* in the *tala* "rounded lateral section" of a *fale tele,* or *fono* house. And it is to this right that the word *tāupou* refers, i.e.: *tau,* particle, denoting continued or repeated activity; *pou,* the post of a house. In marked contrast, *pō* means: night, so that one of the possible connotations of *taupo* (the form preferred by Mead) is, as Krämer pointed out in 1902 in cautioning against this solecism, "to indulge in love affairs at night,"[4] a meaning totally alien to the culturally defined role of a ceremonial virgin, or *tāupou.*

Unfortunately, the emphatically cacographic *taupo,* because of the prominence given to it by Mead in *Coming of Age in Samoa* (1928 and all subsequent editions) and in *Social Organization of Manu'a* (1930 and 1969), has—despite Krämer's warning—become an established solecism in the literature of anthropology.[5] One can only hope that the correct form of this fundamentally important Samoan word will in time become known—at least among anthropologists; and that this and other consequences of Margaret Mead's inadequate knowledge of the Samoan language will gradually be eliminated.

Recently, Dr Mead has written of the "rights" of people who "only recently lived a self-sufficient life without script or relationship to script. . . ."[6] One of the rights of all peoples, I would venture to suggest, is the right to have their language correctly recorded—and especially by professional ethnographers.

The people of Samoa, whose orators are among the most accomplished and sophisticated users of words to be found anywhere in the world, take an intense pride in their language. Thus, it was the late Tupua Tamasese Mea'ole, Joint Head of State (with Malietoa Tanumafili II) of the Independent State of Western Samoa, who was the "moving spirit"[7] in arranging for a modern study of the Samoan language to be made in succession to the studies of the Rev. George Pratt and the other missionary scholars of the nineteenth and early twentieth centuries), by G.B. Milner, Reader in Oceanic Languages in the University of London. And, at this juncture in the history of the Samoan people (a number of whom are university graduates), it is difficult to discern any extenuating circumstances for the failure of both Mead and the Bishop Museum Press to check the orthography of the Samoan words that appeared in the text of *Social Organization of Manu'a* as it was published in 1930, before this monograph was reproduced in 1969 and announced

## 7.8—Social Organization of Manu'a by Margaret Mead: Some Errata

as a "revised edition."[8] This is particularly the case in view of the availability from 1966 onwards of Dr G.B. Milner's superbly scholarly *Samoan Dictionary*. Yet, this most notable contribution to Samoan studies (based on research in all parts of the Samoan archipelago) is not even mentioned in the list of *Later Publications on Samoa Used in Preparation of 1969 Edition,* which is appended (pp. 231-234) to the reprinted version of *Social Organization of Manu'a*.

In the following list of errata, errors (even when they occur repeatedly in the text) are noted once only. Numerous minor imprecisions (especially instances in which glottal stops or macrons are not shown) and a few usages which I have been unable to identify, have been passed over. Errata in English, German, Latin and Fijian are not included. A few mistranslations have been noted. The errata in the language of Samoa which I have listed are to be found in both the 1930 and the 1969 editions of *Social Organization of Manu'a* by Margaret Mead, Bernice P. Bishop Museum Bulletin 76, Honolulu, Hawaii..[9]

| PAGE | | | ERRATA | |
|---|---|---|---|---|
| 12 | for | *vai po* | read | *vāipou* |
| 28 | for | Sili a | read | Silia |
| 31 | for | *laloga* | read | *lalaga* |
| 48 | for | *tapa 'aos* | read | *tapa'au* |
| 49 | for | *talolos* | read | *ta'alolo* |
| 50 | for | Samataafe | read | Sauma'iafe |
| 52 | for | *Ua uso ne i le malaga?* | read | *'Ua usu nei le malaga?* |
| 57 | for | *Mapu* | read | *Ma'upū* |
| 58 | for | *vai atu* | read | *vāe atu* |
| 58 | for | *vai ane* | read | *vāe ane* |
| 58 | for | *alala* | read | *alaala* |
| 58 | for | *Talofai* | read | *Tālofae* |
| 58 | for | *faina* | read | *āfaina* |
| 58 | for | *Ua sua le vai* | read | *'Ua sua le tai* |
| | (Note: the meaning of these words is "the tide is rising" not "the tide is out," as stated by Mead.) | | | |
| 60 | for | *alala* | read | *afioga* |
| 61 | for | *malīe* | read | *mālie* |
| 64 | for | *taiga* | read | *ta'iga* |
| 65 | for | *mauaoloa* | read | *mau'oloa* |
| 68 | for | *aga'e tupu* | read | *agaiotupu* |
| 70 | for | *tui paepae* | read | *tu'i paepae* |
| 71 | for | *tamaita'i* | read | *tama'ita'i* |
| 81 | for | Tama Paia | read | Tama Pa'ia |
| 82 | for | *tautala lai titi* | read | *tautala la'itiiti* |
| 87 | for | cord (*pito*) | read | umbilical cord (*uso pito*) |
| 89 | *failele* means "nursing mother" (cf. Milner, 1966:56), not "a birth feast." | | | |
| 94 | for | *maile* | read | *ma'ilo* |

## Section 7: Publication: Responsibilities and Liabilities

| PAGE | | ERRATA | | |
|---|---|---|---|---|
| 94 | for | 'aiava | read | 'aiavā |
| 95 | for | ao moega | read | aumoega |
| 98 | for | taipoga | read | tautōga |
| 99 | for | ausoga | read | auosoga |
| 103 | for | tui | read | tu'i |
| 103 | for | fa'aoga | read | fa'aaogā |
| 103 | for | soli | read | sōloi |
| 103 | for | to'e au mai | read | toe 'aumai |
| 104 | for | Ua use | read | 'Ua usi |
| 104 | for | fa's soasoa | read | fa'asoasoa |
| 104 | for | fesilafaiga | read | fesilafa'iga |
| 107 | for | ili | read | fili |
| 107 | for | a'alavelave | read | fa'alavelave |
| 107 | for | ai | read | 'ae |
| 107 | for | fou'i | read | foa'i |
| 107 | for | matou te'a 'ai'ai | read | mātou te 'a'ai |
| 107 | for | ina o'o le ma'i | read | ina 'ua o'o le ma'i |
| 107 | for | toaina | read | toea'ina |
| 108 | for | olua | read | 'oulua |
| 109 | for | vavaloa | read | vāvāloloa |
| 109 | for | paū | read | pa'ū |
| 114 | for | vai | read | vāe |
| 115 | for | masiofi | read | masiofo |
| 115 | for | gasoloao | read | gāsoloao |

(Note: *gāsolo* means "to pass along," while *gasalo*, means "to slip down.")

| | | | | |
|---|---|---|---|---|
| 120 | for | malo | read | mālō |
| 121 | for | aui | read | 'aui |
| 121 | for | fa'a sa ina | read | fa'asāina |
| 121 | for | o le silo'i logi | read | 'o le sila'ilagi |
| 122 | for | tigisami | read | atigi sami |
| 122 | for | ugi | read | uga |
| 124 | for | o'a | read | 'o'a |
| 124 | for | faufa sa | read | lama |
| 124 | for | O musu | read | 'A musu |
| 125 | for | o le sol iga | read | 'o le soliga |
| 126 | for | 'o le afafine | read | 'o le afafine |
| | | ("daughter," woman speaking) | | ("daughter," man speaking) |
| 127 | for | toa'ina | read | toea'ina |
| 127 | for | olamatua | read | 'olomatua |
| 127 | for | si'au | read | sio'u |
| 128 | for | tausoga | read | tauusoga |
| 128 | for | laititi | read | la'itiiti |
| 128 | for | toalua | read | to'alua |
| 129 | for | 'o lau alo | read | 'o lou alo |

## 7.8—Social Organization of Manu'a by Margaret Mead: Some Errata

| PAGE | | | ERRATA | | |
|---|---|---|---|---|---|
| 129 | for | *paia* | read | *pa'ia* | |
| 129 | for | *'o lau alo afafine* | read | *'o lou alo fafine* | |
| 130 | for | *ila mutu* | read | *ilāmutu* | |
| 130 | for | *ava* | read | *āvā* | |
| 130 | for | *si'ou* | read | *sio'u* | |
| 131 | for | *tina* | read | *tinā* | |
| 131 | for | *a'u'o* | read | *'o a'u 'o* | |
| 131 | for | *'o lo'o uso* | read | *'o lo'u uso* | |
| 133 | for | *ua uso moni maua* | read | *'ua uso moni mā'ua* | |
| 133 | for | *suna* | read | *suga* | |
| 147 | for | Saumata'afi | read | Sauma'iafe | |
| 148 | for | Tu'i Manua | read | Tui Manu'a | |
| 150 | for | Ga'ogaooletai | read | Gaogaoletai | |
| 150 | for | Fatu (Rock) was the female | read | Fatu (Rock) was the male | |
| 150 | for | Ele'ele the male | read | 'Ele'ele the female | |
| 155 | for | *fale ua* | read | *fale 'ua ato* | |
| 156 | for | Mauna | read | Manu'a | |
| 157 | for | Taū | read | Ta'ū | |
| 157 | for | Fuilelagi | read | Fuailagi | |
| 158 | for | *fai tui* | read | *fai tu'i* | |
| 158 | for | Foisia | read | Fo'isia | |
| 158 | for | *fofoa* | read | *foafoa* | |
| 158 | for | *mali'e* | read | *laumei* | |
| 158 | for | Mafue | read | Mafui'e | |
| 159 | for | Pili vave | read | Pilitavave | |
| 159 | for | Pili pa'u | read | Pilipa'ū | |
| 159 | for | Pili tama tagi | read | Pilitaimatagi | |
| 159 | for | Tiitii | read | Ti'eti'e | |
| 159 | for | *o le 'ate* | read | *'o le ate* | |
| 160 | for | Saumatafi | read | Sauma'iafe | |
| 160 | for | *saua ali'i* | read | *sauali'i* | |
| 161 | for | o le Fafa | read | 'o le Fafā | |
| 162 | for | *fai le aso* | read | *faiaso* | |
| 166 | for | *fa'anoa* | read | *fa'anoanoa* | |
| 166 | for | *lo'u uso ua sou* | read | *lo'u uso 'ua sau* | |
| 166 | for | *pea* | read | *pe'ā* | |
| 167 | for | Soatoa | read | Sotoa | |
| 168 | for | *muao* | read | *muā'au* | |
| 168 | for | *talaiga* | read | *talā'iga* | |
| 168 | for | *talita* | read | *talitā* | |
| 168 | for | *lalafi tagata* | read | *lamalama* | |
| 168 | for | *lalama* | read | *fasioti* | |
| 169 | for | *soli le tulafono* | read | *solitulāfono* | |
| 170 | for | *mati* | read | *mata* | |
| 170 | for | *fatefea* | read | *fa'ate'a* | |

## Section 7: Publication: Responsibilities and Liabilities

| PAGE | | ERRATA | | |
|---|---|---|---|---|
| 170 | for | *fatauto* | read | *fa'autō* |
| 173 | for | Maleetoa | read | Malietoa |
| 173 | for | Manua Tale | read | Manu'a Tele |
| 174 | for | Fitiuamua | read | Fiti'aumua |
| 174 | for | *lupu le tai* | read | *tupu le tai* |
| 174 | for | *olo* | read | *'olo* |
| 174 | for | Agae | read | Aga'e |
| 176 | for | Raratonga | read | Rarotonga |
| 177 | for | Laamaomoo | read | La'amaomao |
| 177 | for | *mamoo* | read | *mamao* |
| 177 | for | Alia | read | 'Ali'a (or Li'a) |
| 178 | for | *aupola* | read | *'aupolapola* |
| 179 | for | puáa | read | pua'a |
| 179 | *fa'ai* is a dish of baked coconut cream not of "cooked bananas." | | | | |
| 180 | for | Tauānuu | read | Tauanu'u |
| 181 | for | *Solesole* | read | *sōlisōli* |
| 182 | for | *aufata* | read | *'aufata* |
| 183 | for | *fale toa* | read | *fale to'a* |
| 184 | for | Lia | read | 'Ali'a (or Li'a) |
| 185 | for | *aluali'i* | read | *atuali'i* |
| 185 | for | Etisela | read | Elisara |
| 186 | for | *Ua tua le malo o Tui Manua* | read | *'Ua tū'ua le mālō 'o le Tui Manu'a* |
| 186 | for | Sili vi vao | read | Sili'aivao |
| 187 | for | Tuiologono | read | Tuiologona |
| 190 | for | *tuloaga* | read | *tulouna* |
| 190 | for | *afia mai* | read | *afio mai* |
| 191 | for | Sama'au'ulu | read | Samala'ulu |
| 192 | for | Salaese | read | Salelesi |
| 192 | for | *'ausoga* | read | *auosoga* |
| 195 | for | *Asoau* | read | *Aso'au* |
| 196 | for | *Taapi* | read | *Ta'ape* |
| 196 | for | *fa'igata* | read | *faigatā* |
| 198 | for | Taniiliili | read | Tau'ili'ili |
| 198 | for | Mapū | read | Ma'upū |
| 198 | for | Lapui | read | La'apui |
| 198 | for | Laie | read | Lealaie'e |
| 198 | for | Galeai | read | Galea'i |
| 198 | for | Lautitlaulelei | read | Lautīlaulelei |
| 198 | for | Lapu | read | La'apui |
| 198 | for | Fale ula | read | Fale 'Ula |
| 199 | for | Lapue | read | La'apui |
| 199 | for | Alii | read | 'Ali'a (or Li'a) |
| 200 | for | *ulu* | read | *'ulu* |

## 7.8 – Social Organization of Manu'a by Margaret Mead: Some Errata

| PAGE | | | ERRATA | | |
|---|---|---|---|---|---|
| 200 | for | *fa'ava* | | read | *faiāvā* |
| 201 | for | *paoga* | | read | *paogo* |
| 201 | for | *ti'a* | | read | *tia* |
| 203 | for | Sae | | read | Sai |
| 203 | for | Lei | | read | Le'i |
| 203 | for | Taloaauau | | read | Talo'au'au |
| 203 | for | Laolagi | | read | La'olagi |
| 203 | for | Talaaoao | | read | Talo'au'au |
| 203 | for | *fetala'iga* | | read | *fetalaiga* |
| 204 | for | Taloau | | read | Talo'au'au |
| 204 | for | Leui | | read | Le'i |
| 205 | for | *itu tua* | | read | *itū i tua* |
| 205 | for | Aluuluu | | read | Ālu'ulu'u |
| 206 | for | *iu* | | read | *i'u* |
| 206 | for | *sogo* | | read | *gogo* |
| 207 | for | *fai le tui* | | read | *fai le tu'i* |
| 208 | for | *lalauili* | | read | *malauli* |
| 208 | for | Sasa | | read | Asaasa |
| 209 | for | Malemu | | read | Malemo |
| 209 | for | Malelena | | read | Malelega |
| 209 | for | Niutao | | read | Niuatoa |
| 210 | for | Laulagi | | read | La'olagi |
| 213 | for | *aiga* | | read | *'āiga* |
| 213 | for | *'aittagi* | | read | *'aitagi* |
| 213 | for | *fa'atu'uiga* | | read | *fa'atuiga* |
| 214 | *mamalu* refers to the dignity of a chief (cf. Milner, 1966:127), not to property given to validate a title | | | | |
| 214 | for | *tafolo* | | read | *taufolo* |
| 214 | for | *talolo* | | read | *ta'alolo* |
| 214 | for | *tapua* | | read | *tupua* |
| 214 | *tāpua'i* refers to the giving of sympathy (cf. Milner, 1966:243); the word for to pray is *tatalo* | | | | |
| 214 | for | *taupo* | | read | *tāupou* |
| 214 | for | *tulafona* | | read | *tulāfono* |

## NOTES

1. I wish to thank those European scholars with an expert knowledge of the Samoan language, as well as the Samoan authorities resident in Upolu, Tutuila and Manu'a who commented on sections of this paper while it was being prepared for publication. For this present version, however, I alone am responsible.
2. Announcement, of Bulletin 76 (revised), by Bishop Museum Press, 1969.
3. In her "Publisher's Preface" to the 1969 edition of *Social Organization of Manu'a,* the editor of the Bishop Museum Press states (p. vii) that "traditions in printing style change through the years," and "authors and editors feel today that the addition of the indication of the glottal stop aids the reader in pronunciation of the words in which they appear." This statement is scarcely accurate, for the importance of the correct indication

of the glottal stop in Samoan words had been firmly established by Pratt (the first edition of whose *Dictionary* was published in 1862) some years before the founding of the Bishop Museum Press, and the correct and consistent use of the inverted comma to indicate the glottal stop in Samoan words is to be found not only in the various editions of Pratt's *Grammar and Dictionary of the Samoan Language*, but also in such scholarly works of the late nineteenth and early twentieth century as Tregear's *Maori-Polynesian Comparative Dictionary*, Wellington N.Z., 1891, and Krämer's *Die Samoa-Inseln*, Stuttgart, 1902. In the main text of *Social Organization of Manu'a* (1969), the glottal stop is represented by a raised comma ('); while in the Introduction and Conclusion an inverted comma (') is used to represent this same phoneme. In this present paper, the glottal stop is represented by an *inverted* comma, the convention to be found in both Pratt's *Grammar and Dictionary of the Samoan Language* (1911) and G.B. Milner's *Samoan Dictionary* (1966).

4. Cf. Krämer 1902:32, "Wenn Miss Fraser stets von einer *taupo* oder gar *tapo* erzählt, so sollte sie doch vorsichtiger sein, denn dies heisst bei einem Mädchen 'in der Nacht Liebeshañdel treiben,' was gerade für eine *taupou* sehr unpassend ist."
5. Cf. Keesing 1934:53; Honigmann 1954:188; Sahlins 1958:30.
6. Mead 1967:304.
7. Cf. Foreword by Malietoa Tanumafili II, C.B.E., Head of State of Western Samoa, and H. Rex Lee, Governor of American Samoa, in Milner 1966:vii.
8. In October, 1967, when I first heard that a new edition of Mead's *Social Organization of Manu'a* was to be published by Bishop Museum Press I at once wrote to the Director of the Bishop Museum from Sa'anapu in Western Samoa (where I was then resident) warning him that the text of the 1930 edition contained numerous errors. The receipt of my letter was formally acknowledged, but the warning contained within it was entirely ignored.
8. In this communication I have dealt only with certain of the literal errors in Samoan which are to be found in *Social Organization of Manu'a*. I am, however, preparing for publication a general appraisal of Margaret Mead's anthropological writings on Samoa.

## REFERENCES

Honigmann, J.J., 1954. *Culture and Personality*. New York, Harper and Brothers.
Keesing, F.M., 1934. *Modern Samoa*. London, George Allen and Unwin.
Krämer, A., 1902. *Die Samoa-Inseln*. Erster Band. Stuttgart, E. Schweizerbartsche Verlagsbuchhandlung (E. Nägele).
Mead, M., 1930. *Social Organization of Manu'a*. Honolulu, Bernice P. Bishop Museum Bulletin, 76.
────── 1967. "The Rights of Primitive Peoples." *Foreign Affairs*, 45:304-18.
────── 1969. *Social Organization of Manu'a*. (Second Edition.) Honolulu, Bernice P. Bishop Museum Bulletin, 76.
Milner, G.B., 1966. *Samoan Dictionary*. London, Oxford University Press.
Pratt, G., 1911. *Grammar and Dictionary of the Samoan Language*. (Fourth Edition.) Samoa, Malua Printing Press.
Sahlins, M.D., 1958. *Social Stratification in Polynesia*. Seattle, University of Washington Press.
Tregear, E. 1891. *The Maori-Polynesian Comparative Dictionary*. Wellington, Lyon and Blair.

# SECTION 8
# RELATIONS AND RESPONSIBILITIES TO FUNDING AGENCIES

**INTRODUCTION**

To what degree does the source of funding influence the direction of research, its results, and their dissemination? These are important questions. Just as important are questions concerning how the researcher uses these funds. Despite several attempts, I was unable to obtain even disguised case materials from the government and the private foundations I approached on the ethical issues and moral dilemmas involved in funding research and the management of such funds by the recipients of grants.

Supplementary readings on the dilemmas of funding can be found in Beals (1969), Berreman (1969, 1971), Johnson (1966), Orlans (1967), and Record (1967). The Camelot affair and the problems of anthropologists working in Thailand present certain related issues. References to these can be obtained in Appendix 2.

**RELATED CASE MATERIALS IN OTHER SECTIONS**

*Section 5: Relations with Other Social Scientists and Responsibilities to the Profession:* Politics, Permits, and Professional Interests: The Rose Case.

*Section 9: Issues in Teaching:* Whether to Write a Recommendation; A Recommendation for a Fellowship.

## 8.1 – SHOULD FUNDING BE ACCEPTED?

I edit a small regional journal that is supported by subscriptions, contributions from anthropologists interested in keeping the journal alive, and an occasional small grant. The journal's subscribers reside in the various countries of the region, as well as in a number of economically developed countries. The subscription price for those in the economically developed countries is higher than for those in the underdeveloped region. This pricing arrangement is in response to the fact that the academic community in many of the countries in the region have extremely low salaries and the cost of foreign exchange is high. As a result, regional subscribers do not pay their share of the publishing and distribution costs of the journal. Their subscriptions are subsidized by the other subscriptions, as well as by grants and contributions.

As a result of this financial structure, the journal has never been able to publish as many articles as the board of editors would like, and it has never reached its potential audience in the region. There was some concern among the board of editors as to just how long the journal could survive on this basis. Consequently, when I learned the Smith Foundation was supporting the distribution of journals, textbooks, and other educational materials in the region, I approached its representative with regard to funding our journal. My idea was that the Smith Foundation might subsidize individual subscriptions in the region so that we could recapture our costs. I also suggested the foundation pay for subscriptions for libraries and other institutions in the region to insure that the journal reached a wider audience.

When I asked our board of editors for approval of this plan, one member expressed strong opposition on the basis that the Smith Foundation had served, and might still be serving, as a conduit for CIA funds. This accusation was made several years ago with allegations that the foundation had subsidized research in a country of a neighboring region that served military more than academic purposes.

At the time that I presented the funding plan to the board, however, the Smith Foundation was operating openly out of local offices in all the capitals of the countries in our region, funding a number of government-supported projects, as well as others. It thus appeared to be welcome in the various countries of the area. Since the local governments seemed to approve of its activities, and since our

## 8.1—Should Funding be Accepted?

request would provide greater access to our journal by educational institutions and the academic community, I could see no reason to refuse the foundation funding. Furthermore, it would ensure our survival as an important source of scientific intercommunication both within the region and between the regional and Western academic communities.

Should the board of editors accept funding from the Smith Foundation?

## 8.2 – DISSEMBLING ON SOURCES OF FUNDS

Henry Smith was a graduate student at the State University. His studies were supported by a program funded by the Agency for International Development. As part of his graduate training, Smith planned to conduct research on a local minorty group in a particular country. His field work would also be supported by funds from this program. Smith's supervisor cautioned him against mentioning the AID funds when applying for a visa or replying to any questions in the field. He was told to state only that his research was funded by the university program. Smith thought that inasmuch as he had a fellowship from the program he should abide by his supervisor's wishes, particularly since any revelation of AID funding of the program could jeopardize other research projects of which he might not be aware. On the other hand, this type of deception was personally distasteful to him and, in the long run, he thought it unwise. He wondered how to resolve this problem.

## 8.3–THE PROFESSOR'S DILEMMA OVER RESEARCH FUNDS

Robert Jenkins had spent a number of years doing research in a little known region in Southeast Asia among a group of hill tribes. He now had a small group of graduate students who wanted to do field work in the same region to help fill in the ethnographic map and to resolve certain anthropological problems that the region presented. Jenkins was quite concerned, however, that he might not be able to finance this research because of the current scarcity of funds.

A solution to this problem was presented to him during the recent visit of a representative from a private corporation which conducted research on contract for the government. This representative said that the corporation was interested in this area because so little was known about it and because it was believed that it might be subjected to Communist influence in the near future. Consequently, the representative said that his corporation might supply the funds necessary to support his graduate students in the field with "no strings attached." Also, there would be no restriction on the publication of results, and Jenkins could be completely open about this source of funds.

The corporation would require periodic reports on the progress and results of the research, but these should contain no information that could not be published elsewhere. The researchers would also be interviewed on their return by a representative of the corporation, but they would not have to answer any questions they did not wish to. Finally, the corporation wanted information relating to the aspirations of the people in the area, but this material should also be publishable in scholarly journals.

Jenkins weighed the problem in his mind, trying to decide whether or not to accept the funding. He wondered what his responsibilities were in this matter and to whom.

## 8.4—A FAILURE TO PREPARE FOR THE FIELD

George Farley planned to study a village in the Middle East. As the village was Muslim, he decided to take a female graduate student along to work with the women of the community. His selection of a field worker was not difficult; for the past two years he had been training a young woman who showed unusual capabilities. When he approached Emily Brown with his research plans, she eagerly agreed to join Farley's project since she would be able to use some of the material for her dissertation.

Farley applied for and received a grant to conduct his two-year study. Part of the grant was to cover a three-month period of preparation during the summer in which Brown would learn the local language and review the available literature on the region. Farley arranged for Brown to work with a language informant and directed that her support allowance be paid from the grant starting in June. Farley, meanwhile, lectured at another university during the summer.

When Farley returned in September, he learned that Brown had become romantically entangled with a man and had failed to follow through on her language lessons or her other studies. She had, however, continued to draw her stipend from the grant. Thus, not only was there no time to locate another assistant, there were no funds to pay another assistant, even if Farley could find one. Farley wondered what his responsibilities were to the granting agency and what he could do to rescue the situation.

## 8.5 – A REQUEST FROM THE NATIONAL FOUNDATION TO REVIEW A RESEARCH PROPOSAL

Eight years ago I returned from field work in a country in Africa. I had lived for eighteen months in a small village inhabited by a minority ethnic group. At that time, the village was in the process of moving into a money economy, and I was interested in returning at a later date to see what long-term social changes accompanied this change in economy. However, I was unable to obtain leave from my teaching commitments until I was scheduled for a sabbatical year.

At that time, I made plans to spend nine months studying the changes which had occurred in the village. I also looked forward to seeing my close friends and informants there. I applied to several foundations for funds to cover my field expenses. Meanwhile, I heard some disquieting news. A graduate student, Walter Stone, was planning to do research in the same village over the same period of time. Stone had worked for an international community development group and had spent almost a year in the village a few years before, helping the agricultural officer who was stationed there.

I talked the situation over with a friend who knew Stone; he offered to talk to Stone about his plans. My friend reported that Stone was not disturbed about the possibility of working in the same village with me and perhaps competing for informants. In fact, he apparently thought it offered him a good opportunity to learn field-work techniques by watching me at work in the field. He refused to consider relocating his research to any other of the nearby villages of the ethnic group. However, Stone did seem to indicate that if necessary he could delay his field work for six to nine months, since he had not yet completed all his curriculum requirements for a Ph.D.

I met Stone at a regional meeting of African specialists. I told him about my research plans and explained that this would be my only chance to return for a number of years. I also told him that I would find it awkward to have another anthropologist in residence in such a small village, where we would be competing for the same informants and could end up working at cross purposes.

But my argument did not sway Stone. He replied that he did not see any reason for conflict, and he was very excited about working in the same village with me and learning from my field work. He was now unwilling to consider any delay in order to minimize or prevent the overlap of our research.

A month later I received a request from the National Foundation to review Stone's research proposal and give my recommendations on it. I wondered what I should do.

# SECTION 9
# ISSUES IN TEACHING

**INTRODUCTION**

The instructor-student relationship can be rich and rewarding. It can also be full of moral dilemmas and liable to abuse. This is largely because this relationship involves multiple, overlapping roles all of which are structured in terms of dominance and subordination. When this is concentrated in one social relationship, tyranny is often fostered and creativity inhibited (Appell 1973a; cf. Harris 1971). I refer here to the roles concerned with evaluating course performance, raising funds for dissertation research, evaluating qualifying examinations, reading dissertations, writing recommendations, etc.

This multiple role structure is not necessary for the teaching of the social sciences. In fact, many foreign universities segregate these roles. Outside instructors are required for oral examinations, one of whom is there to represent the student's interests; and outside readers are required for dissertations. This procedure minimizes the impact of personal biases which may affect a student's entire career.

The adaptation required of the student to deal with this multiple role set is not conducive to the development of ethical concern. For the student may resort to manipulating his instructors opportunistically and behaving in such a way as to create a favorable image. Thus, it is his hope that he can escape with his degree before he reveals aspects of this personality that might be detrimental to his professional advancement and before his instructors learn that the interest he evinces in their work is not as deeply seated as he may have indicated.

On the other hand, there are instructors who are afraid to reveal themselves to their students and yet may inadvertently do so. They are wary of developing a friendship with a student, fearing that the student may merely be motivated by the wish to achieve good grades and professional recognition. Some instructors retreat to a formal pedagogical position because of the ambiguities in the relationship.

As a result, it is not unusual for students to escape with a feeling of having been personally abused as a result of the mercurial temperment of their major advisors.

But the crises of moral leadership in the social sciences do not stem only from the potential risks and abuses inherent in the instructor-student relationship. They can also be attributed to the overriding demand for intellectual performance at the cost of developing moral intelligence and ethical concerns. We need to devise a measure of moral development and encourage its growth as we do intellectual development.

Certain issues in the teaching of the social sciences are not covered in the cases in this section. For example, I believe that the social scientist teaching at the undergraduate level should stress the humanistic interpretation of social experience to avoid contributing to the growing dehumanization which characterizes many of our social relationships. Thus, courses should not provide students with the perspective or the tools that would encourage them to attempt the manipulation of social systems and their members (cf. Myers 1969 for a discussion of the dangers in this but with a different conclusion). Instead, such approaches should be largely confined to the graduate level, where proper safeguards can and should be instituted. Graduate training in ethical decision making should be required to teach the researcher to weigh the deleterious uses to which his research might be put against its possible contribution toward human welfare (Appell 1973a, p. 22).

Finally, the common practice in American anthropology of sending graduate students into the field with minimal training, preparation, and supervision should raise considerable professional concern. It is this aspect of teaching that has its clearest relevance to professional responsibilities. Far too often, the unsupervised neophyte creates a situation in the field which makes future social inquiry there unwelcome.

**RELATED CASE MATERIALS IN OTHER SECTIONS**

*Section 5: Relations with Other Social Scientists and Responsibilities to the Profession:* Dealing with Animosity Arising from a Previous Study.

*Section 8: Relations and Responsibilities to Funding Agencies:* A Failure to Prepare for the Field.

## 9.1 – THE INTRODUCTION OF DEVIANT IDEAS BY THE INSTRUCTOR

The researcher, who, as an outsider, enters a community and begins to ask certain questions, may unwittingly be introducing new, discordant ideas into the community or bringing to consciousness sentiments which before were only latent, as with regard to racial prejudice. An instructor faces a similar kind of problem. In the process of teaching he may not only be introducing new ideas to his students, he may act as a catalyst in their adoption of these ideas. This is a particularly difficult problem when dealing with deviancy.

As part of a graduate course in deviancy which I taught, I asked my students to focus on a particular form of deviancy and interview a sample of deviants. One young woman had read a book on wife swapping and asked my permission to investigate that subject, which I granted. At the end of the semester, she gave me a paper on the subject and told me she wanted to talk with me about it. In our conversation, she told me how the research was carried out. When she went to interview a couple, she took her husband along. In one of these interviews, the couple argued so convincingly in favor of wife swapping that she and her husband decided to try it. They subsequently joined a wife-swapping group.

My moral dilemma as an instructor is that, as a result of my course in deviancy, one of my students became involved in a situation which is defined by our society as immoral and certainly illegal, since it involves adultery. To what degree am I responsible for this behavior as a teacher? Also, what was this student's responsibility as a researcher to remain objective in the face of persuasion by informants to deviate from her own normal behavior?

## 9.2—A PROFESSOR FAILS IN HIS PROMISE

Janet Osgood knocked hesitantly on Dr. Peter Musgrave's door—as she had a rather unusual request. During the summer she wanted to do a social-anthropological study of the Indian community from which Musgrave drew the labor for his archaeological dig. Musgrave however seemed to respond enthusiastically to her research plans and encouraged her to join his dig the following summer. He suggested that she write up a research proposal and submit it to him for the necessary formal approval. Osgood was excited by Musgrave's backing of her research and quickly prepared her proposal and sent it to him.

Two weeks later, when she had heard nothing further from Musgrave, Osgood wondered if department funds were insufficient to support her research. She mentioned her worry to a fellow student and got a rude jolt. The student, who was a member of a radical group in the department, told her that he regularly wandered past the secretaries' desks in the department office to see if he could pick up any information. About a week ago, he had been in the department office and had read her proposal, which was lying on a secretary's desk. Musgrave had appended a note to her application stating that it was not to be approved.

Osgood was furious, largely because she felt powerless in this situation. Later, when her initial anger had somewhat subsided, she wondered what courses of action, if any, were open to her.

## 9.3 – WHETHER TO WRITE A RECOMMENDATION

Professor Patterson of State University was Larry Green's supervisor. Green had been unable to find funds to support his graduate research. At a meeting to discuss various ways out of this predicament, Green proposed a plan for Patterson's approval.

Green would enroll in the Ph.D. program of a university in another country. He would assume immigrant status in the country and apply to the Government Research Institute for funds to carry out his research. However, Green assured Patterson that he really planned to return to State University to write his Ph.D. dissertation for Patterson's department. Green described his research plans and asked Patterson, "Would you recommend me to the department at National University and to the Government Research Institute with regard to my field project?"

## 9.4—A STUDENT RECOUNTS HIS NATIONAL FOUNDATION INTERVIEW

Ray Davidson listened in amazement as his student, Frank Sawyer, recounted his reactions to his National Foundation interview. Sawyer had applied for funds to support research for his dissertation and had just recently been interviewed by a foundation representative with regard to his application. He sat across the desk from Davidson, laughing and obviously enjoying his success in "faking out the National Foundation people." Sawyer had flunked his oral exams during the spring term but did not reveal this to his interviewer. Instead, Sawyer told him that he was scheduled to take his orals in the late autumn. The interviewer hinted that Sawyer was very likely to receive funding if he passed his orals.

After Sawyer left the office, Davidson wondered what he should do. Although Sawyer had failed his oral exams the first time, he was a good student, and Davidson felt that he would pass the next time. However, he was concerned whether a student with this attitude toward the truth would become a reliable scientist, and whether he might be tempted to skew his data to support his hypotheses. Should Davidson inform the National Foundation representative of Sawyer's deception?

## 9.5 – A CASE OF UNCREDITED EDITORIAL WORK

Early in my graduate studies, I was asked to do some editorial work for one of the faculty members in my department, with whom I am quite friendly. This professor had submitted a lengthy paper to a journal. It was accepted on condition that it be reduced to half its present length and substantially reorganized, with grammatical errors corrected. The professor asked me if I would help him since I had a reputation in the department for being able to write well.

I agreed to help with the paper. In reorganizing it, cutting its length, and correcting the errors, I literally rewrote it. The resubmitted paper was then accepted for publication, but when it appeared I discovered that I had received no credit for having assisted in editing.

I now wondered whether I should have received credit in a footnote for my work on the paper, and if so, what should I now do.

## 9.6 – A MATTER OF A TEACHING CONTRACT

The chairman of the Department of Anthropology at State University was talking with the head of the sociology department at Stone College, a small, four-year institution with no graduate program. The anthropology chairman learned from his colleague that Stone College had given a former anthropology student, Sam Norwood, a teaching contract, with the understanding that Norwood would soon take his oral exams as part of his Ph.D. requirements at State University.

The chairman did not know how to respond to his colleague's remarks. The previous year they had given Norwood a terminal M.A. Normally, the chairman would have corrected the misconception in regard to Norwood's academic status. However, he had just heard that Norwood had lost one of his children in a tragic fire. And he suspected that Norwood would be an excellent teacher even if he was not qualified to handle the complexities of research and theory formation that a Ph.D. program required.

## 9.7 – A RECOMMENDATION FOR A FELLOWSHIP

During my third year in graduate school, my advisor, David Johnston, suggested that I apply for an important fellowship in a foreign university that would permit me to carry on my planned field work. He said that he would provide a strong recommendation.

The fellowship application was extensive, including several questions about activities outside of my graduate studies and means of financial support. I replied truthfully, noting the part-time work I was engaged in. This fulfilled an obligation I had to manage and settle the small estate of my mother's late husband, and it also provided me with financial support for my studies. I sent the completed application to the fellowship committee and gave a copy to Johnston.

Several days later, Johnston called me into his office and demanded that I recall my application and delete the information about my part-time employment. Otherwise, he said, he would refuse to recommend me for the fellowship. He appeared highly agitated and would not explain his reasons for this ultimatum.

I wrote the fellowship committee to request that they return my application so I could make certain amendations to it. I resubmitted the application with the mention of outside work deleted, as Johnston had requested. I knew I was not being completely honest, but I felt I had little choice in the matter. I needed the fellowship to support my field research and knew of no other sources of funds which were available at that time.

I received the fellowship and was able to pursue my research. The fellowship committee found my work of sufficient value to suggest that I consider extending my time at the university and return to the field for another period. However, I had planned to return home at the end of the original fellowship to complete my obligations with regard to settling my stepfather's estate. I now found I was in an awkward position. Before I could continue my research on the extension of the fellowship, I had to apply for a leave of absence to deal with these personal matters. Yet these activities had been carefully hidden from the fellowship committee. I wondered how I should now proceed.

## SECTION 10
## MISCELLANEOUS

## 10.1—ETHICAL DILEMMAS IN ANTHROPOLOGICAL FIELD WORK

In 1952, in the early months of my first fieldtrip to South India, a group of my neighbors captures a suspected rapist, tied him to a post about twenty feet from my window, and began slapping him and spitting in his face. Awakened at three o'clock in the morning by the shouts of the crowd and the cries of the victim, I lay in the security of my mosquito tent wondering what to do. My options seemed to be (1) to pretend to be asleep, (2) to adopt the Sahib role and rush out to stop the violence, and (3) to observe the events dispassionately entering a meticulous account in my notebook. Although the third option is only weakly supported by the ethic of the neutral scientific observer, the first two options appeared to me to be supported by strong moral imperatives. The option of pretending to be asleep appeared to conform to the moral imperative that a stranger and guest should not meddle in events which do not concern him and which he does not understand. The option of active intervention seemed supported by moral imperatives shared by both South Indian and United States cultures and having to do with the immorality of violence and the importance of human life.

In the end, I adopted the option of pretending to be asleep. This, I felt, made the point that I disapproved of what was going on, but at the same time expressed the view that I had no intention of acting as moral arbiter in the village. The next morning, the suspected rapist was still alive and the case entered more normal channels of adjudication. This case appears to bear on the general question of the extent to which the social responsibility of the anthropologist in the field applies to the welfare of individuals who are clearly in need of help. Is it, in fact, immoral to do research when there are individuals who need help, or is it, in fact, immoral to expend resources on individuals when they might be expended in the search for general solutions to the problems which cause individual suffering?

In another village, I was quartered in a building adjoining a room occupied by a family of transient laborers. Their baby had recently fallen into a fire and its face

---

By Alan R. Beals. Reprinted from *The Piltdown Newsletter* Vo. 3, No. 3, Spring 1972, pp. 1-3, with permission of the author and publisher.

was severely burned. Although the baby urgently required medical treatment, the parents were doing nothing and were, in fact, systematically starving it to death. Over several nights, as I listened to the baby cry, I entertained the idea of snatching it up and taking it sixty miles away to the nearest hospital. Because, in the end, I would have no option but to return the scarred baby to its parents, I delayed my decision and the baby died. Although I often think of my behavior on that occasion as callous and inhuman, a violation of a deeply held ethical principle, I sometimes rationalize my behavior on the grounds that any action on my part would have had the effect of prolonging death rather than saving life.

One of the reasons that cases of this sort constituted moral dilemmas, at least for me, was that I was never able to formulate clear-cut policies concerning appropriate ways of handling them. At other times, I found medical assistance for individuals and I intervened in village affairs in order to prevent injustices or what I thought were injustices. In some of these cases of intervention, my efforts were greeted with considerable success. In other cases, I am not so sure. For example, one of my ways of helping others was to provide free aspirin tablets. In one village, I was disconcerted when I discovered that the aspirin tablets were regarded as a cure for malaria. I have no way of knowing to what extent my efforts as a medical practitioner led particular individuals to delay or avoid medical treatment they should have had. In a few cases, where individuals were suffering from leprosy or tuberculosis, I forced them to go to the hospital and paid in advance for their treatment. In almost all of these cases, the individuals involved halted the course of treatments too soon and eventually died. Although the picture of the anthropologist standing silently by the bedside of a dying man with his hands folded is horrifying, the picture of the anthropologist playing doctor or social worker is not much more encouraging.

For those who feel that anthropology is worth doing, the solution to this particular moral dilemma would appear to involve some sort of balance between the carrying out of fieldwork, especially fieldwork that might ultimately prove useful in solving problems as the delivery of medical care, and the carrying out of welfare activities designed to help those in need. But the middle way between the adoption of an attitude of callous professionalism and the development of an incompetent sentimentality is difficult to follow.

A second variety of moral dilemma has to do with the fieldworker's response to the question: "Which side are you on?" In a village located within a national forest, which I visited in 1952, a group of village leaders, allied with rapacious forest officials, were systematically exploiting, in fact looting, the village. In this case, the guilt feelings of the forest officials and their strong hostility toward me and my field assistants automatically placed me on the side of the underdog, but it still left me with the choice of doing nothing or taking some kind of action. I accumulated a list of a variety of cases of looting, bribe-taking, and extortion and forwarded the list to the government official in charge of the region. Having fulfilled my duty in this manner, I promptly left India leaving my friends and informants to face the consequences of my action. Because my detailed notes clearly revealed the identity of the village and concealed only the names of my informants, it was easy for me, after I returned home, to imagine that there would be retaliation against the village and my informants. When I returned to India seven years later, I discovered that high ranking government officials had visited the village and, on the basis of formal hearings, had administered punishment to the guilty forest officials and permanently halted the practice of looting forest villages. Perhaps coincidentally, the village had been given a government school with an outstanding school teacher, a post office had been established in a nearby town, and the village had become involved in a highly profitable dairy industry.

Here, a violation of the moral imperative that requires us to conceal the identity of those we study led to results that some would find morally unchallengeable. I would not consider repeating such an action, and I firmly believe that my success was the result of that special providence that watches over lunatics and mental incompetents.

In 1952, in search of an urban influenced village to study, I selected Namhalli, largely because of the warm welcome given to me by a group of young men who referred to themselves as the "educated class." I had no way of knowing that these young men represented a faction in a village riven with conflict. Despite this poor introduction, I managed to maintain a certain semblance of neutrality. Finally, on an August evening, a question arose as to whether or not the village deity, being carried in procession by members of the "educated class," should be permitted to pass a tamarind tree belonging to the opposed faction. There were threats on both sides and one man came screaming from his house swinging an enormous two-handed sword. At this point a group of village women began urging me and my two field assistants, one of whom was a prestigious man from outside the village and one of whom was a member of the "educated class," to take some action to stop the conflict. While we argued, my field assistant's older brother raised the branches of the tamarind tree with a rope and the deity passed safely beneath it. In this case, fears for my personal safety and a determined desire to maintain a professional neutrality caused me to adopt a do-nothing stance.

Continuation of the factionalist dispute was harmful to a number of individuals and costly to the village as a whole. Perhaps, at the cost of choosing sides, I could have brought the dispute to an early end. At that time I was convinced that the members of the "educated class" were underdogs, progressives and generally good guys. It was much later that I discovered that they were no more educated, no more progressive, and no more worthy of support than their opponents.

In 1960, I was welcomed to the village of Gopalpur by its wealthy headman or *gavda*. When it became clear that my wife's prolonged illness, which later turned out to be pregnancy, would make it necessary for us to employ a servant, the *gavda* sent a young man to work for us suggesting that we pay him a low wage and make sure that he did not go home at night to visit his wife. We found out later that the young man had been accused of stealing from the *gavda's* tamarind tree and that he had been assigned to work for us as a punishment. When it turned out that we were generous employers, our servant's brothers-in-law, who belonged to a different lineage and were friendly with the *gavda*, became intensely jealous.

Our servant now became one of the central figures in a developing and village-wide conflict. Because of my wife's pregnancy, I attempted to develop a situation in which our servant, ourselves and our property would be left alone by the warring factions. In recent history, factional conflict (in Gopalpur) had led to three deaths. A few days after we had secured solemn promises from both parties regarding the sanctity of ourselves and our servant, the enemy faction beat our servant and several members of his faction in the course of a religious ritual (Moharrum) that my wife and I were attending.

Out of simple paranoia, I now openly assisted my servant and his faction in reporting the incident to the police and obtaining written contracts from both factions promising an end to the dispute. There was no further violence during our stay in the village, but the conflict was resumed the moment we left.

In reviewing these three incidents of conflict, it is apparent that the presence of an anthropological fieldworker can vitally affect both the intensity of conflict and its outcome. Although on balance it seems probable that people are less violent in the presence of a person who might be considered a reliable witness, it must also be accepted that some of my deliberate or unwitting activities might have exacerbated or even created conflicts. In two of the cases, my presence decisively affected the balance of power between conflicting groups. In all three cases, my identification with one side or the other was determined by forces I did not control. It might also be noted that these conflicts, which I did not seek and which were unrelated to the research I had in mind, had a profound influence upon the data that I collected and upon the theoretical perspectives that I later developed. From a moral or ethical standpoint, the fieldworker who chooses sides or is compelled to choose sides must always consider his knowledge of the situation and the possible productivity or counter-productivity of his actions. The fieldworker who abandons a conflict situation to study another village or group behaves ethically if his departure mitigates the conflict, but what if it makes it worse?

A third variety of moral dilemma has to do with the kinds of responsibilities acquired by the fieldworker with regard to the groups and individuals who help him with his fieldwork. Here, an absence of compensation can be regarded as exploitation, while the presence of compensation may be regarded as a disruptive force or as an ineffective gesture. As the case from Gopalpur, in which we overcompensated our servant, indicates, payment to individuals can seriously disrupt social relationships. If it fails to do so, it may be because the intended recipient of the gift or payment didn't get it. Particularly in Gopalpur, but to some extent in Namhalli and the forest village, we discovered that gifts of cash generally ended up in the hands of those who were already wealthy. Gifts of clothing and other valuables, while they did not move so far up the social scale, were generally transmitted to older brothers or more prestigious members of the recipient's family. In the end, we found that the only personally useful gifts or payments that we could make to individuals were gifts that could be consumed on the spot or that were of such negligible value that nobody else wanted them.

In each of the three villages where I have worked, there has been an expectation that I would render some sort of regular contribution to the village. This has usually taken the form of a distribution of photographs, medicines, petition typing services, free advice and so on. I have also been asked to make normal contributions, sometimes rich man's contributions, to such projects as temple construction, treats for the school children or supplies for festivals. Such gifts have sometimes been stolen or sometimes lined the pockets of the already wealthy, but, on the whole, as long as my gifts reflected local custom, they seem to have been regarded as helpful and adequate compensation. The total value of my gifts never approached the value of the services that people performed for me, and I cast about for a means of providing just compensation for value received.

In the forest village in 1966, I was asked to help with a petition which would give people permanent title to the forest lands which they were then cultivating. The petition was never answered. When I returned home and looked at a map, I discovered that unbeknownst to me or to them, Salem District had been divided into two new districts. The petition had been sent to the wrong place and had probably ended up in the wastebasket.

In Namhalli, the "educated class" decided that I should donate a library to the village. Shortly after I left, the books belonging to the Berkeley Union Library were stolen. Just before I returned, six years later, the "educated class," now labelled "factory workers," subscribed to a number of magazines and established a reading room. Thus, the Berkeley Union Library may not have been completely in vain.

In Gopalpur in 1966, at the height of the worst drought in nearly a hundred years, I was prevailed upon to participate in a scheme to pump water to the dessicating rice fields of the village. The scheme cost me a great deal of time and money and the village sacrificed a great deal of free labor. With my experience of irrigation in California, I anticipated that the project would be a success and was bitterly disappointed when it failed. People in Gopalpur, with their experience of irrigation in India, were delighted when the project almost succeeded. I found little pleasure in their praise of my failure.

It is difficult to estimate the value of the information which people give to the anthropologist and it is difficult to estimate the value of the anthropologist's services to those he studies. It is not clear whether fair payment to those being studied should be calculated in terms of the going wage or in terms of the possible benefits to the anthropologist. A payment which cannot be retained by the recipient or which may even be injurious to him is no payment at all. The fact that the middle class life style of the anthropologist is supported by some of the most poverty stricken people in the world can hardly be a source of satisfaction to us even though we may often claim to be the only advocates they possess. How can we reward those whose life circumstances guarantee that any significant reward will be ineffective, disruptive or a source of their further exploitation? May we resign ourselves to the faint hope that our future publications will somehow help to lead them to utopia?

In reviewing the moral dilemmas connected with helping individuals, choosing sides, and paying dues, I do not wish to suggest that we can forget about ethics because real-life situations are too complicated. The written and unwritten codes of professional ethics which govern the conduct of anthropologists in the field contain moral absolutes which are worthy of respect. I would not engage in clandestine research; I would not lie to my informants about my activities; and I would not knowingly publish research that would be harmful to them. At the same time, the fact that there are some things which a professional anthropologist should never do, and some things that should be done only under the most bizarre and extreme circumstances, should not lead us to the innocent conviction that there are simple solutions to the ethical problems of anthropological fieldwork.

There undoubtedly exist many more kinds of ethical and moral dilemmas than I have mentioned here, and it seems to me that the problem of ensuring ethical professional conduct among anthropological fieldworkers rests more importantly upon our ability to cope with the moral dilemmas which affect us all than with our ability to handle those malign or insensitive individuals who knowingly violate ethical codes.

For most fieldworkers, the question is not whether one should injure one's informants or not, but what to do in situations where almost any conceivable action, including abandonment of the research project, seems likely to produce injury. Although a genuine moral dilemma does not admit an easy solution, I am convinced that my own conduct in the field, and presumably that of others, would have been much improved if I had had a greater awareness of the kinds of moral dilemmas that others had encountered and a knowledge of the kinds of solutions to such dilemmas that other fieldworkers had attempted. While it is exciting and sometimes instructive to consider the errors of the past or cases involving the deliberate violation of professional ethics, practical improvements might best be accomplished through the accumulation of case materials designed to instruct future anthropologists concerning the moral dilemmas they are likely to encounter in the field. As Joseph Jorgensen has suggested, " . . . a normative ethic for anthropologists can be based only on the understanding we develop from our experiences in human encounters."

## 10.2—WHEN A RESEARCH PROPOSAL TURNS OUT TO BE A FLOP

This case deals with the problems encountered in undertaking work among the Bororaminga, a widely dispersed Muslim group in West Africa. The Bororaminga have attracted the interest of development specialists because, until recently, the regions they occupy have been relatively untouched by modern civilization. During the last decade, however, international development agencies and national community development authorities have initiated a large number of projects in the area.

### PREPARATION FOR FIELD RESEARCH

Although the Bororaminga themselves have not been studied by an ethnographer, several closely related groups have been investigated extensively. Therefore, I did not believe that a general ethnography need be the primary focus of my research. As the Bororaminga were undergoing extensive technological acculturation and American Protestant missionaries were active in their region, my research interests were to determine whether there was any relationship between technological acculturation and religious acculturation.

Initial library research indicated that a group of American Protestant missionaries had undertaken the establishment of a colony among the Bororaminga. All sources reported the nature of the colonizing effort quite clearly. American colonists would be brought in to live with acculturated Bororaminga. The Americans agreed to construct a school, hospital, and agricultural station; provide other public services; and train the natives in the maintenance and operation of these facilities. In addition, the missionaries agreed to survey and prepare a railroad right of way up the escarpment isolating the Bororaminga from the coast. My letters to the evangelizing sect remained unanswered.

I obtained a research grant from the University Institute of International Studies, which, in turn, was funded by a private foundation. The grant was specifically earmarked for studies of administrative assistance given by any United States source (private, governmental, or otherwise) on the African continent; the mission colony satisfied both the requirements of the grant and my own interests.

## INITIAL FIELD EXPERIENCES

In the national capital, a French anthropologist warned me that the missionaries working in the colony were likely to be uncooperative. However, my discussions with others in the capital were more encouraging.

I spent several days in the district capital of the Bororaminga region, establishing a temporary home for my family. At the end of my first week there, I traveled to the missionary settlement sixty miles away to make initial contacts and to begin preparations for settling in the new community. In the colony, however, I found that the Frenchman's predictions were accurate. The only person who talked freely with me was a German cattleman who had taken the job of caring for the colony herds out of economic motive rather than missionary zeal.

The colony contained only three Americans and their families—all temporary administrative and technical personnel. In the five years since the colony was begun, only one American family had chosen to live there permanently, and they had been asked to leave in less than a year because they were more bother than they were worth. No Bororaminga colonists had been given land. No hospital had been established. Agricultural experimentation had been abandoned as soon as it appeared that only cattle raising could rapidly repay the funds expended on the railway roadbed.

However, a school had been built to teach the mandatory first three grades to the children of the 200 Bororaminga men employed in clearing and planting pasturage and tending the cattle. Contact between Americans and Bororaminga was minimal, and even missionizing had stopped. It became clear that all previous reports were hoaxes or were based on misinformation perpetuated by the mission group in an effort to hide their failure, lest they be asked to leave the country before they could recoup their large investments. Whatever the reasons for the false reports, it was clear that the colony was not suitable for study.

## THE PREDICAMENT AND ITS SOLUTION

The feelings of frustration that I experienced were nearly devastating. The discovery that months of planning and effort and the problems and dangers of bringing a family into a field situation were all for nothing can destroy a man's confidence. I also realized that unless I could soon begin a project that fell within the purview of a study of United States administrative assistance, my grant would be withdrawn. I was panicked. I point this out because a field worker's emotional condition is of immense importance in determining the likelihood of his success. I knew I had to act in order to stay in the field. In my case, action—the active search for a substitute project—also proved to be the best medicine for depression.

I considered several alternative projects. I met and talked with an American who knew of another group of American missionaries operating medical stations among the more remote non-Bororaminga in the bush. He indicated that about twenty-five or thirty American families were living near the administrative and supply station of this group; perhaps something might be found there. I had no liking for missionaries, but for several reasons I decided to check into the situation. First, my project had been largely concerned with religious acculturation, and I wished to salvage as much of the original research plan as possible. Second, nearly a month

## 10.2 – When a Research Proposal Turns Out to be a Flop

had gone by since my arrival in the country, and I felt that I had accomplished nothing. If I could obtain data from English speakers, my field work might be accomplished according to the original schedule.

I visited the supply station and discussed my new research plans openly with the administrators of this group. They were willing to do what they could to help. They also told me of two neighboring Bororaminga villages that I might find interesting to investigate. On closer inspection, it turned out that one of these villages was not inhabited by Bororaminga but by members of other communities who had recently become "Bororamingafied." The village had recently been established by immigrants who performed menial tasks for the missionaries at the supply station. These people were openly hostile to white people. I was quite confident, however, that eventually I could establish sufficient rapport to carry out field work in this community. But first I decided to visit the other village near the mission supply base.

This second village was an old Bororaminga community that had preceded the missionaires in the area by at least two generations. The members of this village also worked at the supply station, but as a rule they were occupied in more technically skilled jobs. They were friendly and cooperative, indicating that they would welcome an anthropologist in their midst.

A study conforming to the requirements of my grant could be carried on in either village. In the case of the non-Bororaminga village, the study would focus on community development: How had these immigrants from several different communities achieved internal order in their new setting? Was there extensive influence from the American mission station or were organizational patterns strictly indigenous? A study in the second village would be only slightly different than originally planned, since acculturation was readily apparent to the villagers and missionaries alike. I chose the Bororaminga village to work in because of several factors that would facilitate the field work. First, the Bororaminga village was more receptive to my presence as a researcher. Second, the physical conditions of the village were more conducive to my study plans. There was more vegetation than in the other village and the houses were larger. Finally, the location of the Bororaminga village on a river meant that transportation in and out would be easy and my family could enjoy themselves more there.

The research advantages were significant as well. I knew little about the aboriginal organization of the tribes which the members of the first village came from. I could not be sure which patterns were aboriginal, which had been picked up from the Bororaminga and which were a result of interaction with the missionaries. This problem was not present in the second village. The latter met all the grant requirements. Administrative changes had taken place within the community; they were a direct result of contact with the American community; and, in many cases, they were copies or modifications of American patterns. One feature that would make the study especially interesting was the fact that no attempts had been made by the Americans to bring these changes about. The administrative assistance in this case was strictly unintentional.

I completed plans to move into this village and rented a large hut for myself and my family. I began to attend public meetings and celebrations in the Bororaminga village in order to conduct preliminary research and give the villagers the chance to get used to my presence. I also began to establish friendships with some of the people and participated in their work parties and other social events. In addition, I began a census of the community.

Within a week, my work was proceeding smoothly and I had regained what confidence I had lost as a result of the earlier setbacks. However, during the second week, when I was asking an old man about the history of the community, I was told that "somebody had asked these questions before." I soon had confirmed that another anthropologist had visited the community in the recent past.

After extensive questioning of village authorities and missionaries, I finally learned the identity of the anthropologist who had preceded me. Not that the information was secret; rather, the villagers could remember only her first name, and although many of the missionaries knew that "someone" had been doing "something" over there, no one seemed to know who the someone was. She turned out to be a young Bororaminga graduate student at the National University, who was temporarily working at an office job in the district capital. I called on her, and she was obviously pleased to meet an American anthropologist. She had conducted sporadic preliminary research in the village, she told me, and intended to continue her work until she could obtain enough material for a thesis. However, she encouraged me to pursue my studies in the village, noting that our interests were somewhat different.

I decided that despite her encouragement, it would be professionally unethical to continue my research in the village. Therefore, I stopped working there and began to search elsewhere for a suitable project, one that would match my own interests and the limitations of my grant. By this time—nearly two months after my arrival in the field—I was so disappointed at having to change my project a second time, that I completely overlooked the possibility of studying the other community located near the mission supply station. I began a new approach to locating a place to study.

Fortunately, the first two months had not been a complete waste of time. I was learning much about the general characteristics of Bororaminga culture, becoming reasonably proficient in the language, and meeting a number of people who could give me valuable assistance in resolving my problems. Especially important in this regard were government representatives in the Bororaminga District Office.

One of these officials was a young agronomist who was responsible for carrying out community development programs in the region. He had been enthusiastic about my research plans. When he learned of my new predicament, he suggested two villages which I might wish to study. One was an isolated village which was being reorganized as a commercial cooperative—its initial experience with Westernization. Because reorganization was being carried out by a national agency almost wholly financed by the Agency for International Development, the situation met most of the requirements of my grant. The other village was a recently established colony which was also being reorganized and by the same government agency. The primary difference between the two communities lay in the fact that this second village was composed of highly Westernized Bororaminga rather than unacculturated natives.

## 10.2—When a Research Proposal Turns Out to be a Flop

Again I weighed the alternatives. Should I work among the unacculturated group, producing a basic ethnography as well as collecting data to meet the requirements of my grant? Or should I work among the Westernized group, focusing on the formation of the cooperative structure and the impact of the national development agency—the aim of the grant—with the collection of general ethnographic data as a secondary aim? The latter course was taken for several reasons, again, including those associated with personal and family comforts. However, by this time we had all become accustomed to life in the field, so that personal considerations seemed less important than they had at the outset. The time factor was most significant at this point. With less than ten months left to spend in the field, I thought it best to concentrate on a narrow topic. Also, it seemed likely that another anthropologist would be studying a group of isolated Bororaminga before long. It seemed more important to study the effects of rapid Westernization occurring in that region. This choice was admittedly influenced by my concern with international political developments.

## 10.3 – DIFFICULT CHILDBIRTH IN AFRICA

In 1960 I was a community development officer in an African country. While visiting a village located about ninety miles from the nearest hospital, I was approached one evening by the local medical aide who ran a small dispensary. He asked my assistance in trying to persuade some people that they must send a woman to the hospital at once; he also asked me to drive her to district headquarters where the hospital was located.

After walking over rough terrain for half a mile, we arrived at the sick woman's hut, where several people were clustered outside. The situation soon became clear. The woman had been in labor since the day before but had not yet been delivered of the child. I offered to take her to the hospital, but the husband and relatives were adamantly opposed. She had had four children before this, they said, why should she have trouble with this one? In vain the medical aide and I argued that the child might be twisted or jammed. This did not help at all; on the contrary, it was a further argument for them. Why should there be any problem unless the woman had been guilty of some offense? We continued to argue, but to no avail. It would have been almost impossible to carry the woman in the dark over the rocky route we had traversed and then drive the ninety miles over badly rutted roads. Therefore, I told the family that I would return at four in the morning so that we could get her to the car and begin the trip to the hospital just before dawn. I hoped that in the meanwhile, and in my absence, they might decide to send her. At four o'clock I returned, but she was dead.

Several years later I was carrying out research on a village settlement scheme in the eastern section of the country. On a visit to the mountains to see the home area of one of the settlers, I was approached by a man who asked if I could take his daughter to the hospital. His daughter was about fifteen and had been married some months; she had been in labor for a day. The rest of the girl's family were opposed to her going to the hospital, but after pressure from her father, they relented. She was accompanied by her maternal uncle (this was a matrilineal society), her mother, and her husband. We traveled eighty miles over bad roads to the district hospital, where a dead child was delivered by Caesarean section.

---

Contributed by Dr. James L. Brain, State University of New York College, New Paltz.

A similar event occurred later in the year. A girl had been in labor for a day. Finally her father persuaded the rest of the family to agree to send her to the hospital, along with her father and his sister and the girl's mother. On the way she was delivered of a dead child. It is significant that in each of these cases the father of the girl was Christian.

A fourth event, similar to the others, took place in 1966. I was summoned by the educated chairman of the youth league, who said that his brother's wife had been in labor for a day and a half. He had finally persuaded the family to allow her to be taken to the hospital. The girl was accompanied by her mother, father, maternal uncle, and husband. It had been raining hard all day, and the road was almost impassable. Darkness fell and we struggled on, only to find the road blocked by a fallen tree. The family concluded that the tree was an omen and that we should turn back. I refused to do this, instead borrowing axes at a house nearby. The men reluctantly joined me in trying to cut away the trunk of the tree. While we were engaged in this activity, the girl died. I was so angry that I accused the parents of having killed their daughter. Afterwards, I reproached myself, but I think it was unnecessary; they were all so lost in grief that they probably hadn't heard me. The mother's constant refrain was "My child was so beautiful; all the men desired her; this child killed her, bewitched her; it was no child; it bewitched her."

This reluctance to seek medical help is the result of various explanations of difficult childbirth, depending on the society involved. One is that the woman concerned has been guilty of adultery, and therefore the child kills her. Another is that she had a lover to whom she subsequently refused favors; he retaliated by practicing magic against her. Finally, in some societies, it is believed that any offense against the moral code can result in prolonged labor or difficult childbirth. I have been told that in a southern region of the country women having difficulty in childbirth are brought to the hospital with bruised faces; their families beat them in order to force them to confess the name of the lover.

Should the outsider intervene in these cases? If so, when and how?

## 10.4—COSPONSORING TOURISTS

World Travel, Inc.
New York, New York

Dr. Alan Carruthers
Journal of a Regional Association of Anthropologists

Dear Dr. Carruthers:

We are organizing a wildlife trek to Bahadur [the country in which Carruthers had done field work]. We plan to visit the areas outlined in the enclosed itinerary. The trip will be led by Mr. Gregory Johns, a naturalist who spent two years working for the national parks in the country and who is now completing a Ph.D.

We were wondering if your group would be interested in cosponsoring the trip with us and offering it to your members and subscribers. We also plan to offer the trip to the general public. We would be willing to compensate you in the amount of $75 for every member or subscriber who you recruit.

Please let me know at your earliest convenience whether your group would be interested in cosponsoring this trek.

Sincerely yours,

James J. Johnson

Carruthers read the letter carefully and perused the literature that was enclosed. The trip was to take four weeks and was promoted as a unique opportunity to see "the impressive natural history of the country," "observe rare fauna," and visit "tribal villages and local markets, observing the scenery and the people firsthand." There were to be mountain climbing opportunities and "contact with unique mountain villages and colorful native cultures." For the last two weeks, the group would live in a remote native village in the interior of the country so that they could explore the surrounding jungle, observing the flora and fauna.

Carruthers wondered how to respond to the invitation and what his primary responsibilities were.

## 10.5 – INTERVENTION IN A MATTER OF BELIEF

I was working on a scheme designed to increase cotton productivity in an African country. While on tour in one area, I was asked by a local instructor to visit the fields of an older woman who had done everything by the book and, consequently, had a superb crop of cotton. As we approached her fields, we heard sobs and found her crouched with her clothes over her head in a corner of the field. We asked her what was wrong and she answered, "I shouldn't have tried to make myself better than other people." When we asked why, she pointed to a small hole at the edge of the field which was filled with magical objects, including some human hair. This was clearly an example of what George Foster has called "the concept of limited good"; that is, some people apparently felt that she had produced more at their expense.

What should one do to allay anxiety in this kind of situation? I told her not to worry, that I possessed powerful magic and I would place a curse on the person who had tried to work magic on her. At first she was dubious, but when I went into the gruesome details of what would happen to her assailant, she was reassured and went on happily with her work. Later, I wondered whether someone might indeed have suffered the fate which I had described.

## 10.6—ARCHAEOLOGISTS, MUSEUMS, AND INDIANS

The disturbance of graves is often seen as the archaeologist's *raison d'être*, and archaeologists have done virtually nothing to alter this image. Furthermore, the double standard of the all-white archaeological corps and museum staffs is all too evident in the exhuming of thousands of Indian graves and the display of Indian bones, whole skeletons, mummies, and grave goods. Where, the Indians ask, are the white man's bones? The answer is, of course, safely buried with all kinds of laws to keep them there. Moving a white cemetery is a very complicated procedure, requiring approval by a multitude of officials. Digging up a white man's grave is called "grave robbing" and considered despicable. In contrast, digging up an Indian grave is lucrative for the archaeologist and pot hunter alike.

However, archaeologists, like other social scientists, like to think of their discipline as "scientific" and, therefore, above humanistic considerations. It is just this attitude which fosters negative reactions to archaeology and other social sciences. An editorial in *Akwesasne Notes* (1971, p. 1), entitled "Don't Exploit Our Dead," read as follows:

> You encourage digging in the name of science, starting many other diggings in the graves of our Grandfathers and Grandmothers, exposing their bones for the gawking public eye and their rude comments.
>
> You say you want to learn more about the Indians. There are still plenty of alive ones around to talk. If Indians molested white men's graves they would be thrown in jail.
>
> Indians, even if they are dead, have the right to remain Indians. We demand the removal of Indian bones from museums—both public displays and in their storerooms—and their proper reburial by Indian medicine people.
>
> Until that comes to pass, no one will rest.

These remarks were made in reaction to a recent incident in Iowa, where an unmarked cemetery was uncovered by highway workers. Twenty-six white bodies were recovered and reburied in a nearby cemetery. The bones of a young Indian girl from the same cemetery were turned over to Marshall McKusick, a state archaeologist. Mrs. Maria Thompson-Pearson, a Yankton Sioux, demanded proper

---
Contributed by Michael Scullin, Mankato State College.

reburial of the bones. McKusick claims, "He must keep the remains under an Iowan law which entrusts him with *articles of historical significance"* (emphasis mine). Mrs. Thompson-Pearson notes that were she to dig up a white person's grave she would be arrested. McKusick says:

> I don't want that woman to think in any way that if she raises a fuss, I'll give her a couple of bones.
>
> I just can't go giving remains to private individuals. It sounds nice to say just give [the bones] back to the Indians so the girl can be reburied, but I have to follow the Code of Iowa.

Mrs. Maria Thompson-Pearson, who also happens to be a chairwoman of the Indian Woman's Action Council, a national organization, promises to continue her fight (O'Shea 1971).

McKusick may still have the bones but archaeology has lost the battle. The fact that the Iowa incident was the object of an editorial in *Akwesasne Notes,* with a nationwide circulation of 22,000, means that a local dispute has become a national dispute and the activist readers of *Akwesasne Notes* have documentation of their darkest suspicions. Local news may no longer be local.

In the summer of 1971, another dispute occured in Minnesota; it, too, received coverage in *Akwesasne Notes.* Here the problem originated from poorly handled public relations and a misunderstanding on the part of the American Indian Movement (AIM). A group of high school students, under the direction of two professional archaeologists, was excavating a thousand-year-old village site at Welch, Minnesota, on land slated for construction. Thus, they were engaging in salvage archaeology.

AIM believed that the students were "exhuming graves and that they had no legal right to do so," as Daniel Dalton, assistant AIM program director for youth, explained. There were other remarks about "digging up our sacred burial grounds." In retaliation the AIM group "burned notes and archaeological tools, carried away arrowheads and other artifacts unearthed by the students, and exposed rolls of film taken on the site." Said one of the archaeologists, "As far as I'm concerned it's ruined. You can only do an excavation once. If it's done once and messed up, it's ruined." As of that moment, he wouldn't "touch the site with a 29-foot pole." Many of the students were bewildered. "We wanted to preserve their past not destroy it." But nobody explained this to the Indians (*Minneapolis Tribune* 1971).

A meeting between Indians and students the next day began with AIM explaining that they halted the dig to stop "grave robbing" and that, in their opinion, the Indians owned the land, which was taken in violation of a treaty. AIM offered to reimburse the group for the loss of their equipment. The artifacts were to be reburied at the site with appropriate ceremony (Ponsor 1971).

The director of the Minnesota Indian Affairs Commission, Artley Skenandore, deplored the destruction of private property, but was adamant that "we will not stand for the desecration of our Indian burial grounds." Both Clyde Bellecourt, executive director of AIM, and Skenandore said that "no work should be allowed on former Indian land without full prior consent from Indians" (Ponsor 1971).

Because of this dispute, archaeologists from St. Cloud State College halted their excavation in the Sherburne National Wildlife Refuge in Minnesota. The nature of their dig was discussed with Skenandore. A few days later, the president of the college announced, "Now that the information has been provided we are resuming the project on a limited scale. Survey work and excavation of village sites will continue. However, there will be no new excavation of burial mounds, at this time" (Associated Press 1971c).

However, others learned absolutely nothing from the Welch incident, and Charles Coruson, director of the Twin Cities Institute for Talented Youth, which sponsored the Welch dig, said it was "a lesson in inhuman relationship." Indeed it was, although apparently not in quite the same terms that Coruson meant (Associated Press 1971b).

Newspaper articles, although not sympathetic with the rough-house tactics employed by AIM, were sympathetic to AIM's objections, and letters to the editor in the *Minneapolis Tribune* were almost entirely pro-Indian.

"The Welch diggings were done by a group of school kids and young teachers and served no other purpose than to teach the kids to dig. Let them dig up their own yards" (Dodor 1971).

A comment on working through "channels": "Even had the Indians who protested at the Welch, Minnesota, site tried to work through court channels, the artifacts would have been beyond recovery—locked in cases, displayed in museums or even thrown away. Indians have hardly ever been able to recover their property once others get hold of it" (Malmberg 1971).

Archaeologists, who are supported almost entirely by public funds or tax-free foundations, might do well to pay heed to this publicity. It doesn't matter whether it is correct or incorrect, it happens to be there. It is up to archaeologists to make amends or clarify misunderstandings.

The Great Lakes Indian Youth Alliance of Lansing, Michigan, are objecting to: "The display of the bodies of our grandfathers [at Fort Michilimimakinac] and at the burial grounds for tourist dollars." They demand "The right to give our exposed dead decent Indian burials, and the passage of firm laws prohibiting all digs in Indian burial ground wherever they might be" (Great Lakes Indian Youth Alliance 1970). Now they are demanding closure of the fort (run for tourists) until "medical, educational, and cultural centers are established and functioning, operated by Indians" and "until the pageant [presented at the fort] is entirely an Indian affair" (American Indian Press Association 1971, p. 10).

In Albany the New York State Museum, according to Case (1971, p. 37):

> has decided to remove authentic Indian bones from public display as a concession to New York Indians. The action is ringing an alarm bell in similar institutions across the state.
>
> Dr. William A. Ritchie, the state archaeologist, said he did not believe in removing Indian burial displays from all museums. "I think they have a proper place in a popular, scientific institution."

Dr. John C. Broughton, associate education commissioner for cultural education, who oversees the state museum, said that "the museum will stop short of complying with another suggestion sometimes heard from members of the Indian community: that all Indian bones held by museums be turned back to the aboriginal descendents for reburial."

There were suggestions for substituting plastic reproductions for real bones and Broughton agreed that this might well be an acceptable solution.

Ritchie did not think plastic bones were the answer believing that real bones are "more convincing and educational."

"I have sympathy with Indians, or with any people who feel they have received poor treatment, but that's not involved here. If an archaeologist is doing his work, *he has to know about people,* as well as artifacts," explained Ritchie (emphasis mine).

The director of the Rochester Museum and Science Center decided to take a wait-and-see attitude and noted his Seneca associate curator concurred (Case 1971).

Southwest Museum in Los Angeles also found controversy over its displays, resulting in sit-ins by Indians on December 20, 1970, and January 12, 1971. Precipitating the action were displays of a human burial, a medicine bundle, and a scalp. While some Indians picketed with a sign saying "Dig Up Your Own Dead," thirteen others locked themselves in the museum auditorium. Another group sought to meet with the museum director, Carl Dentzel. Dentzel said he was surprised by the demonstration and that he had had no idea that some of the exhibits were considered offensive. He agreed to cover the exhibits and arranged a subsequent meeting with the demonstrators.

In their prepared statement, the demonstrators said (in part): "The objects on display here do not tell our side of the story, but instead help perpetuate the myths and ignorance that still prevail among the modern majority" (Indians of All Tribes 1971, p. 40).

Said Dentzel, "If you'll just read the notations on the exhibits you'll discover that everything done here is to show the greatness of the Indian. I've dedicated my life to such work, so don't tell me this museum is trying to make fun of the Indian" (*Los Angeles Times* 1970).

The displays were apparently not removed and the Indians came back three weeks later; twelve of them chained themselves in again. The museum was closed early, and one hour after closing the Indians were still sitting there. Dentzel had the group arrested—"reluctantly" he said.

According to a newspaper account: "He said he would like to meet with these representatives again, but the meeting must be held in an academic manner. We do not have any immediate solutions to the problems. The museum must tell the story of man, and to do that we must exhibit evidence of his past." Amid constant heckling from the group of Indians outside the museum, he denied their charges that the Indian skeletons were exhumed for purposes of display. "We are not and never have been grave robbers," he said (*Los Angeles Herald Examiner* 1971). In April the twelve Indians were convicted of trespassing (Associated Press 1971a).

Some of the issues were nicely stated in "An Open Letter to a Museum Director," written by Richard O. Clemmer, an anthropology graduate student at the University of Illinois and published in *Akwesasne Notes* (1971, p. 38). In part, the letter stated:

> Perhaps by this time you have reconsidered your Museum's position as an institution of a superordinate society that purports to present a true picture of the peoples which that society has conquered and

subjugated. Perhaps you have realized that those of us "on the winning side" have been inculcated with a bias that is so automatic that we do not see its dehumanizing effects unless they are pointed out to us. For us, the bias seems very subtle; but to those against whom it works, it is as blatant and rank as a festering wound.

Should not all museums seek to educate rather than display? And if a museum is to tell the story of man, should it not attempt to emphasize the story of the conjunction of two cultural systems, rather than just displaying the curiosities and exotica of the subordinate systems? A scalp, whether of a Cheyenne or a white man, whether taken by a Pawnee or an Englishman, is a grisly thing to show. At the museum of Dachau, which documents one of the most tragic sets of atrocities in human history, you do not find the charred bodies of Jews and Russians killed there. . . .

Again, it is not a matter of proving the demonstrator right or wrong. The "facts" don't mean a thing unless each of the participating groups has the same set of "facts." One man's facts are another man's bias and no one should know this better than a social scientist. Archaeology has been self-serving for years. The peoples buried in the earth did not cease to exist in 1492 or 1890. They live, and although the ghosts of the dead may not haunt the pillagers of their graves, the living will.

## BIBLIOGRAPHY

*Akwesasne Notes.* 1970. Editorial comment. *Akwesasne Notes* 2, 6:12.

───────. 1971. Don't exploit our dead. *Akwesasne Notes* 3, 6:1.

American Indian Press Association, 1971. "Death zoo for tourists" protested. *Akwesasne Notes* 3, 6:10.

Associated Press. 1971a. LA museum sit-in nets conviction. *Akwesasne Notes* 3, 3:41.

───────. 1971b. *Indian artifacts given to State Indian Commission.* Mankato Free Press.

───────. 1971c. Sherburne research dig is resumed. *Minneapolis Tribune* 3 August.

Benton, Eddie. 1970. Prayer of thanksgiving. *American Indian Movement Newsletter,* p. 12.

Case, Richard. 1971. Museum ends Indian bones exhibit. *Syracuse Herald American* 17 Jan.:19. Reprinted in *Akwesasne Notes* 3, 2:37.

Clemmer, Richard O. 1971. An open letter to a museum director. *Akwesasne Notes* 3, 2:38.

Dodor, Lorna E. 1971. Letter to editor. *Minneapolis Tribune* 1 August.

Great Lakes Youth Alliance. 1970. Letter to editor. *Akwesasne Notes* 2, 6:35.

Hargrove, Danny. 1971. Letter to editor. *Minneapolis Tribune* 28 July.

Indians of All Tribes. 1971. Statement presented to officials of Southwest Museum. *Akwesasne Notes* 3, 2:40.

*Los Angeles Herald Examiner.* 1971. Twelve Indians jailed over protest at museum here. *Los Angeles Herald Examiner* 13 January.

*Los Angeles Times.* 1970. One hundred Indians protest, museum pledges to remove three exhibits. Reprinted in *Akwesasne Notes* 3, 2:40.

Malmberg, C.L. 1971. Letter to editor. *Minneapolis Tribune* 7 August.

*Minneapolis Tribune.* 1971. Indians break up archaeological dig. *Minneapolis Tribune* 23 July.

O'Shea, James. 1971. Over Indian bones. *Des Moines Register* 11 July. Reprinted in *Akwesasne Notes* 3, 6:13.

Ponsor, Mike. 1971. Indians, student differ on archaeological dig. *Minneapolis Tribune* 24 July.

*Red Wing Republican Eagle.* 1971. Editorial. Reprinted in *Minneapolis Tribune* 29 July.

# APPENDIX 1

# ETHICAL ISSUES AND THE USE OF CASE MATERIALS

There are a number of complex moral dilemmas inherent in social inquiry. I will discuss briefly some of the more salient ones, indicating the relevant case materials and related references. For a more detailed discussion of ethical issues cf. Appell (1973a, 1976), Beals (1969), Berreman, et al. (1968), Kelman (1968), and Jorgensen (1971). Also, consult the materials listed in Appendix 3, which concerns publications by professional societies.

## OBJECTIVITY IN SOCIAL INQUIRY

There are many facets to this issue. First, there is the argument that, unlike the "hard" sciences, there is no way to control in the social sciences the influence of the observer on his results. As a consequence, there is the recurrent problem of the cultural contamination of social inquiry (cf. Appell 1973a, 1973b), which can take various forms.

Some claim that social inquiry and its results are inevitably distorted by ideological bias. This argument has been advanced mainly by the radical and activist social scientists. This controversy has spawned a vast literature, which I will only briefly touch on here.

The claim has been made by Mills (cf. Horowitz 1967) and Gouldner (1962, 1968) that social inquiry is not value free, is not ethically neutral, but that it is ideologically contaminated in that it reflects the values and goals of those in power. In anthropological inquiry, there is the related claim that anthropology has been the handmaiden of colonial interests. The case for this can be found in Asad (1973), Berreman, et. al (1968), Maquet (1964), and Stavenhagen (1971). Firth (1972) and I.M. Lewis (1968) disagree.

The claim of ideological contamination has also been put in terms of the question of whose side the investigator is on in the pursuit of his inquiry (Becker 1967). In the context of these claims is the call for greater involvement with and commitment to the welfare of the people being studied, which is sometimes phrased in terms of more "relevant research" (cf. Berreman, et al. 1968; Jorgensen and Lee 1973; Huizer 1975; Hymes 1972; and Stauder 1972). Also see Appell

(1973a) and Kaplan (1974) for an evaluation of this issue. One aspect of this problem is discussed below in the section dealing with "The Feedback of the Results of Social Inquiry."

Batalla (1966) discusses conservative thought in applied anthropology, and Boguslaw (1967) carefully analyzes the values that have informed his scientific career and in particular his association with Project Camelot. For a discussion of the politicization of science, see Haberer (1972). An interesting case is made by Weigert (1970, p. 111) that "If a sociologist practices rhetoric, but identifies himself ... as a scientist, he renders his rhetoric immoral, the immoral rhetoric of identity deception."

Szwed (1972) and Moskos and Bell (1967) discuss some of the effects of the ideological and value contamination of social inquiry among American social scientists, providing useful examples of the unintended consequences of such contamination. In Section 2, "The Ethical Problems of Doing Field Work in a Setting of Intense Sociopolitical Conflict" presents the case of an investigator who must deal with a polarized community in which the members of both factions assume that his results will be biased by his ideological position.

A distinction must be made between the contamination of research results by explicit political values and by deep-seated values that the investigator usually is not conscious of. This is a critical issue in that contamination by these implicit values can be almost more damaging and pervasive. This is discussed further below.

Another facet of the issue of objectivity is the intrusion of personal bias into social inquiry. Devereaux (1967) provides an insightful analysis of this problem, and many of the case materials here can be studied from this aspect (also cf. Nash 1963).

Finally, another aspect of the issue of objectivity is the charge that the social scientist treats the subjects of their research as objects rather than human beings. A number of cases in this book can be approached from this perspective. For discussions of this facet see Appell (1973a), Hymes (1972), Kaplan (1974), and Wolff (1964). Kelman (1968) presents an extended discussion of the problem with respect to social psychological research. Bernard, Ottenberg, and Redl (1971) provide an excellent analysis of the processes that lead to such dehumanization in research and in the society at large.

## CONFLICT OF VALUES IN RESEARCH

In cross-cultural inquiry in particular, a number of moral dilemmas arise for the investigator as the result of conflicts between his system of values and that of the society he is studying, or between his values and those of the host government. These problems indicate the difficulty of trying to prevent the intrusion of values into the social inquiry (cf. Appell 1973a). Bennett (1946), Colfax (1966), Radin (1939), Kelman (1968), Nash (1963), and Devereaux (1967) have all attempted to demonstrate how an inquiry and its conclusions can be contaminated as a result of the set of values held by the investigator (cf. also Golde 1970).

In every piece of field work there seems to come a time when the value system of the anthropologist crashes head on into the value system held by the members of the host community. These value conflicts often seem to tell us more about the values held by the social scientist than those of the host society. An anthropologist, by his very training, is willing to compromise his own values for the sake of his research. When he is drawn up short by a conflict of values, it usually is with those values that he has never examined because they tend to be the most basic to his view of the world.

The case materials seem to indicate that the core values of the social scientists center around health and disease, the value of life, social justice, freedom of choice, and violation of the law. Thus, participation by the investigator in illegal activities, both those that are illegal for the members of his host community and those which are illegal in the investigator's own system, raises many dilemmas (cf. Yablonsky 1968). Graft, or "speed money," as it is frequently called, also poses difficult problems for American social scientists.

With regard to health and disease, it is quite clear that anthropologists subscribe to the germ theory of disease along with the concommitant materialist view that only Western drugs can provide adequate cures. When Elenore Bowen (1964) stalks off in frustration because she believes she can do nothing for a dying woman, she displays her commitment to the value of materialistic intervention and ignores the life-sustaining values of *agape,* empathy, and sympathy. For an example of the apparent efficacy of these latter values, see "The Efficacy of Faith Healing" in Section 1.

The following cases deal with conflicts concerning social justice and the value of life:

*Section 1: Relations and Responsibilities to Host Community:* To Take a Wife; A Problem in Political Identification and Co-option; Whether to Intervene in Infanticide.

*Section 2: Relation and Responsibilities to Respondents and Informants:* An Act of Compassion; Embarrassing Informants.

*Section 3: Relations with Host Government:* Political Ramifications of Field Work Among the Klee.

*Section 4: Relations with Representatives of Outside Agencies and the Public with Respect to the Host Community:* The Priest, the Manaoans, and the Role of the Anthropologist; On the Horns of a Dilemma: A Problem of Intercession; Playing the Role of Intercultural Mediator; The Local Mission and its Priest; The Trader and his Monopoly.

*Section 7. Publication: Responsibilities and Liabilities:* The Possible Effects of Publication on the Society Studied.

Cases dealing with conflicts in values related to disease and health are:

*Section 1: Relations and Responsibilities to Host Community:* The Efficacy of Faith Healing; Whether to Intervene in Infanticide.

*Section 2: Relations and Responsibilities to Respondents and Informants:* A Medical Emergency; Disease and Death: Research in the Uguru District; Death from a Wound; Intervention in a Curing Session.

*Section 10: Miscellaneous:* Difficult Childbirth in Africa.

Cases dealing with participation in illegal activities are as follows:

*Section 1: Relations and Responsibilities to Host Community:* How Does a Foreign Researcher Interfere to Stop Illegal Activities.

*Section 2: Relations and Responsibilities to Respondents and Informants:* Participation in Illegal Activities.

*Section 7: Publication: Responsibilities and Liabilities:* Problems in Urban Ethnic Research; The Problem of Publishing on Illegal Activities.

Cases involving "speed money" are:

*Section 3: Relations with Host Government:* Field Work in a Climate of Governmental Suspicion.

## ISSUES IN PRIVACY, CONFIDENTIALITY, AND THE PROTECTION OF HUMAN SUBJECTS

These issues are also multifaceted. For example, the resolution of certain of these issues results in the reflection of their image in another area of ethical concern. Thus, disguising a community to protect the subjects of the study can not only lead to a form of dehumanization, it also creates what I have called the "dilemma of ethnography" (Appell 1973a). While disguise protects a community, it produces a loss of explanatory power because the ethnographer in his explanation of sociocultural phenomena includes a consideration of historical events and the structure of the local environment.

Then there is the conflict between the society's "right to know anything that may be known or discovered about any part of the universe" and the individual's right to privacy (Panel on Privacy and Behavioral Research 1967a, p. 536). The Panel on Privacy and Behavioral Research (1967a, p. 536) states that: "The individual has an inalienable right to dignity, self-respect, and freedom to determine his own thoughts and actions within the broad limits set by the requirements of the society. The essential element in privacy and self-determination is the privilege of making one's own decision as to the extent to which one will reveal thoughts, feelings, and actions."

Discussion of the legal protection of privacy can be found in Ruebhausen and Brim (1965 and 1966). Lundsgaarde (1971) provides both a legal and an anthropological perspective on these issues. A survey of the legal protection of privacy in ten countries can be found in Lengyel (1972b). In 1967 there appeared two reports from the Panel on Privacy and Behavioral Research, appointed by the President's Office of Science and Technology (also cf. Privacy Protection Study Commission 1977). Also see Weaver (1974) for a discussion of this conflict and Edsall (1975), "Report of the AAAS Committee on Scientific Freedom and Responsibility," for an argument on the importance of not limiting scientific freedom in research.

However, confidential relationships with informants, argue Rainwater and Pittman (1967), are not always desirable. And Galliher (1973) maintains that ethical codes protecting privacy and the confidentiality of data help maintain the status quo, protect the powerful, and prevent critical information on the functioning of the society from becoming available.

A classic controversy over the right to privacy and the society's right to know arose as a result of Humphreys's study of homosexual behavior in public restrooms (1970a and 1970b; particularly cf. 1970a, postscript). In addition to this issue, the issues of social stimulation, disguised research, and the potentiality of this research for abridging human freedoms were involved (cf. Warwick 1973 and Golann 1973 for a discussion of these issues).

With regard to anthropological inquiry Paddock provides a review of the alleged invasion of privacy by Oscar Lewis's research and the impact that this controversy has had (cf. Paddock's several articles in Halovorson and Moser 1965).

The problem is that much of the discourse over the protection of privacy occurs in the context of the United States legal system; it thus ignores these problems of social inquiry in cross-cultural contexts.

Problems related to the confidentiality of research sources frequently arise in the context of a government or its agency attempting to obtain information about informants and communities. In essence, this presents a conflict between two aspects of the public's right to know. The public has a right to inquire as to whether a crime has been committed and by whom. But the public also has a right to know all that it can about the conditions of its society and the operations of its government. If the informant's right to privacy is violated—that is, if the confidentiality of the social scientist's sources is not protected—the public's right to knowledge about the conditions of its society and its government will be threatened to the extent that the social scientist will have difficulty enlisting the help of informed sources in his research. This confrontation between social science researchers and the agencies of government is causing increasing concern in the scientific community because of the possibility of harassment when engaging in research on deviant populations (see Yablonsky 1968; also cf. Anonymous 1971 for suggestions on methods to protect the confidentiality of data). But the demand for protective legislation also raises other significant issues, such as a growing state control over researchers which might ensue (cf. Oromaner 1968; Symonds 1968; also cf. Green 1971 for a discussion of the implications of the involvement of social scientists with the government). Carroll's (1973) discussion of the Popkin case brings into focus many of the issues over the confidentiality of data with respect to the rights, duties, privileges, and responsibilities of a researcher to society, to the group he is studying, to the government, and to the scientific community.

A related issue in the protection of subjects is the potential psychological and physical harm that might be incurred through participation in a research project. This is a major problem in medical research, but certain social psychological experiments raise similar questions. For example, see Milgram's "Eichmann experiments" (Appendix 2). The feedback of research results to the host community also can be potentially harmful, and I discuss this issue in a later section. However, Reynolds (1972) argues that there has been no evidence of any permanent harm to any individual as a direct result of participation in social science research (1972, p. 695). Certain case materials in this book (for example, Section 3: "Political Ramifications of Field Work Among the Klee") would seem to cast doubt on his conclusion. I have also obtained cases describing instances in which association with the anthropologist has put informants into such political jeopardy that permanent harm has occurred. Unfortunately, these are too sensitive for publication. Cora DuBois reports that several of her former informants on Alor were beheaded by the Japanese when they claimed that they were under United States protection as the result of her research.

The Department of Health, Education, and Welfare (HEW) has published guides to HEW policy on the protection of human subjects. These requirements have made the whole process of obtaining research approval for inquiries involving participant observation more difficult. A National Commission for the Protection of Human Subjects of Biomedical and Behavioral Research has been formed to inquire into this subject and issue periodic reports. Also see Wolfensberger (1967), Freund (1969), Parsons (1969), and Katz (1972) for discussions of ethical issues in experimentation with human subjects. Gray (1975) reports on his study of institutional review committees and procedures for the protection of human research subjects.

Cases which involve ethical issues related to privacy and the protection of subjects and informants are:

*Section 1: Relations and Responsibilities to Host Community:* Using a Disguised Role.

*Section 2: Relations and Responsibilities to Respondents and Informants:* A Case of Privileged Communication; Conflict in the Roles of Friend and Informant During the Feedback of Research Results; The Consequences of Investigating a Sensitive Subject.

*Section 3: Relations with Hose Government:* A Request for Informant Names by a Government Official; Political Ramifications of Field Work Among the Klee.

*Section 6: Dilemmas in the Use and Misuse of Social Science Knowledge:* Misuse of the Anthropologist's Information; Whether or Not to Deposit Field Notes in an Archive.

*Section 7: Publication: Responsibilities and Liabilities:* A Problem of Publishing on Identifiable Communities and Personalities; Problems in Urban Ethnic Research; The Possible Effects of Publication on the Society Studied.

## ISSUES OVER INFORMED CONSENT AND DISGUISED RESEARCH

Closely related to the former issues is that of informed consent. This problem is particularly difficult in cross-cultural inquiry, where the subject of research cannot really comprehend the impact of the research and publication of its results. This issue appears in a number of cases.

Disguised research eliminates the freedom of informed consent. Barnes (1963) in his discussion of ethical issues takes a stand against disguised research, as do Beals (1969) and Erikson (1967). Arguments in favor of disguise often point to the fact that, with certain research topics, it is a necessary device in assuring society's right to knowledge (cf. Galliher 1973), for example, in the study of sexual deviancy (cf. Humphreys 1970a, postscript).

Deception is a major strategy in social psychological experiments. Bonacich (1970) argues against these procedures, and Kelman (1968) discusses these issues at length. Gans (1968) claims that deception is an integral part of participant observation.

Cases dealing with the problem of informed consent and disguised research are as follows:

*Section 1: Relations and Responsibilities to Host Community:* Using a Disguised Role; Imposition of the Anthropologist on the Community.

*Section 2: Relations and Responsibilties to Respondents and Informants:* Embarrassing Informants.

*Section 4: Relations with Representatives of Outside Agencies and the Public with Respect to the Host Community:* On the Horns of a Dilemma: A Problem of Intercession.

*Section 5: Relations with Other Social Scientists and Responsibilities to the Profession:* Tensions in a Northern Community.

*Section 6: Dilemmas in the Use and Misuse of Social Science Knowledge:* Differential Access to the Results of Anthropological Inquiry: A Dilemma in Professional Responsibiltity.

*Section 7: Publication: Responsibilties and Liabilities:* A Problem of Publishing on Identifiable Communities and Personalities; The Possible Effects of Publication on the Society Studied.

## PARTICIPANT OBSERVATION

In the Introduction to Sections 1 and 2, I discuss many of the dilemmas and ethical issues involved in participant observation. Here I shall consider only four aspects: the growth of friendship; dealing with aggression; dealing with deviants; and social stimulation.

*The Growth of Friendship.* If involvement in a community is genuine (cf. Wolff 1964), and if friendship is not used in cold blood as a counter to establish reciprocities for the gathering of data, the field worker develops emotional bonds with members of the host community. Eventually, lasting and deep friendships may develop. These can produce dilemmas when they conflict with other relationships or other goals. But this is the inevitable consequence of participant observation. I have listed the literature dealing with this problem in the introductions to Sections 1 and 2. The dilemmas of friendship are described in many cases in Sections 1 and 2. Here I shall only list those which most clearly present the problem:

*Section 2: Relations and Responsibilities to Respondents and Informants:* Conflict in the Roles of Friend and Informant During the Feedback of Research Results; Intervention in a Curing Session.

*Section 3: Relations with Host Government:* Political Ramifications of Field Work Among the Klee.

*Section 4: Relations with Representatives of Outside Agencies and the Public with Respect to the Host Community:* The Priest, the Mamaoans, and the Role of the Anthropologist.

*Dealing with Aggression.* The problem of dealing with aggression is seldom considered in discussions of field work. Yet the participant-observer role, by its very nature, puts the field worker in situations where he will have to deal with aggressive behavior, sometimes in direct response to his investigation, sometimes displaced from other targets. Case materials that deal with this problem are:

*Section 1: Relations and Responsibilities to Host Community:* Firearms in the Field.

*Section 2: Relations and Responsibilities to Respondents and Informants:* Dealing with Theft; Dealing with Threats of Aggression.

*Section 5: Relations with Other Social Scientists and Responsibilities to the Profession:* Dealing with Animosity Arising from a Previous Study.

*The Problem of Deviants.* The participant-observer role is one that seems to attract deviants, some of whom may turn out to be the field worker's best informants. Others may not only prove troublesome but also dangerous, particularly the more emotionally unstable deviants. Paul (1953) gives an interesting example of the type of unstable individual drawn to the field worker and the difficulties which result. Cases in this book that deal with the problem are:

*Section 1: Relations and Responsibilities to Host Community:* Firearms in the Field.

*Section 2: Relations and Responsibilities to Respondents and Informants:* Dealing with Theft.

*Section 4: Relations with Representatives of Outside Agencies and the Public with Respect to the Host Community:* The Priest, the Mamaoans, and the Role of the Anthropologist; On the Horns of a Dilemma: A Problem of Intercession; The Local Mission and Its Priest.

*Social Stimulation.* The role of participant observer by its very nature involves social stimulation; that is, the presence of the field worker and his activities will tend to encourage or discourage certain behaviors and beliefs, and reinforce or destroy social stereotypes. The classic example of this is the use of a disguised role by Festinger and his associates (1956) to study a millenarian movement. The bogus recruitment of disguised field workers to the movement provided reinforcement for its belief system. In one instance of field work, it is reported that the anthropologist by his presence and questioning helped precipitate the development of a cargo cult movement.

But instances of social stimulation are not always so explicit. For example, an interest in recording old beliefs threatened by social change can make these more valuable to the society in question, thereby prolonging their existence.

Cases that illustrate the problems of social stimulation are:

*Section 1: Relations and Responsibilities to Host Community:* Whether to Intervene in Infanticide; The Efficacy of Faith Healing; Using a Disguised Role; Providing a Storage Place for Weapons.

*Section 2: Relations and Responsibilities to Respondents and Informants:* Participation in Illegal Activities; Disease and Death: Research in the Uguru District.

*Section 3: Relations with Host Government:* Political Ramifications of Field Work Among the Klee; The Anthropologist as a Political Catalyst.

*Section 9: Issues in Teaching:* The Introduction of Deviant Ideas by the Instructor.

## TRUST AND INTERPERSONAL GOODWILL

One of the least understood and least studied aspects of social life is the nature of trust and interpersonal goodwill. These qualities form the foundation of social intercourse and comprise social assets critical to the functioning of any social system. As the level of trust and goodwill in a social system decrease, social relationships tend to become eroded and collective action impeded. How does social inquiry, which depends on trust and interpersonal goodwill, affect these social assets within a society? We know very little about this. But we can assume that if a particular social investigation lowers the level of trust and interpersonal goodwill in the society, it will contribute to social disorganization. And the avoidance of this should be one of the ethical tenets of all social inquiry.

The problem of trust has arisen more frequently in social psychological experiments where deception is the rule. See Kelman (1968) for a discussion of this. However, Gans (1968) argues that all participant observation involves the use of deception.

The feedback of research results can also have deleterious effects on trust and interpersonal goodwill. This will be discussed in the following section on feedback.

Cases relevant to these problems are:

*Section 1: Relations and Responsibilities to Host Community:* Using a Disguised Role.

*Section 2: Relations and Responsibilities to Respondents and Informants:* The Ethical Problems of Doing Field Work in a Setting of Intense Sociopolitical Conflict.

*Section 5: Relations with Other Social Scientists and Responsibilities to the Profession:* Mind Assault.

*Section 8: Relations and Responsibilities to Funding Agencies:* Dissembling on Sources of Funds.

## FEEDBACK OF THE RESULTS OF SOCIAL INQUIRY TO THE HOST COMMUNITY

It has been suggested that the responsible anthropologist has the duty to communicate the results of his research to the community being studied. As a result, it is argued, the community will be better informed and better prepared to cope with the problems of cultural change and with outside forces attempting to exploit it. Certainly this approach prevents outside, special-interest elites from having a monopoly on the published results of any investigation.

However, the appropriateness of this approach depends on the degree to which the social system is organized for effective action, which may not be the case with many social systems studied by anthropologists. This view also assumes that the ideology of participatory democracy will grow, or should grow, in environments where it may in fact be totally inappropriate. In the absense of such democracy, there is no control of the use of the feedback, and it could conceivably fall into the hands of special-interest groups within the host community.

This approach also ignores two sources of dysfunctional stress that may occur as the result of feedback. First, feedback can expose cultural defense mechanisms in the society. Braroe (1965) gives an example of the use of such mechanisms and how their destruction can contribute to increased aggression in a factionalized society. Also to be considered is the social function of ignorance (Moore and Tumin 1949). Until we know more about this, we must carefully weigh the potentially disruptive and dangerous consequences of feedback.

Second, this approach ignores the fact that feedback can also unveil personal defense mechanisms such as those used in the presentation of self and as a basis for social strategems. As such, feedback can threaten the whole fabric of social exchanges that make up a society.

It is understandable, therefore, why the communication of research results back to the host community can be so disturbing and produce such strong emotions. The experience of social scientists in instances of inadvertant feedback illustrates this, as in the Springdale case (see Appendix 2 for references). Other experiences are recorded by Frazier (1964) and Gallaher (1964).

Until we know more about the nature of cultural and social defense mechanisms, feedback can only be viewed as a potentially dangerous action which should be used cautiously, if at all. However, with the increasing accessibility by informants to the published results of research, all investigators must consider what the impact of feedback on his host community might be and what his responsibilities are in this.

*Feedback of Extrinsic Valuations.* Feedback can also affect the host society by subjecting its members to the extrinsic valuations of the observer's culture.

Each society has its own unique set of values and related social behavior by means of which basic needs are met, drives satisfied, and meaning given to experience and existence. However, to the outside observer, to the social scientist, the behaviors and values that provide social and cultural identity may be and usually are valued in different terms. At a minimum, the possible latent functions are posited, and their costs to the society evaluated. In some instances, it is clear, even where the anthropologist has no explicit intent, that certain values and behaviors are subtly demeaned in terms of the investigator's own cultural system; or the folk explanation is debunked as irrational in terms of scientific materialism, although perhaps alleged to provide certain latent functions. This can result in erosion of meaning to the informant's way of life and devaluation of his identity (cf. Metraux 1969, p. 381).

Cases involving feedback are:

*Section 2: Relations and Responsibilities to Respondents and Informants:* Conflict in the Roles of Friend and Informant During the Feedback of Research Results.

*Section 6: Dilemmas in the Use and Misuse of Social Science Knowledge:* The Inadvertant Feedback of Research Conclusions.

*Section 7: Publication: Responsibilities and Liabilities:* The Problem of Publishing on Identifiable Communities and Personalities; Problems in Urban Ethnic Research; The Possible Effects of Publication on the Society Studied.

## THE ISSUES OF OVERCOMPETITION AND THE OVERACHIEVER

The issues of overcompetition and the overachiever are seldom discussed as ethical issues in social inquiry. Yet they are potentially disruptive factors because of the matrix of values in which they are embedded. Clark (1975) describes the set of values that contributes to the basic dilemma of American society: honesty or success. He argues that in a society where too much emphasis is put on success, it is hard to argue as persuasively for honesty when pervasive dishonesties are accepted as the price of success.

This is a question of relative rather than absolute valuation. When the value of success is set too high, moral constraints are eroded. This is a particular problem in scientific inquiry. It is difficult to maintain the basic ethical tenets of truth and honesty—the critical foundations of scientific endeavor—when the rewards are given to those who achieve success through techniques that are dishonest, if not illegal. The Summerlin affair, in which a cancer researcher painted the backs of mice to make it appear as if they had accepted skin grafts, is one example. The Watson-Crick-Franklin affair is another example (see Appendix 2 for references).

Overcompetition in which material rewards are valued above personal satisfaction and integrity has led to the development of an entrepreneurial system in science and the scientific entrepreneur, encouraging opportunism and a subtle erosion of ethical standards. Luria (1973) discusses these issues and their ramifications. Reif (1961) nicely points out how the quest for prestige and material rewards can conflict with the goals of science.

Overcompetition can also lead to the growth of fashion in research and to superficial research. (Cf. Luria 1973; Goldwasser 1965; Krzywoblocki 1965; and McVittie 1964). Wiener (1964, pp. 16-17) states in this respect:

> A man who is to live up to the highest ideas of scientific integrity cannot be led aside by the fact that a piece of work fits the latest style, that everybody's doing it. He's got to be willing to follow it out, even if it doesn't fit the latest style, if it fits his idea of how the field ought to develop. This means, in many cases, that he must consciously forego immediate success for the depth of his own work. It is a gamble he's got to take.

The implications for the major foundations funding research are clear, as they also should be for the social science profession.

Cases related to these issues are:

*Section 5: Relations with Other Social Scientists and Responsibilities to the Profession:* A Case of Poaching?; The Discovery of an Early-Man Site and Its Subsequent Excavation; Field Work Among the Kinani Indians; Competition for Host Communities.

*Section 9: Issues in Teaching:* A Case of Uncredited Editorial Work.

*Section 10: Miscellaneous:* When A Research Proposal Turns Out to be a Flop.

# APPENDIX 2
# SOURCES OF EXTENDED CASE MATERIALS

Several controversies have spawned extensive case materials which provide useful insights into the ethical problems of social inquiry. Some of these are described briefly below.

## THE SPRINGDALE CASE

In the early 1950's, Cornell University organized a project team to study certain social aspects of a small upstate New York village called "Springdale." The overall director of the project was U. Bronfenbrenner; Arthur J. Vidich was the resident field director. After leaving the project, Vidich, in collaboration with Joseph Bensman, who was not a member of the original project, wrote a book on the village (Vidich and Bensman 1958). This was reprinted in 1968, with a new introduction discussing the controversy that arose over publication of the book and a new chapter that included all published articles concerned with the controversy. Involved in the conflict were such ethical issues as the invasion of privacy, the influence of observer bias on research results, and the responsibilities of the researcher to the sponsoring institution, informants, and his profession. Even before the book appeared, there had been a growing controversy over who owned the data in a team project; whether a member could publish data gathered by another team member; methods of disguising individual respondents; and protective measures to avoid damage to informants. Individuals were all given fictitious names, but some identities could be deduced from the roles they occupied. When the book appeared, the community reacted strongly with a public discharge of aggressive feelings toward the project and its personnel in a community parade.

## OSCAR LEWIS'S MEXICO

The work of Oscar Lewis has raised a number of important issues. In regard to his restudy of Tepoztlán, Lewis and Robert Redfield debated the issue of personal bias in field work (cf. Paddock 1965a, Halovorson and Moser 1965 for a review of this). Both observer bias and invasion of privacy were charged in connection with Lewis's studies of Mexican families in *Five Families, The Children of Sanchez,* and *Pedro*

*Martinez.* Publication of *The Children of Sanchez,* in particular, caused a public scandal (cf. Beals 1969, pp. 11-19). Lewis was castigated in the press and at professional meetings in Mexico for misrepresentation of facts, interference with the internal affairs of Mexico, and lack of responsibility to subjects. John Paddock (1965a, 1965b, 1965c, 1965d) in Halovorson and Moser (1965) reviews the history of these controversies.

## MILGRAM'S STUDIES ON OBEDIENCE: THE "EICHMANN EXPERIMENT"

Stanley Milgram's research was concerned with the situation in which one agent commands another to hurt a third (Milgram 1963, 1965, 1974). The laboratory procedure involved ascertaining the amount of electric shock a subject was willing to administer to another when ordered by the experimenter to give the "victim" increasingly severe punishment. As Milgram (1965, pp. 59-60) describes the process:

> The naive subject is told that it is his task to teach the learner a list of paired associates, to test him on the list, and to administer punishment whenever the learned errs in the test. Punishment takes the form of [simulated] electric shock. . . . The teacher is instructed to increase the intensity of electric shock one step on the generator for each error. The learner, according to plan, provides many wrong answers. . . . Increases in shock level are met by increasingly insistent demands from the learner that the experiment be stopped because of growing discomfort to him. . . . The experimenter orders the teacher to continue with the procedure in disregard of the learner's protests.

Milgram's research techniques have produced a number of articles raising the ethical issues involved: Baumrind (1964); Milgram (1964); Kelman (1968, Chapter 8); also cf. Gray (1974).

## THE CAMELOT AFFAIR

Project Camelot and the public outcry that accompanied its revelation probably need no introduction. This international social science research project was sponsored by the Army Research Office of the Department of Defense. It was concerned with developing rapid methods for analyzing the nature and causes of social and political unrest, determining the circumstances under which this unrest develop into armed conflict, and identifying effective ways of averting as well as resolving conflicts (Beals 1969, p.4). For discussions of this controversy, see Horowitz (1965, 1967); El Mercurio (1965); United States House of Representatives (1966); Vallance (1966); Silvert (1965); Johnson (1966); and Sjoberg (1967a).

## THE STRUCTURE OF DNA AND THE WATSON-CRICK-FRANKLIN AFFAIR

While the events related to the discovery of the structure of DNA do not involve social inquiry, they raise many ethical issues in the behavior of scientists with respect to each other, funding agencies, the general public, and their profession as a whole. In my view, it is a classic case of the intrusion of uncontrolled competition and opportunism into the domain of scientific inquiry with all their corrupting influences on character and the very structure of scientific inquiry itself. A basic tenet in science is that scientific inquiry and its results should be available to all. Yet, when competition and opportunism are so rampant that investigators fear that their research results will be stolen, then the profession is in real difficulty. Materials on this controversy can be found in Watson (1968), Chargaff (1968), Merton (1968), Sayre (1975), Snow (1975), Shapley (1975), and Berman (1965).

## ANTHROPOLOGICAL INVOLVEMENT IN THAILAND

During the Vietnam War, anthropologists were accused of participating in anti-insurgency work and contributing to the cenral government's repression of tribal peoples in the northern part of Thailand. It is hard to delineate the ethical issues involved in this situation because the controversy became a political *cause célèbre*. There are no clear, dispassionate discussions of the conflicts; and many of the facts have probably not yet been made public. However, for those wishing to pursue the matter, see Jones (1971); Wolf and Jorgensen (1970), and related letters in subsequent issues of *The New York Review; The Student Mobilizer* (1970); and the American Anthropological Association (1971).

## EXTENDED DESCRIPTION OF FIELD WORK

A few anthropologists have published extended descriptions of their field-work experiences. These provide examples of many ethical issues that arise. See Berreman (1962), Maybury-Lewis (1965), Powdermaker (1966), Read (1965), Malinowski (1967), Golde (1970), Diamond (1964), Bowen (1964), and Wax (1971).

# APPENDIX 3

# MATERIALS FROM PROFESSIONAL SOCIETIES

All professional societies have published codes of ethics. However, these are frequently presented as stark statements of rules of conduct, without informative discussion. There are two exceptions. The American Political Science Association (1968) has published a 28-page booklet on the *Ethical Problems of Academic Political Scientists*. Also, the *Ethical Principles in the Conduct of Research with Human Participants*, published by the American Psychological Association (1973), is unusually helpful and informative. Following a brief statement of ethical principles, the authors discuss them in detail and provide abbreviated cases to illustrate the ethical issues addressed.

# BIBLIOGRAPHY

Adams, Richard M. 1967. Ethics and the social anthropologist in Latin America. *American Behavioral Scientist* 10, 10:16-21.
———. 1971. Responsibilities of the foreign scholar to the local scholarly community. *Current Anthropology* 12:335-39.
American Anthropological Association. 1971. *Report of Ad Hoc Committee to evaluate the controversy concerning anthropological activities in relation to Thailand.* Washington.
———. 1973. *Professional ethics: statements and procedures of the American Anthropological Association.* Washington.
American Anthropological Association, Committee on Ethics. 1973. Ethics Committee rules and procedures. *Newsletter of the American Anthropological Association* 14, 6:20-23.
American Orthopsychiatric Association. 1969. Code of ethics on human experimentation adapted from the Helsinki Declaration of the World Medical Association. *American Journal of Orthopsychiatry* 38: 589-90.
American Political Science Association. 1968. *Ethical problems of academic political scientists. Final report of the Committee on Professional Standards and Responsibilities.* Washington.
American Psychological Association, 1968a. Ethical standards of psychologists. *American Psychologist* 23: 357-61.
———. 1968b. Rules and procedures: Committee on Scientific and Professional Ethics and Conduct. *American Psychologist* 23:362-66.
American Psychological Association, Ad Hoc Committee on Ethical Standards in Psychological Research. 1973. *Ethical principles in the conduct of research with human participants.* Washington.
American Sociological Association. 1968. Toward a code of ethics for sociologists. *The American Sociologist* 3:316-18.
———. 1971. *Code of ethics.* Washington.
Andrews, Kenneth R., ed. 1953. *The case method of teaching human relations and administration: an interim statement.* Cambridge: Harvard University Press.
———.1954. The role of the instructor in the case method. In *The case method at the Harvard Business School: papers by present and past members of the faculty and staff,* ed. Malcolm P. McNair. New York: McGraw-Hill.
Annas, G.J.; Glantz, L.H.; and Katz, Barbara F. 1977. *Informed consent to human experimentation: the subject's dilemma.* Ballinger.
Anonymous. 1971. Confidentiality of research data. *Socio-Log.* 1, 4:2.
Appell, G.N. 1971. Comments on Adams and Jorgensen: toward an ethics for anthropologists. *Current Anthropology* 12:340-41.

———. 1973a. Basic issues in the dilemmas and ethical conflicts in anthropological inquiry. Module 19. New York: MSS Modular Publications.
———. 1973b. The distinction between ethnography and ethnology and other issues in cognitive structuralism. *Bijdragen tot de Taal-, Land- en Volkenkunde* 129:1-56.
———. 1976. Teaching anthropological ethics: developing skills in ethical decision-making and the nature of moral education. *Anthropological Quarterly* 49:81-88.
Asad, Talal, ed. 1973. *Anthropology and the colonial encounter*. Atlantic Highlands, N.J.: Humanities Press.
Bailey, Joseph C. 1953. A classroom evaluation of the case method. In *The case method of teaching human relations and administration: an interim statement*, ed. K.R. Andrews. Cambridge: Harvard University Press.
Barnes, J.A. 1963. Some ethical problems in modern field work. *British Journal of Sociology* 14:118-34. Reprinted 1967 in *Anthropologists in the field*, ed. D.G. Jongmans and P.C.W. Gutkind. Assen: Van Gorcum.
———. 1977. *The ethics of inquiry in social science: three lectures*. Delhi: Oxford University Press.
Batalla, Guillermo Bonfil. 1966. Conservative thought in applied anthropology: a critique. *Human Organization* 25, 2:89-92.
Baumrind, Diana. 1964. "Some thoughts on ethics of research: after reading Milgram's "Behavioral study of obedience." *American Psychologist* 19:421-23.
Beals, Ralph L. 1967. Background information on problems of anthropological research and ethics. *American Anthropological Association Fellow Newsletter* 8, 1:1-13.
———. 1969. *Politics of social research: an inquiry into the ethics and responsibilities of social scientists*. Chicago: Aldine.
Beck, Robert N., and Orr, John B. 1970. *Ethical choice: a case study approach*. New York: Free Press.
Becker, Howard S. 1964a. Problems in the publication of field studies. In *Reflections on community studies*, ed. Arthur J. Vidich, Joseph Bensman, and Maurice R. Stein. New York: John Wiley and Sons.
———. 1964b. Letter to editor: against the code of ethics. *American Sociological Review* 29:409-10.
———. 1967. Whose side are we on? *Social Problems* 14:239-47.
Becker, Howard S., and Greer, Blanche. 1960. Participant observation: the analysis of quantitative field data. In *Human organization research: field relations and techniques*, ed. Richard N. Adams and Jack J. Preiss. Homewood, Ill.: Dorsey Press.
Becker, Howard S., and Horowitz, I.L. 1972. Radical politics and sociological research: observations on methodology and ideology. *American Journal of Sociology* 78:48-66.
Beiser, Morton. 1977. Ethics in cross-cultural research. In *Current perspectives in cultural psychiatry*, ed. Edward F. Foulks, et al. New York: Spectrum Publications.
Bennett, John W. 1946. The integration of Pueblo culture: a question of values. *Southwestern Journal of Anthropology* 2:361-74.
Berman, Helen. 1975. A restitution: review of *Rosalind Franklin and DNA* by Anne Sayre. *Science* 190:665.
Bernard, Viola W.; Ottenberg, Perry; and Redl, Fritz. 1971. Dehumanization. In *Sanctions for evil*, Nevitt Sanford, et al. San Francisco: Jossey-Bass.
Berreman, Gerald D. 1962. *Behind many masks: ethnography and impression management in a Himalayan village*. Monograph 4. Ithaca: The Society for Applied Anthropology.
———. 1968. Is anthropology alive? In Social responsibilities symposium, Gerald D. Berremen, et al. *Current Anthropology* 9:391-96.

———. 1969. Academic colonialism: not so innocent abroad. *The Nation* November 10, 1969, pp. 505-8.
———. 1971. Ethics, responsibility and the funding of Asian research. *Journal of Asian Studies* 30:390-99.
Berreman, Gerald D., et al. 1968. Social responsibilities symposium. *Current Anthropology* 9:391-435.
Blair, Calvin P.; Schaedel, Richard P.; and Street, James H. 1969. Responsibilities of the foreign scholar to the local scholarly community: Studies of U.S. Research in Guatemala, Chile and Paraguay. In *Council on Educational Cooperation with Latin America*, ed. Richard N. Adams. Washington: Education and World Affairs.
Blok, Anton. 1973. A note on ethics and power. *Human Organization* 32:95-98.
Boguslaw, Robert. 1967. Ethics and the social scientist. In *The rise and fall of Project Camelot*, ed. I.L. Horowitz. Cambridge: M.I.T. Press.
Bonacich, P. 1970. Letters: deceiving subjects: the pollution of our environment. *The American Sociologist* 5:45.
Bowen, Elenore Smith (Laura Bohannan). 1964. *Return to Laughter*. Garden City, N.Y.: Doubleday.
Braroe, Niels W. 1965. Reciprocal exploitation in an Indian-white community. *Southwestern Journal of Anthropology* 21:166-78.
Braroe, Niels Winther, and Hicks, George L. 1967. Observations on the mystique of anthropology. *Sociological Quarterly* Spring, pp. 173-86.
Bronowski, J. 1965. *Science and human values*. Revised ed. New York: Harper and Row.
Brown, Martin, ed. 1971. *The social responsibility of the scientist*. New York: Free Press.
Carroll, James D. 1973. Confidentiality of social science research sources and data: the Popkin case. *PS* 6:268-80.
Casagrande, Joseph B., ed. 1960. *In the company of man: twenty portraits of anthropological informants*. New York: Harper and Row.
Cain, Leonard D., Jr. 1967. The AMA and the gerontologists: uses and abuses of "A profile of the aging: USA." In *Ethics, politics, and social research*, ed. Gideon Sjoberg. Cambridge: Schenkman.
Chargaff, Erwin. 1968. A quick climb up Mount Olympus: review of *The double helix. A personal account of the discovery of the structure of DNA* by James D. Watson. *Science* 159:1448-49.
Chomsky, Noam. 1967. The responsibility of intellectuals. In *American power and the new mandarins*, ed. Noam Chomsky. New York: Random House.
Clark, Kenneth B. 1975. The American dilemma. *The New York Times* February 16, 1975, p. 15.
Clemmer, Richard O. 1969. The fed-up Hopi: resistance of the American Indian and the silence of the good anthropologists. *Journal of the Steward Anthropological Society* 1, 1:18-40.
Cochrane, D.G. 1970. Anthropologists in the field: an administrative view. *Journal of the Polynesian Society* 79:349-53.
Cohen, Burton, and Schwab, Joseph J. 1965. Practical logic: problems of ethical decision. *American Behavioral Scientist* 8:23-27.
Colfax, J. David. 1966. Pressure toward distortion and involvement in studying a civil rights organization. *Human Organization* 25, 2:140-49.
Colvard, Richard. 1967. Interaction and identification in reporting field research: a critical reconsideration of protective procedures. In *Ethics, politics, and social research*, ed. Gideon Sjoberg. Cambridge: Schenkman.
Condominas, Georges. 1973. Ethics and comfort: an ethnographer's view of his profession. In *Annual Report of the American Anthropological Association, 1972*. Washington.

Crocombe, R.G., and Spate, O.H.K. 1969. Pacific research: the need for reciprocity. *The Australian National University News* 4, 3:1-4.
Davenport, William H., et al. 1968. No research anthropologist for psychological warfare in Vietnam. Duplicated.
Davis, Shelton H. 1976. The Yanomamo—ethnographic images and anthropological responsibilities. In *The geological imperative: anthropology and development in the Amazon Basin of South America,* Shelton H. Davis and Robert O. Mathews. Cambridge: Anthropology Resource Center.
Deloria, Vine, Jr. 1969. *Custer died for your sins: an Indian manifesto.* New York: Avon Books.
_____. 1970. *We talk, you listen.* New York: Macmillan.
Department of Health, Education, and Welfare. 1971. *The institutional guide to DHEW policy on protection of human subjects.* Bethesda, Md.
_____. 1977. *Code of Federal regulations title 45—public welfare, revised as of November 6, 1975: part 46—protection of human subjects.* Bethesda, Md.: PRR Reports.
De Solla Price, Derek. 1964. Ethics of scientific publication. *Science* 144:655-57.
Devereux, George. 1967. *From anxiety to method in the behavioral sciences.* The Hague: Mouton.
Dewing, Arthur Stone. 1954. An introduction to the use of the cases. In *The case method at the Harvard Business School: papers by present and past members of the faculty and staff,* ed. Malcolm P. McNair. New York: McGraw-Hill.
Diamond, Stanley. 1964. Nigerian discovery: the politics of field work. In *Reflections on community studies,* ed. Arthur J. Vidich, Joseph Bensman, and Maurice R. Stein. New York: John Wiley & Sons.
Dunphy, Dexter C. 1967. Planned environments for learning in the social sciences: two innovative courses at Harvard. *The American Sociologist* 2:202-6.
Eckel, Malcolm. 1968. *The ethics of decision-making.* New York: Morehouse-Barlow.
Edgerton, Robert B. 1965. Some dimensions of disillusionment in culture contact. *Southwestern Journal of Anthropology* 21:231-43.
Edsall, John T. 1975. Scientific freedom and responsibility: report of the AAAS Committee on Scientific Freedom and Responsibility. *Science* 188:687-93.
Erikson, Kai T. 1967. A comment on disguised observation in sociology. *Social Problems* 14:366-73.
Fabian, Johannes. 1971. On professional ethics and epistemological foundations. *Current Anthropology* 12:230-31.
Festinger, Leon; Riecken, Henry W.; and Schachter, Stanley. 1956. Methodological appendix. In *When prophecy fails,* Leon Festinger, Henry W. Riecken, and Stanley Schachter. Minneapolis: University of Minnesota Press.
Fichter, Joseph H., and Kolb, William L. 1953. Ethical limitations on sociological reporting. *American Sociological Review* 18:544-50.
Firth, R. 1972. The sceptical anthropologist? Social anthropology and Marxist views on society. Inaugural Radcliffe-Brown Lecture in Social Anthropology, 1972 (pamphlet). *Proceedings of the British Academy* Vol. 58.
Fletcher, Joseph. 1966. *Situation ethics: the new morality.* Philadelphia: The Westminster Press.
_____. 1967 *Moral responsibility: situation ethics at work.* Philadelphia: Westminster Press.
Fox, John B. 1953. A note on counseling as an adjunct of the case method. In *The case method of teaching human relations and administration: an interim statement,* ed. Kenneth R. Andrews. Cambridge: Harvard University Press.
Frankena, William L. 1963. *Ethics.* Englewood Cliffs, N.J.: Prentice-Hall.
Frazier, E. Franklin. 1964. Black bourgeoisie: public and academic reactions. In *Reflections on community studies,* ed. Arthur J. Vidich, Joseph Bensman, and Maurice R. Stein. New York: John Wiley and Sons.

Freund, Paul A., ed. 1969. *Experimentation with human subjects.* New York: George Braziller.
Friedrichs, Robert W. 1968. Choice and commitment in social research. *The American Sociologist* 3, 1:8-11.
―――. 1970. Epistemological foundations for a sociological ethic. *The American Sociologist* 5:138-40.
Fuller, Frances Mulhearn. 1953. The use of the lecture in a case-method course. In *The case method of teaching human relations and administration: an interim statement,* ed. Kenneth R. Andrews. Cambridge: Harvard University Press.
Gallaher, Art, Jr. 1964. Plainville: the twice-studied town. In *Reflections on community studies,* ed. Arthur J. Vidich, Joseph Bensman, and Maurice R. Stein. New York: John Wiley and Sons.
Galliher, John F. 1973. The protection of human subjects: a reexamination of the professional code of ethics. *The American Sociologist* 8:93-100.
Gans, Herbert J. 1968. The participant-observer as a human being: observations on the personal aspects of field work. In *Institutions and the person: essays presented to Everett C. Hughes,* ed. Howard S. Becker, et al. Chicago: Aldine.
Gjessing, Gutorm, 1968. The social responsibility of the social anthropologist. *Current Anthropology* 9:397-402.
Glass, Bentley. 1965a. The ethical basis of science. *Science* 150:1254-61.
―――. 1965b. *Science and ethical values.* Chapel Hill: The University of North Carolina Press.
Glazer, Myron. 1972. *The research adventure: promise and problems of field work.* New York: Random House.
Glover, John D., and Hower, Ralph M. 1953. Some comments on teaching by the case method. In *The case method of teaching human relations and administration: an interim statement,* ed. Kenneth R. Andrews. Cambridge: Harvard University Press.
Golann, Stuart E. 1973. Ethical problems of research in the community. In *Current ethical issues in mental health,* ed. Milton F. Shore and Stuart Golann. Rockville, Md.: National Institute of Mental Health.
Gold, Raymond L. 1958. Roles in sociological field observations. *Social Forces* 36:217-23.
Golde, Peggy, ed. 1970. *Women in the field: anthropological experiences.* Chicago: Aldine.
Goldner, Fred H. 1967. Role emergence and the ethics of ambiguity. In *Ethics, politics, and social research,* ed. Gideon Sjoberg. Cambridge: Schenkman.
Goldwasser, Edwin L. 1965. Letter: fashion and competition in science. *Science* 147:237-38.
Gough, Kathleen. 1967. World revolution and the science of man. In *The dissenting academy,* ed. Theodore Roszak. New York: Vintage Books.
―――. 1968. New proposals for anthropologists. *Current Anthropology* 9:403-7.
Gouldner, Alvin W. 1962. Anti-minotaur: the myth of a value-free sociology. In *Sociology on trial,* Maurice R. Stein and Arthur J. Vidich. Englewood Cliffs, N.J.: Prentice-Hall.
―――. 1968. Disorder and social theory: review of *American sociology: perspectives, problems, methods* ed. by Talcott Parsons. *Science* 162:247-49.
Gragg, Charles I. 1954. Because wisdom can't be told. In *The case method at the Harvard Business School: papers by present and past members of the faculty and staff,* ed. Malcolm P. McNair. New York: McGraw-Hill.
Gray, Bradford H. 1975. An assessment of institutional review committees in human experimentation. *Medical Care* 13:318-28.
Gray, Jeffrey. 1974. The "Eichmann" experiment. Review of *Obedience to authority* by Stanley Milgram. *The Times Higher Education Supplement* June 21, 1974, p. 18.
Green, Philip. 1971. The obligations of American social scientists. *The Annals* 394:13-27.

Gusfield, Joseph R. 1960. Field work reciprocities in studying a social movement. In *Human organization research: field relations and techniques*, ed. Richard N. Adams and Jack J. Preiss. Homewood, Ill.: Dorsey Press.
Haberer, Joseph. 1972. Politicalization in science. *Science* 178:713-24.
Hackbursch, Florentine. 1948. Professional ethics in institutional practice. *American Psychologist* 3:85-87.
Halovorson, James, and Moser, Chris L., eds. 1965. *Mesoamerican Notes* 6. Mexico City: Department of Anthropology, University of the Americas.
Hanna, William John. 1965. Image-making in field research: some tactical and ethical problems of research in tropical Africa. *American Behavioral Scientist* 9:15-20.
Harris, Richard N. 1971. Intellectual despotism in graduate school. *The American Sociologist* 6:35-36.
Henry, Frances. 1966. The role of the fieldworker in an explosive political situation. *Current Anthropology* 7:552-59.
Henry, Frances, and Saberwal, Satish, eds. 1969. *Stress and response in fieldwork.* New York: Holt, Rinehart, and Winston.
Henry, Jeannette, ed. 1971. Anthropology and the American Indian. *The Indian Historian* 4:10-18, 63.
Hessler, Richard M., and New, Peter Kong-Ming. 1972. Research as a process of social exchange. *The American Sociologist* 7:13-15.
Hicks, George L. 1977. Informant anonymity and scientific accuracy: the problem of pseudonyms. *Human Organization* 36:214-20.
Hobbs, Nicholas. 1968. Ethical issues in the social sciences. *International encyclopedia of the social sciences* 5:160-67.
Horowitz, Irving Louis, ed. 1939. *Power, politics and people: the collected essays of C. Wright Mills.* London: Oxford University Press.
_____. The life and death of Project Camelot. *Trans-action* 3:3-7, 44-47.
_____, ed. 1967. *The rise and fall of Project Camelot: studies in the relationship between social science and practical politics.* Cambridge: M.I.T. Press.
Huizer, Gerrit. 1975. The a-social role of social scientists in underdeveloped countries; some ethical considerations. In *Current anthropology in the Netherlands,* ed. Peter Kloos and Henri J.M. Claessen. Rotterdam: Anthropological Branch of the Netherlands Sociological and Anthropological Society.
Humphreys, Laud. 1970a. *Tearoom trade: impersonal sex in public places.* Chicago: Aldine.
_____. 1970b. Tearoom trade: impersonal sex in public places. *Trans-action* 7:11-25.
Hymes, Dell, ed. 1972. *Reinventing anthropology.* New York: Pantheon Books.
Jacobs, Glenn, ed. 1970. *The participant observer.* New York: Braziller.
Jansen, William H., II. 1973. The applied man's burden: the problem of ethics and applied anthropology. *Human Organization* 32:325-29.
Jarvie, I.C. 1969. The problem of ethical integrity in participant observation. *Current Anthropology* 10:505-8.
Johnson, Dale L. 1966. Letter: ethics of the nature, procedures, and funding of research in other countries. *American Anthropologist* 68:1016-17.
Jonas, Hans. 1969. Philosophical reflections on experimenting with human subjects. *Daedalus* 98:219-47.
Jones, Delmos J. 1971. Social responsibility and the belief in basic research: an example from Thailand. *Current Anthropology* 12:347-50.
Jongmans, D.G. and Gutkind, P.C.W., eds. 1967. *Anthropologists in the field.* Assen: Van Gorcum.
Jorgensen, Joseph. 1971. On ethics and anthropology. *Current Anthropology* 12:321-34.

Jorgensen, Joseph G., and Lee, Richard B., eds. 1973. *The new native resistance: indigenous peoples' struggles and the responsibilities of scholars.* Module 6. New York: MSS Modular Publications.

Kaplan, David. 1974. Review article: the anthropology of authenticity: everyman his own anthropologist. *American Anthropologist* 76:824-39.

Katz, Jay. 1972. *Experimentation with human beings: the authority of the investigator, subject, professions and state in the human experimentation process.* New York: Russell Sage Foundation.

Kelman, Herbert. 1968. *A time to speak: on human values and social research.* San Francisco: Jossey-Bass.

Kloos, Peter. 1969. Role conflicts in social fieldwork. *Current Anthropology* 10:509-11.

Kluckhohn, Florence R. 1940. The participant-observer technique in small communities. *American Journal of Sociology* 46:331-43.

Krzywoblocki, M.Z. von. 1965. Letter: fashion and competition in science. *Science* 147:237.

Landis, Benson Y., ed. 1955. Ethical standards and professional conduct. *The Annals* Vol. 297.

Langton, P. 1972. Politics, oppression, and anthropology: the implications of research in a politically volatile area. *!Kung* pp. 30-36.

Lengyel, Peter. 1971a Introduction: ethics, institutionalization and policies. *International Social Science Journal* 24:635-47.

_____, ed. 1972b. The protection of privacy. *International Social Science Journal* 24:417-602.

_____, ed. 1972c. Ethics and institutionalization in social science. *International Social Science Journal* 24:635-719.

Lewis, I.M. 1968. Comment to Berreman, Gjessing, and Gough: Social responsibilities Symposium. *Current Anthropology* 9:417.

Lewis, Oscar. 1951. *Life in a Mexican village: Tepoztlan restudied.* Urbana, Ill.: University of Illinois Press.

_____. 1959. *Five families: Mexican case studies in the culture of poverty.* New York: Basic Books.

_____. 1961. *The Children of Sanchez: Autobiography of a Mexican Family.* New York: Random House.

_____. 1964. *Pedro Martinez: a Mexican peasant and his family.* New York: Random House.

Liebow, Elliot. 1967. *Tally's Corner: a study of Negro street corner men.* Boston: Little-Brown.

Long, Joseph K. 1968. The case study of a do-gooder among the Wisconsin Indians: philosophical implications for applied anthropology. *Transactions of the Conference on Social Issues.* Part 1. University of Wisconsin Center System.

Lundsgaarde, Henry P. 1971. Privacy: an anthropological perspective on the right to be let alone. *Houston Law Review* 8:858-75.

Luria, S.E. 1973. On research styles and allied matters. *Daedalus* 102:75-84.

MacIver, R.M. 1955. The social significance of professional ethics. In Ethical standards and professional conduct, ed. Benson Y. Landis. *The Annals* 297:118-24.

Malinowski, Bronislaw. 1967. *A diary in the strict sense of the term.* New York: Harcourt.

Maquet, J.J. 1964. Objectivity in anthropology. *Current Anthropology* 5:47-55.

Markovic, Mihailo. 1972. Ethics of a critical social science. *International Social Science Journal* 24:672-85.

Maybury-Lewis, David. 1965. *The savage and the innocent.* London: Evans Brothers.

McCall, George J., and Simmons, J.L., eds. 1969. *Issues in participant observation: a text and reader.* Reading, Mass.: Addison-Wesley.

McNair, Malcolm P., ed. 1954. *The case method at the Harvard Business School: papers by present and past members of the faculty and staff.* New York: McGraw-Hill.

———. 1971. McNair on cases. *Harvard Business School Bulletin* 47, 4:10-13.

McVittie, G.C. 1964. Letter: fashion and competition in science. *Science* 146:341-42.

Mead, Margaret. 1969. Research with human beings: a model derived from anthropological field practice. In *Experimentation with human subjects,* ed. Paul A. Freund. New York: George Braziller.

Mead, Margaret; Chappel, Eliot D.; and Brown, Gordon G. 1949. Report of the Committee on Ethics. *Human Organization* 8, 2:20-21.

Medicine, Beatrice. 1971. The anthropologist and American Indian studies programs. *The Indian Historian* 4:15-18, 63.

Mercurio, El. 1965. *Select committee report on Camelot to the Chilean Chamber of Deputies.* Santiago, Chile. December 29, 1965.

Merry, Robert W. 1954. Preparation to teach a case. In *The case method at the Harvard Business School: papers by present and past members of the faculty and staff,* ed. Malcolm P. McNair. New York: McGraw-Hill.

Merton, Robert K. 1968. Making it scientifically: review of *The double helix: a personal account of the discovery of the structure of DNA* by James D. Watson. *The New York Times Book Review* February 25, 1968, pp. 41-45.

Metraux, Rhoda. 1969. Appendix II: study program in human health and the ecology of man—China: measures taken for the protection of confidentiality in an interdisciplinary study of health and cultural adaptation based on retrospective life histories. *Daedalus* 98:379-81.

Milgram, Stanley. 1963. Behavioral study of obedience. *Journal of Abnormal and Social Psychology* 67:371-78.

———. 1964. Issues in the study of obedience: a reply to Baumrind. *American Psychologist* 19:848-52.

———. 1965. Some conditions of obedience and disobedience to authority. *Human Relations* 18:57-76.

———. 1974. *Obedience to authority: an experimental view.* New York: Harper and Row.

Miller, S.M. 1952. The participant observer and "over rapport." *American Sociological Review* 17:97-99.

Moore, Wilbert E., and Tumin, Melvin M. 1949. Some social functions of ignorance. *American Sociological Review* 14:787-95.

Moskos, Charles C., Jr. and Bell, Wendell. 1967. Emerging nations and ideologies of American social scientists. *The American Sociologist* 2, 2:67-72.

Myers, James E. 1969. Unleashing the untrained: some observations on student ethnographers. *Human Organization* 28:155-59.

Nash, Dennison. 1963. The ethnologist as stranger: an essay in the sociology of knowledge. *Southwestern Journal of Anthropology* 19:149-67.

Native Struggles Support Group. 1974. Anthropologists' world guide to native political movements. Revised edition. In *The new native resistance: indigenous peoples' struggles and the responsibilities of scholars,* ed. Joseph J. Jorgensen and Richard B. Lee. Module 6. New York: MSS Modular Publications.

New, Peter Kong-Ming, and Hessler, Richard M. 1973. Community researchers meet community residents: interpretation of findings. *Human Organization* 32:243-55.

Nooter, Gert. 1975. Ethics and the acquisition policy of anthropological museums. In *Current anthropology in the Netherlands,* ed. Peter Kloos and Henri J.M. Claessen. Rotterdam: Anthropological Branch of the Netherlands Sociological and Anthropological Society.

Orlans, Harold. 1967. Ethical problems in the relations of research sponsors and investigators. In *Ethics, politics, and social research,* ed. Gideon Sjoberg. Cambridge: Schenkman.

Oromaner, Mark Jay. 1968. Letter to the editor: a moral decision. *The American Sociologist* 3, 3:254.
Ortiz, Alfonso. 1971. An Indian anthropologist's perspective on anthropology. *The Indian Historian* 4:11-14.
Paddock, John. 1965a. Oscar Lewis's Mexico. *Mesoamerican Notes* 6:3-34.
_____. 1965b. A review of *Five families* and *The children of Sanchez*. *Mesoamerican Notes* 6:37-48.
_____. 1965c. A review of *Pedro Martinez: a Mexican peasant and his family*. *Mesoamerican Notes* 6:51-55.
_____. 1965d. Private lives and anthropological publications. *Mesoamerican Notes* 6:59-65.
Panel on Privacy and Behavioral Research. 1967a. Privacy and behavioral research: preliminary summary of the report of the Panel on Privacy and Behavioral Research. *Science* 155:535-38.
_____. 1967b. *Privacy and behavioral research*. Washington: Government Printing Office.
Parsons, Talcott. 1967. Editorial: the editor's column. *The American Sociologist* 2:192-94.
_____. 1969. Research with human subjects and the "professional complex." *Daedalus* 98:325-60.
Paul, Benjamin D. 1953. Mental disorder and self-regulating processes in culture: a Guatemalan illustration. In *Interrelations between the social environment and psychiatric disorders: Papers presented at the 1952 annual conference of the Milbank Memorial Fund*. New York: Milbank Memorial Fund.
Pehrson, Robert N. 1966. Preface. In *The social organization of the Marri Baluch*. VFPA 43. New York: Wenner-Gren Foundation for Anthropological Research.
Perloff, Robert. 1964. Problems of method and ethics in interracial research. *American Behavioral Science* 7:7-9.
Petersen, William. 1972. Forbidden knowledge. In *The social context of research*, ed. Saad Nagi and Ronald Corwin. New York: John Wiley and Sons.
Powdermaker, Hortence. 1966. *Stranger and friend: the way of an anthropologist*. New York: Norton.
Privacy Protection Study Commission. 1977. *Personal privacy in an information society*. Washington: Government Printing Office.
Radin, Paul. 1939. The mind of primitive man. *New Republic* 98:300-303.
Rainwater, Lee, and Pittman, David J. 1967. Ethical problems in studying a politically sensitive and deviant community. *Social Problems* 14:357-66.
Read, Kenneth E. 1965. *The high valley*. New York: Scribner's.
Record, Jane Cassels. 1967. The research institute and the pressure group. In *Ethics, politics, and social research*, ed. Gideon Sjoberg. Cambridge: Schenkman.
Reif, F. 1961. The competitive world of the pure scientist. *Science* 134:1957-62.
Reissman, Leonard, and Silvert, Kalman H., eds. 1967. Ethics and social science research. *American Behavioral Scientist* 10, 10:1-32.
Reynolds, Paul Davidson. 1972. On the protection of human subjects and social science. *International Social Science Journal* 24:693-719.
Rogers, Carl R. 1942. *Counseling and psycho-therapy*. Boston: Houghton Mifflin.
_____. 1951. *Client-centered therapy: its current practice, implications, and theory*. Boston: Houghton Mifflin.
Ronken, Harriet O. 1953. What one student learned. In *The case method of teaching human relations and administration: an interim statement*, ed. Kenneth F. Andrews. Cambridge: Harvard University Press.
Ruebhausen, Oscar M., and Brim, Orville G., Jr. 1965. Privacy and behavioral research. *Columbia Law Review* 65:1184-1211.
_____. 1966. Privacy and behavioral research. *American Psychologist* 21:423-44.
Sayre, Anne. 1975. *Rosalind Franklin and DNA*. New York: Norton.

Schoen, Donald R., and Sprague, Philip. 1954. What is the case method? In *The case method at the Harvard Business School: papers by present and past members of the faculty and staff*, ed. Malcolm P. McNair. New York: McGraw-Hill.
Schwartz, Morris S., and Schwartz, Charlotte Green. 1955. Problems in participant observation. *American Journal of Sociology* 60:343-53.
Shapley, Deborah. 1975. Review of *Rosalind Franklin and DNA* by Anne Sayre. *The New York Times Book Review* September 21, 1975, pp. 27-32.
Shils, Edward A. 1959. Social inquiry and the autonomy of the individual. In *The human meaning of the social sciences*, ed. Daniel Lerner. New York: Meridan Books.
Shore, Milton F., and Golann, Stuart E., eds. 1973. *Current ethical issues in mental health: based on a workshop at the 47th annual meeting of the American Orthopsychiatric Association, San Francisco, California, March 1970*. Rockville, Md.: National Institute of Mental Health, National Clearinghouse for Mental Health Information.
Silvert, Kalman H. 1965. American academic ethics and social research abroad. American University Field Staff Reports, West Coast South America Series 12, 3. New York: American Universities Field Staff.
Sjoberg, Gideon. 1967a. Project Camelot: selected reactions and personal reflections. In *Ethics, politics, and social research*, ed. Gideon Sjoberg. Cambridge: Schenkman.
_____, ed. 1967b. *Ethics, politics, and social research*. Cambridge: Schenkman.
Snow, Charles P. 1961. The moral un-neutrality of science. *Science* 133:255-62.
_____. 1975. The corridors of DNA: review of *Rosalind Franklin and DNA* by Anne Sayre. *The New York Review of Books* November 13, 1975, pp. 3-4.
Society for Applied Anthropology. 1963-64. Statement on ethics of the Society for Applied Anthropology. *Human Organization* 22, 4:237.
Stauder, Jack. 1972. The 'relevance' of anthropology under imperialism. *Critical Anthropology* 2, 2:65-87.
Stavenhagen, Rodolfo, 1971. Decolonializing applied social sciences. *Human Organization* 30:333-57.
*The Student Mobilizer.* 1970. Counterinsurgency research on campus exposed. *The Student Mobilizer* 3, 4:1-31.
Symonds, Carolyn. 1968. Letter to the editor: risky and rewarding. *The American Sociologist* 3, 3:254.
Szwed, John F. 1972. An American anthropological dilemma: the politics of Afri-American culture. In *Reinventing anthropology*, ed. Dell Hymes. New York: Pantheon Books.
Thatcher, Sandy. 1975. Opinion: the decline of academic morality. *Princeton Alumni Weekly* October 13, 1975, pp. 10-11.
Tumin, Melvin M. 1968. Some social consequences of research on racial relations. *The American Sociologist* 3:117-24.
Ulrich, David N. 1953. The case method. In *The case method of teaching human relations and administration: an interim statement*, ed. Kenneth R. Andrews. Cambridge: Harvard University Press.
United States House of Representatives. 1966. *Behavioral sciences and the national security*. Washington: Government Printing Office.
Vallance, Theodore R. 1966. Project Camelot: an interim postlude. *American Psychologist* 21:443-44.
Vargus, Brian S. 1971. On sociological exploitation: why the guinea pig sometimes bites. *Social Problems* 19:238-48.
Vidal, Gore. 1974. Real class: review of *A writer's capital* and *The partners* by Louis Auchincloss. *New York Review of Books* July 18, 1974, pp. 10-11, 14-15.
Vidich, Arthur J., and Bensman, Joseph. 1958. *Small town in mass society: class, power and religion in a rural community*. Princeton: Princeton University Press. Revised edition, 1968.

Warwick, Donald P. 1973. Tearoom trade: means and ends in social research. *The Hastings Center Studies* 1, 1:27-38.
Watson, James D. 1968. *The double helix. A personal account of the discovery of the structure of DNA.* New York: Atheneum.
Wax, Rosalie Hankey. 1960a. Reciprocity in field work. In *Human organization research: field relations and techniques,* ed. Richard N. Adams and Jack J. Preiss. Homewood, Ill.: Dorsey Press.
_____. 1960b. Twelve years later: an analysis of field experience. In *Human organization research: field relations and techniques,* ed. Richard N. Adams and Jack J. Preiss. Homewood, Ill.: Dorsey Press.
_____. 1971. *Doing fieldwork: warnings and advice.* Chicago: University of Chicago Press.
Weaver Warren, Jr. 1974. Public's right to know: how much? about whom? *The New York Times* December 15, 1974, p. 11.
Weigert, Andrew. 1970. The immoral rhetoric of scientific sociology. *The American Sociologist* 5:111-19.
Whyte, William Foote. 1969. The role of the U.S. professor in developing countries. *The American Sociologist* 4:19-28.
Wiener, Norbert. 1964. Intellectual honesty and the contemporary scientist. *Technology Review* April, pp. 17-18, 45-47. Reprinted 1964 *American Behavioral Scientist* November, pp. 15-18.
Winthrob, Ronald M. 1969. An inward focus: a consideration of psychological stress in fieldwork. In *Stress and response in fieldwork,* ed. Frances Henry and Satish Saberwal. New York: Holt, Rinehart and Winston.
Wolf, Eric R., and Jorgensen, Joseph G. 1970. Anthropology on the warpath in Thailand. *The New York Review of Books* November 19, 1970, pp. 26-35.
Wolfensberger, Wolf. 1967. Ethical issues in research with human subjects. *Science* 155:47-51.
Wolff, Kurt H. 1964. Surrender and community study: the study of Loma. In *Reflections on community studies,* ed. Arthur J. Vidich, Joseph Bensman, and Maurice R. Stein. New York: John Wiley and Sons.
Wright, Derek. 1971. *The psychology of moral behavior.* Harmondsworth: Penguin Books.
Yablonski, Lewis. 1968. On crime, violence, LSD, and legal immunity for social scientists. *The American Sociologist* 3:148-49.

## ABOUT THE AUTHOR

G.N. Appell, a social anthropologist, was educated at Harvard College (A.B., 1948), Harvard Business School (M.B.A., 1952), Harvard University (A.M. in Anthropology, 1956), and at the Department of Anthropology, Institute of Advanced Studies, Australian National University (Ph.D., 1966).

He and his wife have undertaken extensive research in Borneo among the Rungus Dusun as well as field work among the Dogrib Indians of the Northwest Territories of Canada. He has published on the ethnography of Borneo, social anthropological theory, field-work methods, the human consequences of social change and development, and the ethics of anthropological inquiry. His most recent book is *The Societies of Borneo: Explorations in the Theory of Cognatic Social Structure*, edited by G.N. Appell (Washington: American Anthropological Association, Special Publication 6, 1976).

He is a founder and member of the Board of Directors of the Borneo Research Council, former editor of the *Borneo Research Bulletin*, former president of the Northeastern Anthropological Association, former president and current trustee of the Fund for Astrophysical Research, Inc.

He has been a Research Associate in the Department of Anthropology, Brandeis University, since 1968.